'I SIGNED MY DEATH WARRANT'

MICHAEL COLLINS & THE TREATY

T. RYLE DWYER

MERCIER PRESS

Cork

www.mercierpress.ie

© T. Ryle Dwyer

ISBN: 978 1 85635 526 1

10 9 8 7 6 5 4 3

A CIP record for this title is available from the British Library

To Brian Looney

Contents

Preface

Although I grew up in Ireland from the age of four, my first real introduction to modern Irish history was at University of North Texas in 1965, when I wrote a term paper on the the causes of the Irish civil war. I was staggered to learn that the partition question had essentially nothing to do with that conflict. Ever since I have had a deep and abiding interest in the subject, so this book is the product of an interest stretching over forty years. Some of those involved with the negotiations were still alive when I first became interested and I corresponded with Robert Barton, the last surviving signatory and Sir Geoffrey Shakespeare, an aide and confidant of the British prime minister.

I wrote a master's thesis on the Anglo-Irish Treaty in 1968 and the first article I published was a revision of that thesis under the title of 'The Anglo-Irish Treaty and Why they Signed', *Capuchin Annual*, 1971. Many of the Irish documents relating to the negotiations were not released until the mid 1970s. In 1981, Mercier Press published my third book, *Michael Collins and the Treaty* in conjunction with the sixtieth anniversary of the Treaty.

In the quarter of a century since then a wealth of material has been released, including the papers of Eamon de Valera and Robert Barton. Much of the early material written on the Anglo-Irish negotiations came from a particular perspective. Frank Pakenham's book *Peace by Ordeal* was a brilliant study that threw a phenomenal amount of new light on the subject in 1935, because he had access to the papers of Robert Barton and Erskine Childers and also personal access to Eamon de Valera. But the book did not show as keen an understanding of the role of Arthur Griffith and Michael Collins, because he did not have access to the papers of Collins, especially those that subsequently appeared in the biography by Rex Taylor, which threw considerable new light on the part played by Michael Collins.

My aim is to make an honest appraisal of the part Collins played in the making of the Anglo-Irish Treaty. People on all sides made mistakes, but all too often the history of these troubled time is marred by partisanship. Too many have tried to depict Collins as always right and de Valera as almost always wrong, or the other way around. In reality there were rights and wrongs on all sides.

Ultimately the Treaty provided the stepping-stones to an Irish Republic for twenty-six of the thirty-two counties of Ireland, as Collins had confidently predicted. His views in relation to the partition issue were not justified, but this was not an issue of contention between himself and his republican critics during his lifetime. After his death some of his strongest supporters insisted that they had an obligation to complete the Big Fellow's unfinished work. This kind of thinking led to the Army Mutiny of 1924, but thereafter those of his supporters who retained power behaved as if Collins had died trying to ensure that the Treaty was the ultimate settlement rather than a means to an end. Ironically it was Eamon de Valera who ultimately proved that Collins was right in relation to the Treaty controversy when he said the Treaty 'gives us freedom, not the ultimate freedom that all nations desire and develop to, but the freedom to achieve it'.

TRD
Tralee, 2006

Foreword

'At this moment,' Michael Collins wrote after the Truce came into effect on 11 July, 1921, 'there is more ill-will within a victorious assembly than ever could be anywhere else except in the devil's assembly. It cannot be fought against. The issues and persons are mixed to such an extent as to make discernability an utter impossibility except for a few.'

He and President Eamon de Valera would later pretend that they had trusted each other implicitly at this stage, but that is clearly contradicted by any examination of the true state of relations between them. Michael Collins had come to prominence as a result of his involvement in the Irish Republican Brotherhood (IRB) as a trusted confidant of Thomas Ashe, who took over as the IRB leader following the Easter Rebellion. Ashe was the most successful commandant and the last to surrender during the Easter Rebellion. After his death on hunger strike in September 1917, Collins formed a close relationship with Ashe's Kerry colleague Austin Stack. This relationship developed largely through correspondence while Stack was in prison.

Collins – who was nicknamed the Big Fellow because he was so full of self-importance – came very much to the fore within the movement following the so-called German Plot of May 1918 when most of the Sinn Féin leadership were arrested. He and his friend Harry Boland played a major role in organising the party's successful performance in the 1918 general election, in which Sinn Féin won almost all the seats outside the north-east. In January 1919, Collins was appointed director of intelligence of the Irish Volunteer Force, which was shortly to become known as the Irish Republican Army (IRA).

From the outset, he had a distinct plan. He believed the Dublin Metropolitan Police (DMP) and the Royal Irish Constabulary (RIC) were the eyes and ears of the British administration, and he advocated that the most effective detectives should be killed. Once they were silenced he believed the British would retaliate, but without proper intelligence they would react blindly and hit out at totally innocent Irish people. In the process they would drive the Irish people into the arms of the IRA.

In developing his intelligence organisation, Collins enlisted the help of a number of policemen, the most important of whom were three detectives. Ned Broy was a confidential typist at the Detective Division Headquarters of the DMP. He would insert an extra carbon paper and make a copy of any reports that Collins desired. One night he invited Collins into the headquarters to go through the police records with a colleague for some hours. Liam McNamara and Seán Kavanagh, two detectives based in Dublin Castle, also provided invaluable information.

Collins hoped that de Valera would lead that struggle and he therefore helped to arrange his escape from Lincoln Gaol in February 1919, but de Valera had other ideas when he got out. He believed the movement's best chance of success was to exploit President Woodrow Wilson's promise to make the world safe for democracy when he led the United States into the First World War. He thought that the influence of Irish-Americans would be Ireland's most potent force in persuading the British to make concessions, especially after they had supposedly fought for the rights of small nations in the recent war. De Valera therefore decided to go to the United States, but not before he had frustrated the designs of Collins.

All of those arrested for supposed involvement in the German Plot were released in March and so de Valera was able to return to Dublin before setting out for the United States On 25 March a notice was placed in the newspaper:

President de Valera will arrive in Ireland on Wednesday evening next, the 26th inst., and the Executive of Dáil Éireann will offer him a national welcome. It is expected that the homecoming of de Valera will be an occasion of national rejoicing, and full arrangement will be made for marshalling the procession. The Lord Major of Dublin will receive him at the gates of the city, and will escort him to the Mansion House, where he will deliver a message to the Irish people. All organisations and bands wishing to participate in the demonstration should apply to 6 Harcourt Street, on Monday the 24th inst., up to 6 p.m.

> H. Boland
>
> T. Kelly, Honorary Secretaries.

Such arrangements were usually reserved for royalty, so Dublin Castle banned the reception, and the Sinn Féin Executive held an emergency meeting. Arthur Griffith presided at what was for him and Darrell Figgis, the first meeting since their arrest the previous May. Cathal Brugha had complained privately to Figgis some days earlier that Collins and his IRB colleagues had essentially taken over the movement from within while the others were in jail.

'He told me that he had seen what had been passing, but that he had been powerless to change events,' Figgis wrote. 'It was at this meeting I saw for the first time the personal hostility between him and Michael Collins.'

When the executive met to discuss what to do about Dublin Castle's ban on the planned reception, members witnessed the Big Fellow at his most arrogant. Figgis asked to see the record of the Executive meeting authorising the honorary secretaries to announce the plans to welcome de Valera, but he was told that the issue had never come up. 'I therefore asked Alderman Tom Kelly on what authority he, as one of the signatories, had attached his name as secretary, and he answered with characteristic bluntness that, in point of fact, he had never seen the announcement, and had not known of it till he read it in the press.'

There followed a 'tangled discussion' before Collins rose. 'Characteristically, he swept aside all pretences, and said that the announcement has been written by him, and that the decision to make it had been made, not by Sinn Féin, though declared in its name, but by "the proper body, the Irish Volunteers",' Figgis wrote. 'He spoke with much vehemence and emphasis, saying that the sooner fighting was forced and a general state of disorder created through the country (his words in this connection are too well printed on my memory ever to be forgotten), the better it would be for the country. Ireland was likely to get more out of a state of general disorder than from a continuance of the situation as it then stood. The proper people to take decisions of that kind were ready to face the British military, and were resolved to force the issue. And they were not to be deterred by weaklings and cowards. For himself he accepted full responsibility for the announcement, and he told the meeting with forceful candour that he held them in no opinion at all, that, in fact, they were only summoned to confirm what the proper people had decided.

'He had always a truculent manner, but in such situations he was certainly candour itself,' Figgis continued. 'As I looked on him while he spoke, for all the hostility between us, I found something refreshing and admirable in his contempt of us all. His brow was gathered in a thunderous frown, and his chin thrust forward, while he emphasised his points on the back of a chair with heavy strokes of his hand.'

Arthur Griffith certainly was not impressed. Tapping the table in front of him with a pencil, Griffith emphasised that the decision was one to be taken by the meeting and by no other body.

'For two hours the debate raged fiercely,' according to Figgis. Going ahead with the announced plans would undoubtedly lead to trouble, while abandoning them could have disastrous implications for the morale of the whole movement. Parallels were drawn with the disastrous consequences of Daniel O'Connell's decision to accede to the British decision to ban the monster meeting at Clontarf some seventy years earlier.

De Valera was contacted and he requested the welcoming demonstrations be cancelled. 'I write to request that you will not now persist in your idea,' he wrote. 'I think you must all agree with me that the present occasion is scarcely one on which we would be justified in risking the lives of the citizens. I am certain it would not.'

In the following days de Valera ensured that the Standing Committee of Sinn Féin would have a veto over some of the plans the Big Fellow had been developing. Collins wrote to Austin Stack in frustration, but once de Valera went to the United States Collins soon got his way. At the end of July 1919, five specially selected IRA men shot and mortally wounded Detective Sergeant Patrick Smyth. The British retaliated by banning Sinn Féin, Dáil Éireann and other organisations, thereby undermining the measures that de Valera had put in place to control Collins.

When the DMP raided Sinn Féin headquarters, Collins retaliated by having another detective killed that night. He also went over to Manchester and visited Austin Stack in Strangeways Jail as part of an elaborate escape plan.

Collins helped to spring Stack in October 1919, but thereafter Stack turned out to be a dreadful disappointment as far as the Big Fellow was concerned. In comparison with Collins, who was an administrative genius, Stack was a bungler, yet Collins initially admired Stack greatly. This was probably as result of the latter's friendship with his fellow Kerryman Thomas Ashe, while the latter was president of the IRB. But Stack and Collins could hardly have known each other very well, because Stack had been in jail since Ashe's death in September 1917.

If Collins had known Stack better, he might not have had such confidence in him. Stack had been caught by surprise when Roger Casement showed up near Tralee on Good Friday 1916, but Stack showed no leadership. He made no effort to rescue

Casement even though Head Constable John A. Kearney of the local RIC went out of his way to facilitate his rescue. Stack ruled out a rescue attempt, saying that he was under orders to ensure that nothing happened that might impede the planned landing of guns that Sunday.

On the fateful Friday evening Stack decided to visit another prisoner in custody in the RIC barracks instead. Before going, he was advised to ensure he had nothing incriminating on him. He handed over a revolver but he then went to the barracks with what he wrote to his brother was, 'a large number of letters, i.e. fully 20 or 30 letters I imagine'. Those included letters from Patrick Pearse, James Connolly and Bulmer Hobson. He was duly arrested, which may have been what he desired in order to insure that he would be safely incarcerated when the rebellion began.

Part of Stack's local prowess rested on his reputation as a footballer, having captained the Kerry team to win the All-Ireland championship of 1904. In addition, he had a rebel pedigree, as his father was known locally as a Fenian patriot, having been arrested and jailed in December 1866. Moore Stack initially protested his innocence, but then pleaded guilty in the hope of a lighter sentence. He was sentenced to ten years in jail. The British released him after little over two years, in March 1869. He returned home to a hero's welcome and it would not be for more than a century that documentary evidence would emerge casting a shadow over his patriotic credentials.

It was largely through the influence of Collins that Stack was appointed deputy chief of staff of the IRA, but he never even attended a meeting of the general headquarters staff. It was hardly because he was so busy as minister for home affairs, seeing that he never came to grips with the proper formation of the republican courts either.

The Squad, an assassination team set up by Collins, targeted a number of individuals, including some prominent detectives with the Dublin Metropolitan Police and people who were providing them with information. The British retaliated by killing Tomás MacCurtain the lord mayor of Cork, and Collins revenged this killing by having at least three people suspected of involvement shot. Amid the tit-for-tat killings there was a mass of police resignations. Most of the police considered themselves Irishmen and they had no stomach for a fight against their fellow countrymen. As a result they were quite prepared to turn a blind eye, and many even provided republicans with information.

The British introduced recruits to bolster the police, and they became known as Black and Tans, after a pack of hounds. Minister for War Winston Churchill persuaded the government to recruit an elite force of former military officers as police Auxiliaries. Operating on poor intelligence the Auxiliaries and Black and Tans sacked towns around the country, often striking at innocent people. In the process they drove the bulk of the Irish people into the arms of the republicans, as Collins anticipated.

Meanwhile de Valera antagonised Irish-American elements by indicating that they would support Woodrow Wilson if the president provided official recognition of the Irish Republic. The dispute really centred over who would speak for the Irish-Americans – de Valera or Daniel Cohalan. The whole thing came to ahead when de Valera stated in an interview with the *Westminster Gazette* that the Irish regime would be prepared to provide an assurance that Irish independence would never be used to undermine Britain's security.

Having fought alongside Britain in the Great War, he feared that Americans would be afraid to support Ireland as this would be seen as a betrayal of the recent ally, so he suggested that Britain should declare a kind of Monroe Doctrine in relation to the British Isles and Ireland would provide an assurance to Britain like Cuba gave to the United States in a 1901 treaty. The Cubans said that they would maintain their independence and not allow their territory to be used against the United States. The Americans were also afforded the base that they still hold at Guantanamo

Bay. Irish-Americans denounced de Valera's interview on the somewhat spurious grounds that it would mean that Ireland would side with Britain in the event of a war between Britain and the United States.

'The trouble is purely one of personalities,' de Valera admitted. 'I cannot feel confidence enough in a certain man [Cohalan] to let him have implicit control of tactics here without consultation and agreement with me.' De Valera was insisting on having the final say on policy matters, though he was prepared to consult with Irish-American leaders, but they were insisting that he should have nothing to do with American politics. 'On the ways and means they have to be consulted,' de Valera conceded, 'but I reserve the right to use my judgment as to whether any means suggested is or is not in conformity with our purpose.'

Collins supported de Valera against Cohalan and the Clan na Gael leader John Devoy, going so far as to sever relations between the IRB and its sister organisation in America, Devoy's Clan na Gael, even though Devoy had actually been touting Collins as the real Irish leader in his *Gaelic American* newspaper. But in one matter the Big Fellow's help was probably less than welcome.

Throughout the period that de Valera was in the United States, Collins helped his family, and de Valera's wife, Sinéad, remained deeply appreciative of this help throughout the remainder of her life. As the dispute between de Valera and the Irish-Americans intensified, there were rumours that de Valera was having an affair with his secretary, Kathleen O'Connell, a Kerry woman that he met in the United States. They were travelling about America together, and de Valera later accused a Catholic bishop in Chicago of spreading rumours that he was philandering. Collins arranged for Sinéad to join de Valera in the United States, but he was less than pleased to see her as he felt her place was at home with the children.

'The visit to America was one of the biggest mistakes I ever made,' she later wrote. 'It was a huge blunder for me to go to

America. I derived neither profit nor pleasure from my visit.' Her son Terry wrote that she often remarked that the six weeks there were 'the longest and least profitable part of her life'.

Meanwhile in Ireland the struggle entered its bitterest phase with the Black and Tan and Auxiliaries wreaking havoc around the country, sacking towns like Balbriggan, Carrick-on-Shannon, Tuam, Ennistymon, Miltown-Malby and Tralee, which was closed down for the first ten days of November 1920. No businesses or schools were allowed to open and people were warned to keep off the streets.

The British had infiltrated many intelligence agents into Dublin, and some of those closest to Collins had very narrow escapes. Lloyd George proudly proclaimed that he had 'murder by the throat' during his address at the annual Lord Mayor's banquet at the Guildhall on 9 November. The IRA decided to kill simultaneously as many of those agents as they could at nine o'clock on the morning of Sunday, 21 November 1920. Members of the Squad, backed up the various battalions of the Dublin IRA, targeted as many as thirty-five agents. Sixteen of the agents were shot – eleven fatally. Another officer was killed as a result of mistaken identity and two Auxiliaries were taken prisoner and then shot dead, bringing the total dead for the morning to fourteen.

That afternoon the Auxiliaries retaliated blindly, raiding a football game and firing into the crowd, killing fifteen innocent civilians, including one of the footballers on the field. The dead included a ten-year-old boy who was shot in the head, a fourteen-year-old boy, and a young woman who had gone to the game with her fiancée. They were due to marry five days later. Over sixty people required hospital treatment, and eleven of those were detained in hospital.

The day was remembered as Bloody Sunday. The following Sunday seventeen Auxiliaries were killed in the famous Kilmichael ambush in Cork, and another was taken prisoner and killed a couple of days later. Arthur Griffith, the acting president of the Dáil, was arrested and Collins became acting president.

Lloyd George asked Archbishop Patrick J. Clune of Perth, Australia, to contact IRA leaders in Dublin to sound out the prospects for a settlement. The archbishop met Griffith in jail and Collins in a private house. Terms for a ceasefire were agreed but the whole thing fell through because Dublin Castle contended that the IRA was about to collapse, and Sinn Féin vice-president Fr Michael O'Flanagan made some intemperate remarks that were seen as defeatist. The British also learned that de Valera was secretly returning to Ireland. He had planned to stay in the United States for at least another six months, but on hearing that Collins had taken over at home, he decided to return to Ireland immediately. Upon his return he promptly complained to IRA chief of staff Richard Mulcahy that the war was being waged in the wrong way.

'Ye are going too fast,' he told Mulcahy. 'This odd shooting of a policeman here and there is having a very bad effect, from the propaganda point of view, on us in America. What we want is one good battle about once a month with about 500 men on each side.'

It was insensitive to criticise the way the campaign had been run without, at least, waiting to consult a few people. In the following days, de Valera tried to send Collins to the United States, but the Big Fellow refused to go. 'That Long Whoor won't get rid of me as easy as that,' he complained.

But Collins had lost some of his clout at home, not only with the return of de Valera, but also with the uncovering of his main police spies. Kavanagh had died of natural causes, McNamara had been dismissed on suspicion of leaking material, and Ned Broy was arrested after the carbon copies of some of his reports were found among captured documents.

While Collins had targeted selected individuals, de Valera called for battles in which numbers became more important. A distinct rift widened between Collins and Minister for Defence Cathal Brugha, who revived an old plan to target members of the British cabinet.

'This is madness,' Collins thundered when Seán MacEoin told him that Brugha had asked him to lead an attack on the cabinet in London. 'Do you think that England has the makings of only one cabinet?' He told MacEoin to discuss the matter with Mulcahy, who ordered MacEoin to forget about the operation and return to his battalion. On the way back to Longford, MacEoin was arrested, having being wounded in a shoot-out with crown forces.

De Valera was adopting a two-pronged approach in the quest for negotiations with the British. He was encouraging more activity on the part of the IRA, but at the same time, he was speaking in moderate terms to encourage the British to negotiate. Collins appeared to adopt the opposite approach. He deliberately frustrated what he considered the more irrational plans, such as the scheme to kill members of the British cabinet, or engaging 500 members of the IRA in an open battle with the British. But at the same time he adopted a hard-line approach in his public utterances.

In an interview with the American journalist Carl Ackermann in early April, for instance, Collins said the IRA was going to fight on 'until we win'.

'What are your terms of settlement?' Ackermann asked.

'Lloyd George has a chance of showing himself to be a great statesman by recognising the Irish Republic.'

'Do you mean a Republic within the British commonwealth of Nations or outside?' Ackermann asked.

'No, I mean an Irish Republic.'

'Why are you so hopeful?'

'Because I know the strength of our forces and I know our position is infinitely stronger throughout the world,' Collins explained. 'The terror the British wanted to instill in this country has completely broken down. It is only a question of time until we shall have them cleared out.'

'So you are still opposed to compromise?'

'When I saw you before I told you that the same effort which would get us Dominion Home Rule would get us a Republic. I am still of that opinion, and we have never had so many peace moves as we have had since last autumn.' Off the record, Collins indicated that 'he was much more accommodating', according to Ackerman, who noted that Collins had pointedly indicated that 'No one has ever defined a Republic.'

The British concluded there was a power struggle within Sinn Féin in which de Valera was little more than a figurehead, crying in the wilderness for a negotiated settlement, while Collins, the real leader, wanted to fight it out to the bitter end.

'De Valera and Michael Collins have quarrelled,' Lloyd George told his cabinet on 27 April 1921. 'The latter will have a Republic and he carries a gun and he makes it impossible to negotiate. De Valera cannot come here and say he is willing to give up Irish independence, for if he did, he might be shot.'

Lloyd George's government had the greatest majority ever in the House of Commons, but he was drifting into a precarious position. Of course, he was an extremely talented politician. Born in Manchester in 1863, his family promptly moved to north Wales, where he was reared as a native Welsh speaker. He qualified as a lawyer and was elected to parliament as a Liberal in a by-election in April 1890, and he held the seat for fifty-five years. He was appointed to the cabinet in 1905 and served as chancellor of the exchequer from 1908 to 1915. He then became minister for munitions and secretary for war the following year when, with the help of Unionists and Conservatives, he managed to oust prime minister Herbert Asquith and split the Liberal Party into two factions. Lloyd George enjoyed unprecedented popularity following the successful conclusion of the First World War. He would be dubbed as 'the man who won the war', and the 'architect of victory'.

In the first post-war general election in 1918, Lloyd George led the coalition to a massive landslide victory, winning 473 of the 707 seats throughout Great Britain and Ireland, but the abstention of Sinn Féin with its 73 seats, meant the Conservatives with 322 seats, enjoyed an overall majority of their own in parliament.

The coalition's majority was so big that cracks quickly began to appear, as it was a combination of very different ideologies. The traditional wing of the Unionist Party had little desire for reform, and there was a gulf of suspicion between them and Lloyd George's faction of the Liberal Party. The events in Ireland and the behaviour of the Black and Tans raised serious issues.

Following the general election Lloyd George was preoccupied with the peace negotiations in Paris. He had created problems for himself by promising to squeeze the Germans until the pips squeak, but he was unable to command the kind of influence he would have liked at the Peace Conference in the midst of strong personalities like President Woodrow Wilson of the United States and Premier Georges Clemenceau of France. Asked how he felt he had fared in Paris, Lloyd George replied, 'Not badly, considering I was seated between Jesus Christ and Napoleon.' Such irreverence was symptomatic of another problem. The prime minister was having an affair with his secretary, Frances Stevenson, whom he eventually married after his wife's death. Although this affair had not been publicised, it was well known in political circles and did not go down well with the moralistic element in the Conservative Party that included Stanley Baldwin, especially when there were also rumours of growing sleaze with whispers that Lloyd George was selling knighthoods and peerages.

Rather than strengthening his character, his popularity tended to bolster his weaknesses, such as his passions for intrigue and self-assertion, his indifference to principle and his naked manipulation of public opinion by his adroit handling of the press.

He even endorsed the outrageous tactics of the Black and Tans and Auxiliaries by bragging that he had 'murder by the throat'.

Lloyd George had been sending out peace feelers in Ireland since the autumn of 1920, and de Valera encouraged those by suggesting that Ireland would be prepared to satisfy Britain's legitimate security needs. The Big Fellow's approach was clearly unhelpful as far as de Valera was concerned, and he was naturally annoyed. He later told his authorised biographers that from April 1921 onwards, 'Collins did not seem to accept my view of things as he had done before and was inclined to give public expression to his own opinions even when they differed from mine.'

Collins organised a daring rescue attempt after Seán MacEoin was transferred to Mountjoy Jail, but it failed due to an inopportune change in procedures that day. De Valera's advocacy of major battles seem to bear fruit in late May when the IRA launched an attack on the Custom House. As this was the biggest operation since the Easter rebellion, it seemed to make a mockery of British claims that they were winning the war, as they suffered their heaviest casualties that month since the rebellion, but it was something of a pyrrhic victory for the IRA, especially from the perspective of Collins, as the Squad was virtually eradicated with the arrest of most of its members.

Alfred Cope, known to his friends as Andy, had been a detective in the office of customs and excise when he was sent to Ireland as an assistant under-secretary. His real function was to act as a kind a secret envoy on behalf of Lloyd George, making contact with Sinn Féin leaders as part of a peace initiative. He met with Fr Michael O'Flanagan, Sinn Féin vice-president, and Bishop Michael Fogarty, a strong Sinn Féin supporter, and he even met with Michael Collins. He also arranged meetings between de Valera and Lord Derby in April 1921 and with Sir James Craig the following month.

Cope had talks with senior republicans in Mountjoy Jail, such as Arthur Griffith, Eamonn Duggan and Eoin MacNeill, and he was instrumental in securing their release from prison, along with the release of Desmond Fitzgerald and Robert Barton. He also arranged the release of Erskine Childers, the editor of the *Irish Bulletin*, following his arrest. Cope actually met with Childers while he was being held at Dublin Castle on 9 May 1921. A couple of weeks later when British intelligence raided Collins' finance office in Mary Street, they found a letter from Childers informing Collins of the 'settlement outlined to me by Cope in the Castle a week ago'. Childers noted that Cope 'is probably a good actor, but his ostensible attitude was one of almost feverish anxiety to get something done and the business over'.

The assistant under-secretary's efforts to initiate a negotiated settlement were bitterly resented by the military. One British officer noted that Cope was 'universally detested by everyone in the Castle, it being generally supposed that he was going to sell us all to the rebels'.

Sir John Anderson, the under-secretary for Ireland, warned assistant under-secretary Mark Sturgis that if Cope succeeded in persuading Lloyd George to talk with Sinn Féin that the British military might 'upset the apple cart not because they want to but out of a mixture of personal pride, soldierly prejudice and downright stupidity'.

After the events in Dublin and the heavy crown losses during May, Sir Neville Macready, the general officer in charge of British forces in Ireland, argued that the British had to change their policy in Ireland. If Sinn Féin did not accept the new southern parliament by the deadline of 14 July, he suggested that as many as a hundred men a week should be executed, and that the government could not turn around and say 'this cannot go on' after the first week. 'The Cabinet must understand that any man found with revolvers or bombs would be shot at once,' he said. Sir Maurice Hankey, the chief cabinet secretary, told Lloyd George that General Macready asked him if the cabinet would go through with the coercion.

'Will they begin to howl when they hear of our shooting a hundred men a week?' Macready asked. Maybe his argument was just designed as shock treatment to force the cabinet to think seriously about changing its Irish policy. The Irish Situation Committee of the cabinet was warned on 15 June that it has to be 'all out or get out'.

'Military action to be effective must be vigorous and ruthless,' Anderson told Chief Secretary Hamar Greenwood. 'Dreadful things must happen. Many innocent people must inevitably suffer and the element of human error cannot be eliminated.' He added that resorting to such all-out coercion without the full support of parliament and the country would be 'the wildest folly'.

Collins learned that the British had decided to declare martial law throughout the twenty-six counties and intensify their campaign. British forces, which would be trebled, would intensify their operations, especially their searches and internment. 'All means of transport, from push bicycles up, will be commandeered, and allowed only on permit,' he warned de Valera.

On 24 June de Valera was arrested and Austin Stack was designated to take over from him as acting president. It was Collins who had taken over the previous November, following the arrest of Griffith, so he was obviously being relegated.

At this point Cope succeeded in persuading the British cabinet, which was already shaken by doubts shown by the scenario outlined by Macready, to try to negotiate with the Irish first. 'No British government in modern times has appeared to make so complete and sudden a reversal of policy,' Churchill noted.

Cope organised de Valera's prompt release and asked him to make himself available for a letter from Lloyd George. Cope actually brought this letter from Downing Street. It was an invitation to de Valera and anyone he wished to accompany him to London for discussions with representatives of the British government and Sir James Craig, the new prime minister of Northern Ireland.

Cope arranged for Jan C. Smuts, the South African prime minister, to visit Dublin for secret talks with the president on 5 July 1921.

Chapter One

'I MEAN TO MAKE THEM RESPONSIBLE'

Part of the aim in having Prime Minister Jan C. Smuts of South Africa come to Ireland was for him to get an idea of the kind of peace settlement that Sinn Féin leaders desired, so that he could pass on the information to Lloyd George. De Valera explained that before there could be any talks with the British, there would have to be a truce, and he insisted that he would not take part in three-way talks that included Craig.

'What do you propose as a solution of the Irish question?' Smuts asked

'A republic,' de Valera replied.

'Do you really think that the British people are ever likely to agree to such a republic?'

Such a status was so desirable, de Valera explained, the Irish side would agree to be bound by treaty limitations guaranteeing Britain's legitimate security needs, but he emphasised they would not be prepared to accept any limitations on dominion status. In short, he insisted the Irish people should have the choice between a 'republic plus treaty limitations and dominion status without limitations'.

'We want a free choice,' de Valera emphasised. 'Not a choice where the alternative is force. We must not be bullied into a decision.'

'The British people will never give you this choice,' Smuts replied. 'You are next door to them.' He then talked about the difficulties in South Africa following the Boer War and noted that when the people were subsequently asked if they wanted a republic, 'a very large majority' preferred free partnership with the British empire. 'As a friend,' Smuts added, 'I cannot advise you too strongly against a republic. Ask what you want but not a republic.'

'If the status of dominion rule is offered,' de Valera replied, 'I will use all our machinery to get the Irish people to accept it.'

Smuts reported on his Irish visit to a cabinet-level meeting in London next day. It was decided to accede to de Valera's demands for a truce, and it was left to him to take the initiative for Craig's exclusion. He did this by agreeing to meet the prime minister to discuss 'on what basis such a conference as that proposed can reasonably hope to achieve peace'.

Robert Barton, one of those recently released from jail in order to promote the peace initiative, helped to conclude what he called 'an armed truce. It was, as I understood, agreed to by our side for one reason only, mainly to enable the volunteers to rearm and equip,' he explained. 'I was one of those who negotiated it.'

William Darling, who later became chancellor of Edinburgh University, was serving as Major-General Tudor's secretary in Dublin Castle at the time. He recalled a strange incident one night before the Truce when he was sent out to collect a 'high official' following an accident in Newry. A police car was in collision with the vehicle containing the official. When Darling arrived at the scene he found a group of men standing around with the official. They had been going from Belfast to Dublin, and they piled into Darling's car.

Collins got into the front with Darling and the driver. He could feel the gun that Darling was carrying. 'Are you carrying a gun?' Collins asked.

'I am.'

He then guessed at Darling's name but was wrong, so he said he was one of two other people. This time he was right.

'Do you know me?'

'No,' Darling replied. 'I think I know your friends, but I don't know you.'

'I am Michael Collins.'

'Are you the Michael Collins whom the British police have made famous?'

'What do you mean by that?'

'A police force has a duty to apprehend criminals,' Darling explained. 'If they fail to apprehend criminals one defence is to say that the criminal whom they cannot apprehend is the most astute, remarkable, astonishing criminal in history, and so I say: "Are you Michael Collins whom the British police force have made famous?"'

Collins laughed at that. They talked on the way to Dublin and they were driven to 'an hotel in one of Dublin's squares'. The official went into the hotel with the other two, while Collins and Darling followed and had a couple of bottles of stout and chatted together until the official was ready to leave.

'That was an astonishing thing meeting Michael Collins,' Darling remarked when they got into the car.

'What do you mean?' the official asked.

'You knew that was Michael Collins with whom I sat in the car?'

The man rushed back into the hotel, but Collins was not there. Darling did not identify the official, but it may well have been Cope, because very shortly afterwards, just before the Truce came into effect, Cope and Collins met. Tim Kennedy, who had worked for Collins in Dublin and was the intelligence officer in charge of the Kerry No. 1 Brigade of the IRA, was in Dublin to meet with Collins. He called to Vaughan's Hotel in Parnell Square. Christy Harte, the porter, was rather drunk and he called Collins out to meet Kennedy as he had a companion with him. Collins brought the two of them in.

'When we got inside the door in the hall he told me the

war was over and Sir Alfred Cope of the Castle was in the room to which he was taking me and that I wasn't to disclose anything to him and his two bodyguards. Collins introduced Kennedy under an assumed name to Cope and the two RIC head constables accompanying him. One of the head constables had actually been stationed in Castleisland, County Kerry, so he and Kennedy recognised each other immediately.

'Mick again announced about the Truce', and they drank brandy and champagne to celebrate it. 'Cope and I got talking and we discussed the troubled times,' Kennedy noted. 'I was regretting it was over and said I enjoyed it. Both Cope and I and Mick kept drinking glass after glass and Mick pretended to be drunk but I discovered afterwards he was drinking some coloured liquid.' Kennedy said that he and Cope passed out, and Collins arranged for Kennedy to be taken back to his hotel in a taxi. 'I awoke that evening in a bed fully clothed, with the taxi driver, also fully clothed, outside me,' Kennedy continued. 'Apparently he was warned by Mick to look after me and to stay with me 'til he knew that I was all right and over the shock of the war ending.'

The Truce came into effect at noon on 11 July. The terms were the subject of an honourable understanding with no signed, formal agreement. In the following months each side tended to interpret the terms differently, even though there was a remarkable similarity in their understanding of the Truce. De Valera issued instructions to the IRA to cease all attacks on crown forces and civilians, to prohibit the use of arms, to cease military manoeuvres, to abstain from interference with public and private property, and to avoid any disturbances of the peace that might necessitate military interference.

De Valera selected a delegation consisting of four cabinet colleagues, Griffith, Stack, Count George N. Plunkett and Robert Barton, as well as Erskine Childers, the acting minister for propaganda, to accompany him, along with a number of others.

On the evening of the Truce Kathleen O'Connell noted that 'Collins called out this evening and spent several hours with the President'. He tried to insist on his own inclusion in the team going to London, but the president flatly refused to have him, saying that he feared the negotiations 'might end in a stalemate and that war might be resumed, so he saw no reason why photographers should, at this stage, be given too many opportunities of taking pictures of Collins'. They had an acrimonious meeting, with the Big Fellow refusing to accept the explanation because, for one thing, it could not be squared with de Valera's attempt to send him to the United States earlier in the year. 'Hot discussion,' Kathleen noted. 'President rather upset.'

Having been demoted in favour of Stack of all people, Collins was now being ignored for peripheral figures like Laurence O'Neill, the lord mayor of Dublin, and the Dáil deputy, Robert Farnan, who had been invited along with his wife. In addition, there were two secretaries, Kathleen O'Connell and Lily O'Brennan. The delegation set up headquarters at the Grosvenor Hotel, but de Valera and Kathleen stayed with the Farnans in a private house acquired for them.

It was in the context of these events that Collins wrote the opening words of this foreword about the ill will among members of the Dáil. He was clearly despondent.

'I think you would be warned of the changes here,' he wrote to Harry Boland in the United States some days later. 'There's something about [them] which I don't like, and I have the impression that the whole thing is pressing on me. I find myself looking at friends as if they were enemies – looking at them twice just to make sure that they really are friends after all. I mention no names. After all it may be a wrong impression that's got into me. Frankly, though, I don't care for things as they are now.'

Prior to his arrest in February 1920 'all members of the Cabinet were, as far as I knew, fast friends with complete trust in one another,' Robert Barton noted. 'There was not a sign of disunion, suspicion or ill feeling. I verily believe that had the occasion arisen each of us would have given his life for any other member without a thought. We acted like a one-man team. If we disagreed it was upon matters of detail rather than of policy or principle. Every member appeared to have implicit faith in the integrity of his comrades.'

'Seventeen months later when I returned from imprisonment a great change had come over relationships in the cabinet,' Barton added. 'Michael Collins whom I knew best, for we had worked together every evening in Cullenswood House for more than 6 months, told me that efforts were being made to get rid of him as he and Richard Mulcahy were distrusted by Cathal Brugha and Stack. I soon found this to be true.' Barton found he had difficulty meeting other cabinet colleagues. 'All ministers were too busy with their own departments to meet except for cabinet meetings or when necessity required.' He had 'practically no acquaintance' with either Austin Stack, or W. T. Cosgrave, and he had never even met Kevin O'Higgins before. The cabinet was apparently split. 'There was an obvious rift between Brugha and Stack on one side and Collins and Griffith on the other,' according to Barton. As he saw it IRA chief of staff Dick Mulcahy was 'at loggerheads' with Defence Minister Cathal Brugha, with 'Collins obviously supporting Mulcahy' and 'Stack supporting Brugha'. In fact, the real rift was between Brugha and Collins, with Mulcahy being drawn into the vortex because of his support of Collins.

'I tried to discover from Collins what was the root cause of his antipathy to Brugha,' Barton wrote. 'I failed but learned that he bore resentment to Dev also for the impartial attitude he adopted regarding this quarrel with Brugha. Brugha was, I consider, a difficult man to work with. A man of iron will and scrupulous honesty he often argued fiercely over details that were of little moment and in a manner that was at times offensive though generally unintentionally so. At every meeting Dev exercised self-control and patience that filled me with admiration in his endeavours to prevent an open rupture between Brugha, Collins, Stack and Griffith. Brugha had, I believe, always distrusted Griffith as a Republican.'

Barton would later come to the conclusion that the rift with Collins was at least partly the result of the Big Fellow's 'effort to control the national movement through the IRB of which he was the leader'. The IRB had been 'strengthening its hold upon the Volunteers by appointing its nominees to all the important positions in the Army as vacancies occurred through capture or casualties'.

'De Valera on all occasions played the role of peacemaker and I endeavoured to support him,' Barton added. 'I never spoke to him alone and knew as little about him as I did of my other colleagues.' Barton concluded that his lack of familiarity with cabinet colleagues was partly the result of the circumstances of being in jail for so long, but it was also partly due to his own upbringing as a member of the Protestant landowning class, who were generally unionist in outlook. He had worked with Collins, but their relationship was tempered more by the 'risks to which we were subjected than by temperamental affinity'.

Barton was obviously more sympathetic to de Valera than to Collins, as he was clearly not impressed with the manner in which the Big Fellow was critical of the president. Barton held de Valera in enormous regard. 'He is a patriot without personal ambition,' Barton wrote. 'A supremely honest and conscientious leader.' The faults of other leaders were conspicuously lacking in de Valera.

In the light of history it was absurd to suggest that de Valera had no personal ambition. He grew up as an unwanted child with enormous ambition. He had a driving need to be recognised as somebody, and this was a significant factor in his difficulties in the United States, where he admitted that his problems were largely the result of his personal determination to block Daniel Cohalan, unless the judge was prepared to consult him first. De Valera would demonstrate his ambition by serving as head of government more than twice as long as any other Irish leader in the twentieth century. He also served as chancellor of the National University from 1919 to his death in 1975.

Collins had a different kind of appeal. On Tuesday night, 12 July 1921, Collins sent a message to Brigid Lyons to arrange for him to accompany her to see Seán MacEoin in Mountjoy Jail the following afternoon. He entered the prison with her under the name of James Gill.

'It was a joy to see Seán MacEoin's surprise when he saw Mick Collins walk into Mountjoy that day,' according to Brigid. 'Seán just greeted him as a visitor but there was no hiding his inner delight.'

'I don't know how to explain to you how grateful I am to you for your visit yesterday,' MacEoin wrote to Brigid next day. 'My old heart beat high with joy and all I could do was stare and murmur to myself "Thank God". I am sure you understand how I felt.

'I will be forever grateful to you for that visit,' he continued. 'Never were you so welcome and that welcome will always remain so long as I remain.'

There was no doubting the intensity of MacEoin's appreciation at the gesture by Collins. Part of the loyalty that Collins attracted was prompted by the sense of caring that he generated. Men believed that he was really concerned about them as individuals and that he would go to extraordinary lengths to try to help them.

Even though de Valera brought a whole delegation with him to London, he essentially suggested that he and Lloyd George should meet privately. 'For my own part,' he wrote to the prime minister on 13 July, 'I am quite ready, if you prefer it, to meet you alone.'

Lloyd George would almost inevitably have preferred such a meeting because, despite his personal popularity, he was in a virtually unique position of political weakness. He was in a coalition with the Conservative Party, which had traditionally been opposed to even Home Rule for Ireland, but unlike any normal coalition, the Conservatives actually enjoyed an overwhelming majority in parliament. Thus, they could bring down the government at will and they had the numbers to form a government on their own.

De Valera had the first of four private meetings with Lloyd George at 10 Downing Street on the afternoon of 14 July. Immediately afterwards the prime minister dictated a note to his private secretary, Edward Grigg, indicating that de Valera had been more inclined to listen than he had expected and had 'listened well'. The same evening, however, he gave a very different account to another secretary, Geoffrey Shakespeare, as the latter drove him to an official dinner.

'I listened to a long lecture on the wrongs done to Ireland starting with Cromwell, and when I tried to bring him to the present day back he went to Cromwell again,' the prime minister said. 'It reminded me of a circus roundabout when I was a boy. I used to sit on a rocking horse that raced round and round after the horse in front, and when the roundabout came to rest I was still the same distance from the horse in front as when I started. That's how I ended with de Valera.'

Lloyd George, of course, was not renowned for his honesty. The account dictated to Grigg was probably the more accurate, because on this occasion de Valera had come to listen, but it was the fanciful version given to Shakespeare which found credence and would come back to haunt de Valera in later years.

From the outset of the talks the Irish leader's aim was to show as little of his own hand as possible while trying to get the British to make some definite proposals. 'You will be glad to know that I am not dissatisfied with the general situation,' he wrote to Collins after a second meeting next day. Lloyd George had indicated he would be making a definite offer.

'The proposal will be theirs,' de Valera explained. 'We will be free to consider it without prejudice.'

'You confirm exactly what I was thinking about,' Collins replied in a letter exuding his own arrogant temperament next day. 'Apart from the little unpleasant things on Monday evening, have you got some little value from the talk?' he asked.

He did not record his advice to de Valera, but there can be little doubt that the Big Fellow did not take the president's advice about keeping a low profile himself. 'I have made millions of discoveries,' Collins wrote. 'For instance, their civilian and military heads have said that it would not be wise for Michael Collins to appear too publicly.' He was therefore determined to go right into the lion's den by requesting permission to visit his brother in the internment camp on Spike Island in Cork harbour.

'They said they could not be responsible for my safety in the Martial Law area, which means that they could not and would not be responsible for my non-safety,' he continued. 'The whole thing is an effort on their part to make us believe that they have irresponsible forces. My effort, of course, is the very contrary, and it will be seen later how I mean to make them responsible.'

Although Collins realised the British were unlikely to make an acceptable offer at such an early stage, he warned de Valera not to reject the proposals without allowing the Dáil to consider them. This would afford the Irish side the opportunity of demanding the release of all imprisoned members of the Dáil so that they – the democratically elected representatives of the people – could consider the offer. Several deputies had already been released since the Truce, but Collins was particularly anxious to secure the release of Seán MacEoin, who was under sentence of death. 'No matter how bad the terms are,' Collins wrote to de Valera, 'they would be submitted to a full meeting' of the Dáil.

Rather than adopt a low profile, Collins deliberately kept himself in the news. He had the Republican Publicity Bureau disclose that a literary agent in Southampton had offered him £10,000 for his memoirs.

'Sorry I cannot comply,' Collins responded. 'The time is not yet opportune, but as your offer reached me first, I shall at some time give you the offer of the first refusal.'

De Valera had a third meeting with Lloyd George on 18 July. The prime minister began by observing that the notepaper on which de Valera had written to him was headed 'Saorstát Éireann', which literally translated as 'Free State of Ireland'.

What did *Saorstát* mean? Lloyd George asked.

'Free state,' replied de Valera.

'Yes,' remarked the prime minister, 'but what is the Irish word for republic?'

De Valera was taken aback. Although his own command of the Irish language was not nearly as complete as he liked to pretend to non-speakers, he must have known that the leaders of the Easter Rebellion had used the term *Phoblacht na hÉireann* (Republic of Ireland), but he now played dumb, possibly because he had no convincing explanation as to why the original term had been dropped and *Saorstát* adopted instead in 1919.

'Must we not admit that the Celts never were Republicans and have no native word for such an idea!' Lloyd George exclaimed triumphantly. He was content that *Saorstát Éireann* could be used in any agreement, provided the literal translation – Irish Free State – was used. He promised to send settlement proposals to de Valera before their next meeting.

There was widespread press speculation at this stage about de Valera's willingness to compromise, which was hardly surprising after he had spent six months making conciliatory public statements. *Le Matin*, the Paris newspaper, now quoted him as having supposedly said he would drop the word republic provided Ireland was given 'the substantial equivalent' to it. This was no doubt a leak inspired by somebody close to the talks, but de Valera denied making the statement or anything like it. 'The press give the impression that I have been making compromise demands,' he said. 'I have made no demands but one – the only one I am entitled to make – that the self-determination of the Irish nation be recognised.'

Sir James Craig, the prime minister of Northern Ireland, jumped on this to proclaim that the six counties had already exercised a right of self-determination to separate from the rest of the island and were not therefore involved in the London talks. 'It now merely remains for de Valera and the British people to come to terms regarding the area outside of that which I am Prime Minister,' Craig said.

The formal British proposals, which were delivered to the Irish delegation on the night of 20 July, offered the twenty-six counties a form of dominion status, limited by defence restrictions curtailing the size of the Irish army, prohibiting a navy, and according Britain the right to obtain whatever military or naval facilities might be desired in time of a war or international crisis. The proposals also included an insistence on free trade between Britain and Ireland, as well as a stipulation that the new Irish state should 'allow for full recognition of the existing powers and privileges of the parliament of Northern Ireland, which cannot be abrogated except by their own consent'.

That day Collins returned to Clonakilty. He reported that the local Black and Tans were very provocative and he essentially warned them off. 'I had it conveyed to them that if they were on the streets when I got out, they would be regarded as breaking the Truce.' He added that they were not there 'a few minutes afterwards'.

Collins did not yet know what was in the British offer but 'in the final result,' he wrote to de Valera, 'it would be worthwhile stipulating that, no matter how bad the terms are, they would be submitted to a full meeting. You know my object in this.' His aim, of course, was to be in a position to demand the release of all members of the Dáil so that the offer could be properly considered.

On discussing the British terms with Lloyd George next day, de Valera indicated a willingness to accept unfettered dominion status, as he had in his discussion with Smuts a fortnight earlier in Dublin and with various journalists earlier in the year, but he complained that the latest proposals did not even amount to an offer of dominions status, because the restrictive conditions meant that Ireland would have an inferior status to existing dominions like Canada and South Africa.

'The British Dominions have been conceded to them all the rights that Irish Republicans demand,' de Valera had told *Manchester Guardian* back in February 1921. 'It is obvious that if these rights were not being denied to us we would not be engaged in the present struggle.'

Now he told Lloyd George that he would agree to 'the status of a dominion *sans phrase*, on condition that Northern Ireland would agree to be represented within the all-Ireland parliament', according to the prime minister. 'Otherwise, de Valera insisted that the only alternative was for the twenty-six counties to be a republic.'

'This means war,' Lloyd George warned.

But de Valera was not intimidated. He became quite dismissive of the British proposals. At one point he actually said he would not 'be seen taking these things home'. That stunned the prime minister, who threatened to publish the proposals, even though it had earlier been agreed that neither side would do so without the prior approval of the other.

'Aren't you going to give me a considered reply?' Lloyd George asked.

'I'll give you a considered reply if you keep your part of the bargain.' If the British desired counter proposals in the form of a considered reply, they would have to wait for them and keep their own offer secret in the meantime. With that de Valera departed, leaving the British document behind him. He later sent word to Downing Street to forward the proposals to him in Dublin. In effect, he not only called Lloyd George's bluff but also made good his own threat not to be seen carrying the proposals home with him.

The British had used Smuts to sound out de Valera before the Truce, and now the Long Fellow used the South African prime minister to reinforce his rejection of the British terms. 'I was greatly disappointed with the British government's proposals,' de Valera wrote to Smuts. 'They seem quite unable to understand the temper of our people, or appear not to have the will to realise the opportunity that is now presented to them.'

While de Valera was in London, Collins had engaged in an amount of posturing, and the Long Fellow promptly demonstrated that he was not about to allow himself to be upstaged. Upon his return to Dublin he spoke briefly at a reception at the Mansion House.

'This is not the time for talk,' de Valera told the gathering. 'We have learned one magnificent lesson in the last couple of years, and that is that it is by acts, and not talk, that a nation will achieve its freedom.' The gathering cheered. 'I do not want, therefore, to begin a bad example by starting speech-making. If we act in the future as we have acted in the last couple of years, we will never have to talk about freedom, for we will have it.'

'There is, I fear, little chance of his counter-proposals being satisfactory,' Lloyd George wrote to King George V, 'but I am absolutely confident that we shall have public opinion overwhelmingly upon our side throughout the Empire and even in the United States when our proposals are published.'

The British proposals were a significant advance on anything previously offered to Ireland, so de Valera had to tread carefully. Unless the Irish people were given some alternative other than 'continuing the war for maintenance of the Republic', he later admitted, 'I felt certain that the majority of the people would be weaned from us.' Hence he had to come up with an alternative for which the Irish people would be prepared to fight.

Chapter Two

'FREE TO CONSIDER EVERY METHOD'

The Dáil cabinet gathered in a front room of the Mansion House. De Valera sat at the head of a table facing Dawson Street, while Cathal Brugha was at the foot of the table. Arthur Griffith was on the president's left with Joe McDonagh beside him, while Austin Stack, Robert Barton and Erskine Childers sat on a lounge chair withdrawn from the table, with Eoin MacNeill next on a chair partly facing the president. Richard Mulcahy came next, while J. J. O'Kelly (Sceilg) and Countess Markievicz sat behind Brugha on another lounge chair facing de Valera, and Collins, who came in late, sat partially facing the president on a seat alongside Kevin O'Higgins. Then came Ernest Blythe, W. T. Cosgrave and Count Plunkett sitting well back from the table. Diarmuid O'Hegarty, the cabinet secretary, sat between them and de Valera.

De Valera hoped to persuade all concerned to agree to a settlement in which Britain would acknowledge Ireland's freedom and the Irish people would then freely accept the same *de facto* status as the dominions, without formally being a member of the British commonwealth. He had not yet worked this out fully in his own mind when he presented his idea to the cabinet. He had not even thought of a name for the plan.

It was a thorny meeting at which 'elements of friction were already manifest', according to J. J. O'Kelly, the minister for education. Things were not helped by de Valera's poor chairmanship. His cabinet meetings lacked discipline. Instead of considering one thing at a time, he tended to deal with everything together in the hope of reaching a general consensus. This would have been extremely difficult at the best of times, but it was almost impossible in a cabinet of eleven headstrong ministers, who were often joined by obstinate understudies. As a result the discussions tended to ramble and they were often quite inconclusive. Ministers frequently came away with conflicting opinions about the outcome of discussions.

Griffith and W. T. Cosgrave said the British offer was better than they had expected and MacNeill welcomed it. 'You all know my opinion,' said Collins, who nevertheless described the British proposals as 'a step forward', but Stack was very critical. Childers was also hostile. O'Kelly suggested that relevant documents should be circulated so that everyone could give the issues more consideration, and Constance Markievicz, the minister for labour, agreed with him.

Brugha sat silently until de Valera asked him for his views after everyone else had spoken. A normally quiet, reserved man, he nevertheless had definite views and did not believe in mincing words. Resolute and utterly fearless, he was prone to obstinacy. When he spoke everybody knew exactly where he stood.

'I haven't much to add,' Brugha now said, looking straight at de Valera, 'except to say how glad I am that it has been suggested that we circulate these documents and consider them fully before we meet again, if for no other reason than to give you and the great masters of English you keep at your elbow an opportunity of extricating us from the morass in which ye have landed us.'

'We have done our best,' de Valera replied, 'and I have never undertaken to do more than my best.'

'We have proclaimed a Republic in arms,' Brugha reminded him. 'It has been ratified by the votes of the people, and we have sworn to defend it with our lives.'

'The oath never conveyed any more to me than to do my best in whatever circumstances might arise.'

'You have accepted a position of authority and responsibility in the Government of the Republic,' Brugha said striking the table with his fist, 'and you will discharge the duties of that office as they have been defined. I do not want ever again to hear anything else from you.'

The meeting adjourned shortly afterwards and did not resume until two days later. By this time de Valera had decided to call his plan External Association. He presented his colleagues with a memorandum arguing that 'the Irish people would be ready to attach themselves as an external associate to that partial league known as the British Commonwealth of Nations'. With this he overcame Brugha's objections, and the members of the government unanimously agreed that External Association would be acceptable.

The president sought to use the South African Premier Smuts to explain his position to the British. 'Unless the North East comes in on some reasonable basis no further progress can be made,' he wrote. 'An Ireland in fragments nobody cares about. A unified Ireland can only be happy or prosperous.' He added that the country could readily become friendly with the British commonwealth and Britain itself, 'but it is only in freedom that friendship could come,' he said. 'To the principle of national self-determination our people are devotedly attached, for they recognise in it a principle vital to the peace of the world. The Republic is the expression of that principle in their own regard. These then they will not readily abandon, but they are prepared to make great sacrifices in other directions.'

In the light of what subsequently happened, de Valera added a very pertinent observation. 'The questions of procedure and form as distinguished from substance are very important, as I pointed out to you,' he wrote. 'The British do not seem to realise this at all.'

He had already indicated to both Smuts and Lloyd George that he was prepared to accept the real status of a British dominion, but this did not mean that he would accept dominion status – this was what he meant by the distinction between form and substance. In form the dominions were subject to the British crown, but they were substantially independent. In accordance with External Association, Ireland would be formally independent but it would assume the same substantial responsibilities of the dominions. He was hoping that Smuts would try to influence the British, but the South African leader decided to return home.

Although Collins had been showing moderation within the government, he remained uncompromising in public. Indeed he made another of his unauthorised pronouncements on 8 August when the British announced the release of all members of the Dáil with the exception of MacEoin. Without consulting with the president, Collins issued a statement warning 'there can and will be, no meeting of Dáil Éireann unless and until Commandant Seán MacEoin is released. The refusal to release him appears to indicate a desire on the part of the British government to terminate the Truce.' It was a gross piece of arrogance to issue such a statement without even consulting the president.

De Valera said he was hoping to work quietly behind the scenes, believing it would be easier to secure the prisoner's release if the British were not forced to back down publicly, but Collins' intervention destroyed any chance of this. The president therefore declared publicly that he could 'not accept responsibility for proceeding further in the negotiations' unless MacEoin was freed. The British cabinet promptly backed down and released him.

De Valera essentially acted with the same disregard for the Dáil that Collins displayed towards him. In view of the fuss kicked up over the MacEoin affair, it was ironic that de Valera did not bother to consult the Dáil before formally rejecting the British offer. 'On the occasion of our last interview,' he wrote to Lloyd George on 10 August 1921, 'I gave it as my judgment that Dáil Éireann could not and the Irish people would not accept the proposals of your Government. I now confirm that judgment.' But the Dáil had not even met, and did not convene until the following week when it was presented with a *fait accompli* and simply asked to endorse this reply.

At the time the Dáil was composed largely of people selected by the leadership of Sinn Féin to represent the party. Since independent thinkers could be difficult to handle, the individuals selected were those who would give unquestioning support to party leaders. As a result all initiative was invariably left in the hands of the few recognised leaders. The general body of the Dáil approved decisions rather blindly and took much for granted. As one member observed, 'nothing could well be less democratic in practice than the government which we recognised as the government of the Irish Republic'.

In his letter to the prime minister, de Valera stated that the restrictive conditions proposed for Ireland were unheard of in the case of the dominions. 'A certain treaty of free association with the British commonwealth group, as with a partial league of nations, we would be ready to recommend,' he wrote, 'had we an assurance that the entry of the nation as a whole in such an association would secure it the allegiance of the present dissenting minority, to meet whose sentiments alone this step could be contemplated.' The Irish factions would settle partition among themselves without resorting to force, if the British would just stand aside. 'We agree with you,' he added, '"that no common action can be secured by force".'

Back in 1918 de Valera had concluded that the British undermined the Irish Convention by assuring Ulster Unionists that they would not be coerced. Bolstered by the assurance, unionists insisted on having their own way and, when the nationalists balked, the convention inevitably ended in failure. 'It was evident to us,' de Valera wrote shortly after the convention, that 'with the "coercion of Ulster is unthinkable" guarantee, the unionists would solidly maintain their original position.' Thus when he gave Lloyd George a similar assurance on 10 August 1921, he was obviously accepting that some form of partition would be a part of any settlement.

Following de Valera's formal rejection of their proposals on 10 August, the British decided to publish their offer 'because of the importance of ranging on the side of our proposals all sane opinion, not merely in this country and in Ireland, but throughout the whole world'. Austen Chamberlain, the Conservative leader, was sure that the government would have popular support. 'I feel confident that nothing but the most extreme opinion will support an attitude of refusal on their part,' he noted.

The reaction of the British press justified his optimism, and the cabinet was satisfied. *The Times* noted that the terms represented 'the extreme limit of concession to which the British people is likely to allow this Government or, indeed, any other British Government, to go', while the *Daily Telegraph* observed that the offer might even be too generous. 'If Lloyd George should appeal to the country on the basis of the published correspondence between de Valera and himself and General Smuts, he will win hands down,' the *New Statesman* concluded. 'And he will gain a mandate.'

The Dáil convened in the Round Room of the Mansion House on the morning of 16 August 1921. The hall was crammed as de Valera entered ceremoniously, followed by the rest of his ministry in Indian file. The gathering rose to give them a rapturous welcome.

The president sat facing the general body as the speaker read out the republican oath in Irish, allowing the deputies to repeat it after him. For some, including de Valera, it was the first time they took the oath, obliging them to 'support and defend the Irish Republic, which is Dáil Éireann, against all enemies, foreign and domestic'.

For many of the press this would be their first glimpse of Collins. Bertie Smyllie of *The Irish Times* remembered the previous October when he was sitting in a Dublin restaurant with a friend who seemed to know everybody. 'Suddenly I noticed that my companion had turned very pale.'

'Don't look round yet,' his friend whispered, 'Michael Collins has just come in.'

'I could not resist the temptation to have a look at the elusive "Mike". The man to whom my friend referred was small, thin, with mouse-coloured hair, and looked rather like a jockey. What he lacked in physique, however, he made up in facial ferocity, for a more villainous looking individual I never saw.'

'Are you sure that he is Collins?' Smyllie asked.

'Of course, don't I know him well?'

'For nearly a year, therefore, I guarded the guilty secret of having been within touching distance of the most badly "wanted" man in Ireland,' Smyllie continued. But now he was about to learn the truth.

'I scanned the assembly in vain for the gentleman of the restaurant. None of the members resembled him in the very least, and I was just beginning to be afraid that Collins was a myth after all, when the Clerk of the House began to call the roll by constituencies. As Collins was the only member present who had been elected from Antrim or Armagh, he was the first person to answer the roll call.

'Here was no emaciated little jockey-man, furtive of eye, and hang-dog of look. A big, burly, broad shouldered individual with a shock of pitch-black hair and a broad smile, walked across the floor and signed the register. All my preconceived ideas were shattered. I could not have been more completely taken aback if the Moderator of the General Assembly had answered to that name.

'At first sight Collins is decidedly disappointing. He does not look a bit like a mystery man. And the stories we used to hear about him! One, I remember was that he had slipped up a chimney to escape arrest. I should like to see that chimney, for

Collins does not weigh an ounce under fourteen stone. He is of more than average height, although you would not describe him as tall. He face is round and somewhat O'Connellesque, with a sharpish nose and a largely mobile mouth. A phrenologist would give him good marks for his head, and he has a fine pair of eyes, which are well set off by arching brows. One misses that aggressive firmness that hits you when you look at Mr Arthur Griffith. Collins can be firm enough when he pleases, but it is impulse rather than resolution that makes him dig his heels into the ground.'

A special correspondent of *The Irish Times* wrote that Collins 'gave one the impression of an almost Falstaffian geniality. Unless his looks belie him, Collins has an abundant sense of humour.'

Eamon de Valera delivered a short presidential address. 'Speaking with great emphasis and obvious sincerity, de Valera soared into the realms of pure theory and lofty idealism,' according to *The Irish Times* correspondent. It reminded one reporter of Woodrow Wilson's famous speech at the opening of the Paris Peace Conference in January 1919. 'One had the same impression of moral fervour and passionate sincerity and the same unwelcome convictions that disillusionment lay in store,' the correspondent noted. 'As a shrewd observer of human affairs remarked on that occasion when the American President resumed his seat: "*C'est magnifique*; but it is not hard tacks".'

Speaking off the cuff de Valera caused a bit of a stir when he talked about the unmistakable answer given by the people in the recent general election. 'I do not say that the answer was for a form of government so much, because we are not Republican doctrinaires,' he said, 'but it was for Irish freedom and Irish independence, and it was obvious to everyone who considered the question that Irish independence could not be realised in any other way so suitably as through a Republic.' Yet he had indicated to both Smuts and Lloyd George that the unfettered status of the dominions would be acceptable.

'Great numbers of people were not Republicans,' Robert Barton explained. 'They were sympathetic but not sincere Republicans. They suffered willingly and gave the Republican leadership enthusiastic support because public opinion and patriotism demanded it and because the Irish Army could punish as well as the English. But the resistance of the people was measured by the resistance of the leaders. To the outside observer the demand for complete independence may have appeared to spring from the people; in reality the people were infused by the leaders and the strength of the National demand.'

In a further speech the next day, 17 August, de Valera elaborated by emphasising his personal readiness to compromise on partition and defence, as well as on the issue of association with the British commonwealth. 'I would be willing to suggest to the Irish people to give up a good deal in order to have an Ireland that could look to the future without anticipating distracting internal problems,' he said. The unionists in the six counties were 'Irishmen living in Ireland', so he would be prepared to give up a lot to win them over. 'We are ready,' he emphasised, 'to make sacrifices we could never think of making for Britain.'

The main demands made by the British in the July proposals related to membership of the British commonwealth and defensive measures. De Valera openly indicated a distinct willingness to compromise. 'We are never likely to complete with Britain in armaments,' he said. 'Therefore, we have no hesitation in entering into any agreement on the limitation of armaments, provided it is obvious that they intend it for that good and wise purpose, and not simply for the purpose of disarming us or making us helpless.'

Since the British described their relations with the dominions as 'free and friendly co-operation', he intimated that such a relationship would be acceptable. 'The cooperation of the British dominions is free,' he told the Dáil. 'They have said that as a proof that it was free, they could get out of it if they wanted to. They have not chosen to get out.'

Collins spoke rarely during the session, except in his capacity as minister for finance on financial matters, but one intervention was poignant in a discussion on the operation of the republican courts. There was no doubt that he was getting a dig in at Stack. 'The courts broke down for the reason that the machinery was not held together,' the Big Fellow complained. 'There was not enough work done locally or at headquarters.'

The way Collins crossed the bounds of his own portfolio to express views on other matters might have been more acceptable if he had not been so resentful of similar interference in his own areas. He behaved as if others should abide by certain rules, while he was free to improvise as he went along.

'What the hell do you know about finance?' he snapped at Stack one day, when the latter had the temerity to make some suggestion.

'I know more about finance, than you know about manners!' Stack replied.

On 18 August the Dáil went into a private session from which the press and public were excluded, and de Valera spoke much more candidly. For instance, he stated it was a fact 'that no nation would recognise the Irish Republic, unless that nation was prepared to go to war with Britain'. While he would be very glad of such support, he said 'that was a very vague hope'.

In the course of a rather rambling discussion during a private session on 22 August, de Valera seemed to be almost echoing the *New Statesman* when he told deputies that if they were determined to make peace only on the basis of recognition of the Republic, then they were going to be faced with war, only this time it would be a real war of British re-conquest, not just a continuation of limited military coercive measures 'in support of the civil police' to force some people to obey the law. In short, he was saying the War of Independence had not been a real war at all.

Although de Valera's remarks were couched in terms of out-lining stark realities so the Dáil could decide the best course for itself, there was absolutely no room for doubt about his readiness to compromise, even on important issues like the partition question. He gave the private session an idea of what he had meant when he talked publicly about making sacrifices for a settlement.

'The minority in Ulster had a right to have their sentiments considered to the utmost limit,' he explained, according to the official record. 'If the Republic were recognised he would be in favour of giving each county power to vote itself out of the Republic if it so wished.' The only choice would be to coerce Northern Ireland, and he was opposed to such coercion because it would not be successful and, anyway, he warned, attempting to coerce the majority in Northern Ireland would be to make the same mistake the British had made with the Irish people as a whole.

On the issue of commonwealth membership, he told deputies 'they could not turn down what appeared to be, on the face of it, an invitation to join a group of free nations provided it was based on the principles enunciated by President Wilson'. And he also indicated they would have to make concessions to satisfy Britain's security requirements.

'It was ridiculous of course to say that because Ireland was near Britain she should give Britain safeguards,' de Valera admitted. 'But,' he continued, 'America demanded such strategic safeguards from the small island of Cuba.' If security concessions were refused, Britain would depict the Irish as unreasonable, America would agree, as would the international community generally, and then 'England would be given a free hand to deal with Ireland'. The Irish people's natural moral right to their own island would be eradicated, just as the rights of the American Indians had been trampled on in North America.

'Look at America,' he said ominously, 'where are the natives?

Wiped off the face of the earth.' The same thing could happen in Ireland. 'Unfortunately,' he added, 'they were very far away from living in a world where moral forces counted'; it was 'brute force' that mattered.

If the deputies insisted on securing recognition of the republic as a totally independent country, they would be acting like prisoners in jail going on hunger strike to secure their freedom, he explained. If they won, they would have their freedom, but if they lost, they would be dead and have nothing. His choice of allusion was particularly significant because he had always opposed hunger strikes himself.

De Valera gave only a vague outline of the kind of compromise alternative he had in mind. He demanded what amounted to a blank cheque to negotiate whatever agreement he thought fit, subject only to its subsequent approval by a majority of the Dáil. With the latter due to go back into public session for the formal election of the president, he told the secret session he wanted his own position clearly understood before allowing his name to be put forward.

'I have one allegiance only to the people of Ireland and that is to do the best we can for the people of Ireland as we conceive it,' he declared. 'If you propose me I want you all to understand that you propose me understanding that that will be my attitude.' All questions would be discussed, he said, 'from the point of view absolutely of what I consider the people of Ireland want and what I consider is best from their point of view'.

One deputy interjected to object to the president's stated willingness to allow each of the six counties to vote itself out of the Irish Republic, but de Valera reaffirmed his position. He would be ready to consider allowing counties or provinces to vote themselves out.

'I do not feel myself bound to consider anything,' he emphasised. 'I feel myself open to consider everything.' He would not be confined. 'I will not accept this office if you fetter me in any way whatever,' he declared. 'I cannot accept office except on the understanding that no road is barred, that we shall be free to consider every method.' The policy of his government would be to do what he thought best for the country and 'those who would disagree with me would resign'.

Brugha had said at the cabinet meeting of 25 July that the president had no right to consider anything which was not in line with allegiance to the Irish republic, so the latest remarks were a patent effort to ensure such an argument would have no validity in future. De Valera concluded by proposing the Dáil adjourn for the day. No time was allowed for any debate on what he had said; there was no room for discussion as far as he was concerned. If the deputies wanted him as president they had to accept his terms; otherwise they should elect somebody else.

Before the election for president on 26 August, however, there was a discrepancy to be cleared up about his actual title as president because, as de Valera admitted, 'no such office had been created'. Back in 1919 he had simply given himself the title of president without the authority of the Dáil, which had elected him *priomh aire* (prime minister). Now the discrepancy was somewhat obliquely tackled by slipping the term 'President' into a constitutional amendment limiting the size of the cabinet to seven specified officers – 'the President who shall also be Prime Minister' and the ministers for foreign affairs, home affairs, defence, finance, local government and economic affairs.

Chapter Three

'WE CAN AFFORD TO BE GENEROUS'

De Valera was duly elected president unanimously, and he delivered a short address extolling in mythical terms the supposed unity within the Dáil. 'When I was in America I used to be amused about the talk of extremists and moderates and differences of opinion,' he said. 'There are no differences of opinion amongst us.' He went on to emphasise that this was not only within the cabinet, but also within the whole movement. He then proceeded on to engage in a piece of theatrics to bolster his own carefully cultivated image of passionate sincerity.

It had been agreed to release at noon the text of his latest letter to Lloyd George confirming 'the anticipatory judgment' of the Dáil's rejection of the British offer. As there was still two minutes to go, he waited in silence for the two minutes. He then read the letter, which concluded by intimating that the British should convene a conference to negotiate a democratic peace settlement. 'To negotiate such a peace, Dáil Éireann is ready to appoint its representatives, and, if your Government accepts the principle proposed, to invest them with plenary powers to meet and arrange with you for its application in detail.'

De Valera then nominated the six men who were to make up the new cabinet with him. He began with Griffith, then Stack, Brugha, Collins, Cosgrave and, finally, Robert Barton. The president also named eight 'Extra Cabinet Ministers', who included Kevin O'Higgins, Count George N. Plunkett, Desmond Fitzgerald, Countess Markievicz and Ernest Blythe.

Although Collins had been dropped to fourth place in the

pecking order, he delivered the first ministerial report. 'The President has been sufficiently praised', he declared early in the address in which he went on lavish praise on James O'Mara for his work in America.

De Valera had asked Collins to come out to the United States to organise the bond drive in 1919, but the Big Fellow sent James O'Mara, one of the Dáil's trustees, instead. If it were not for the pioneering work done by O'Mara, they would not have been 'nearly so successful in raising the money abroad', according to Collins. He believed he was voicing the feelings of everyone who worked with, or was associated with him. 'Everyone was particularly grateful to Mr James O'Mara for the work he had done for us,' Collins emphasised.

De Valera was so happy with O'Mara's work that he offered him the post of ambassador to the United States, but O'Mara was far from content with de Valera's performance. He declined the offer because he could no longer 'hold any official position under the government of the Irish Republic whose President claims such arbitrary executive authority, and in whose judgment of American affairs I have no longer any confidence'. He not only refused the post but also resigned as one of the Dáil's three trustees, and he announced he would not stand for re-election to the Dáil itself. Instead of just accepting the resignation, de Valera sent O'Mara a petulant telegram announcing he was being fired. It was a blatant example of de Valera's presumption of the arbitrary authority about which O'Mara had already complained. Even if O'Mara had not already resigned, de Valera did not have the authority to remove him as a trustee, because the Dáil had appointed him.

The effusive praise that Collins heaped on O'Mara was really a figurative shot across the Long Fellow's bows, though few of those present seemed to have realised that at the time. De Valera had been so touchy about O'Mara's criticism, however, he would not have missed the significance of the Big Fellow's remarks.

The same day in some written answers to questions posed by Clyde A. Beals of *United Press*, Collins appeared to adopt a firmer approach than de Valera's much more moderate tone during the Dáil private session of recent days. He essentially dismissed any suggestion of submitting the British offer to a plebiscite of the Irish people. 'There is unanimity in rejecting the present proposals,' Collins explained. 'The proposals constitute no basis that any self-respecting Irish man will consider. Another thing – and the thing that counts – is that nationally there can be no free plebiscite while the English forces are in occupation here.'

Asked by Beals whether any alternative to a republic could be submitted to the people, Collins was evasive, rather like a typical politician. 'No,' he said. 'The issue was the Irish republic – that means Irish freedom. The Irish people stand solidly for that.'

Collins did some of his own posturing in the following days. 'They have asked me to go north to Armagh for a meeting on Sunday. A rally for Ireland! I must do it although I hate a public meeting like I hate a plague,' he wrote. Armagh was one of the two constituencies from which he had been elected to the Dáil and he planned on expressing strong sentiments. 'I'm going to endeavour making such an appeal to them as will make them rock to their foundations,' he continue. 'At least I'm going to try.'

He had little to say about the British offer in his speech in Armagh on 4 September. 'With regard to the terms themselves I have little to add to what has been said in our letters to the British Government,' he said. 'These terms are not acceptable to us. They do not give us the substance of freedom.'

He was speaking to nationalists, but his remarks were really directed at the unionist population. He asked the gathering of some 7,000 in the playing field of the local seminary how Sir James Craig could believe in self-determination and deny it to the people of Fermanagh and Tyrone. 'The Orangemen have been used as a tool in preventing up to the present, what is now inevitable,' Collins said. 'The moment is near when they will no longer be of use as a tool – when they will, in fact, stand in the way of an agreement with Ireland which has now become essential to British interests. Then they will be thrown aside, and they will find their eyes turned to an England which no longer wants them.

'Our proposal is,' he added, 'that they should come in. We can afford to give them more than justice. We can afford to be generous. That is our message to the north, and it is meant for those who are opposed to us rather than for those who are with us. But to those who are with us, I can say that no matter what happens, no matter what the future may bring, we shall not desert them.'

Collins was sharing the platform with Eoin O'Duffy and Harry Boland, among others. 'If they are for Ireland we will extend the hand of welcome as we have done in the past,' O'Duffy said. 'If they decide that they are against Ireland and against their fellow-countrymen, we will have to take suitable action. We will have to put on the screw. The boycott of Belfast – we will tighten that screw, and, if necessary, we will have to use the lead against them.'

Mary MacSwiney complained to Harry Boland that Collins' speech was 'much too "safe" on the only point that matters'. The debate about the forthcoming negotiations had already begun even though it had not yet been agreed to hold negotiations. Boland told Collins what MacSwiney had written and the Big Fellow confronted her and she, in turn, protested to Boland, as the debate went in circles. 'You need not have told your friend Mick that I thought him a compromiser,' she wrote to Boland. 'He says he is not and I believe him but I wish people could realise that the Republic means the Republic and nothing less.'

On the afternoon of de Valera's formal election as president, when the Dáil first discussed in private session the possibility of appointing a delegation to negotiate he gave no hint that he did not intend to be a member of delegation. During the course of a rambling discussion he talked about 'the advisability of not committing this Dáil in advance to anything that the plenipotentiaries might do'. He said that they should do 'the best they could' under the circumstances. Certainly if there were to be any limitations of any kind further than had been stated broadly in their reply, he for one could not retain office.

'Either they gave a free hand to the plenipotentiaries or they tied them up,' he continued according to the official report. 'If they tied them up they would get no one to go.'

'They would have to do the best they could for the country and they could not do that if they tied up the hands of their plenipotentiaries,' he repeated later. He 'would oppose it to the extent of resigning'. He said that all the members of the delegation would have to be ratified by the Dáil. Liam de Róiste formally proposed and Pádraig Ó Máille seconded a motion that the Speaker put to the floor:

> ... that if plenipotentiaries for negotiation be appointed either by the Cabinet or the Dáil, such plenipotentiaries be given a free hand in such negotiations and duly to report to the Dáil.

The motion was passed unanimously.

De Valera stunned his cabinet colleagues with his announcement that he did not intend to take part in the conference with the British. He suggested Arthur Griffith to lead the delegation, with Michael Collins as his back-up.

Griffith, who founded Sinn Féin, was born in 1872. He also established the *United Irishman* newspaper, which he used to promote the idea that Irish members of parliament should withdraw from Westminster and set up their own assembly in Dublin. He advocated the creation of a dual monarchy between Britain and Ireland on Austro-Hungarian lines, so he was not a republican, and he did not believe in the use of physical force.

He took no part in the Easter Rebellion, but the British jailed him anyway. He stepped down as leader of Sinn Féin to allow de Valera become president of party in 1917. Griffith was promptly elected vice-president, and he took over the acting leadership of the party and the movement when de Valera went to the United States in 1919.

The president wished for Collins to accompany Griffith. They had worked well together in the Dáil, but Collins initially refused to go. 'I was somewhat surprised at his reluctance for he had been rather annoyed with me for not bringing him on the team when I went to meet Lloyd George earlier on in July,' de Valera wrote. 'I now considered it essential that he should be on the team with Griffith.

'They by themselves alone, it seemed, would form a well balanced team,' the president continued. 'Griffith would, I thought, have the confidence of the "moderates" and Collins that of the IRB and the Army.' He added that 'with these two as the leaders no one could suggest that the delegation was not a strong and representative one'.

Collins did not want to be a part of the delegation, especially when de Valera was staying at home, but he was urged to go by his friend Harry Boland. He and Boland discussed the whole thing for hours at de Valera's home on the night of 30 August.

'For three hours one night, after the decision had been made to send a delegation to London, I pleaded with de Valera to leave me at home and let some other man take my place as a negotiator,' Collins recalled. 'The point I tried to impress on de Valera was that for several years (rightly or wrongly makes no difference) – the English had held me to be the one man most necessary to capture because they held me to be the one man responsible for the smashing of their Secret Service organisation, and for their failure to terrorise the Irish people with their Black-and-Tans.' It really did not matter whether the legend was true, or was simply the product of press sensationalism.

'The important fact,' he emphasised, 'was that in England, as in Ireland, the Michael Collins legend existed. It pictured me as the mysterious active menace, elusive, unknown, unaccountable, and in this respect I was the only living Irishman of whom it could be said.'

In effect, Collins was arguing that he was seen as the real leader; so he would be in a better position to influence republicans to accept a compromise if he was not involved in the negotiations. Back in April and May, for instance, Lloyd George had ruled out talks with Sinn Féin because he did not wish to talk with Collins, whom he considered the real Irish leader. The delegation could always delay in order to consult him or demand further concessions to placate him. The Irish delegation would thereby be able to get better terms from the British without him.

De Valera was not impressed. 'His argument,' according to Collins, 'was that aside from whatever truth might be in my view the menace I constituted was of advantage to us.' That was how de Valera explained the situation, but his insistence on the inclusion of Collins was motivated not so much by the belief that he would be an asset to the delegation as the realisation that it would be too risky not to include the real architect of the Black and Tan war.

Collins, after all, had been questioning the president's judgment on military and political matters in the lead up to the Truce and had bitterly resented his exclusion from the delegation that went to London in July. Moreover, he had deliberately stampeded the president in the matter of demanding MacEoin's release, and de Valera – with his acute sensitivity to criticism – was no doubt suspicious of the implied criticism in the Big Fellow's lavish praise of James O'Mara in the Dáil on 26 August. Very few in the Dáil would have thought there was any sinister significance in those remarks, but de Valera and Collins were aware. From the president's standpoint the best way of committing

Collins to any settlement terms was to ensure that he was part of the negotiating team.

When the supreme council of the IRB discussed the issue on 1 September, some members were deeply suspicious of de Valera's motives and they told Collins. 'There were certain members of the Supreme Council who thought there was something sinister behind the suggestion, and we had the temerity to tell him that he was likely to be made a scapegoat in the matter,' Seán Ó Muirthile, the secretary of the IRB's Supreme Council, noted.

'From what I have learned since I came back from America you will not succeed in overthrowing the British militarily,' Harry Boland argued. 'If it is a question between Peace and War, I'm for Peace. If there are negotiations I think "Mick" should go, and I'll tell you why. In my opinion a "Gunman" will screw better terms out of them than an ordinary politician.'

'When we argued the matter further with Collins,' Ó Muirthile noted that they were unable to convince him.

'Let them make a scapegoat or anything they wish of me,' Collins said. 'We have accepted the situation as it is, and someone must go.'

'It was a job that had to be done by somebody,' he explained later. In the past he had not shirked responsibility and now was no different, even though he was warned by several people not to trust de Valera. On the other hand, however, the president had courageously confronted the Dáil hard-liners by emphasising his unwillingness to exclude the possibility of any kind of settlement.

On 7 September Lloyd George wrote to de Valera 'for a definite reply as to whether you are prepared to enter a conference to ascertain how the association of Ireland with the community of nations known as the British Empire can best be reconciled with Irish national aspirations'. The British proposed that the conference should begin in Inverness, Scotland, on 20 September 1921.

The Dáil cabinet selected the delegation for the negotiations on 9 September. Although de Valera had told his colleagues a couple of weeks earlier that he was not going to be part of the delegation, Griffith insisted that the president should go and the cabinet debated the issue at length. De Valera gave several reasons for not going. If Lloyd George tried the strong-arm tactics he used in July, the delegation could, he said, always use the necessity of consulting him as an excuse to prevent it being rushed into any hasty decisions. There were, however, much broader considerations.

'There seemed, in fact, at the time to be no good reason why I should be on the delegation,' he later wrote. 'There was, on the other hand, a host of good reasons why I should remain at home. One had, above all, to look ahead and provide for the outcome of the negotiations. They would end either in a "make" or "break" – in a settlement based on the accepted cabinet policy of External Association, or in a failure of the negotiations with a probable renewal of war. In either case I could best serve the national interest by remaining at home.

'If the outcome were to be the settlement we had envisaged, that based on External Association,' he continued, 'it was almost certain that it would be no easy task to get that settlement accepted wholeheartedly by the Dáil and by the Army.' He had already got a taste of the kind of bitterness such a proposal could generate, not only from Brugha's vitriolic outburst at the cabinet meeting on 25 July, but also in the United States during a controversy that erupted following an interview he gave the *Westminster Gazette* in January 1920. External Association was essentially a more developed version of the ideas he first propounded in that controversial interview.

By not taking part in the negotiations, de Valera argued he would be in a better position to influence radical republicans to accept a compromise agreement. 'My influence,' he said, 'would be vastly more effective if I myself were not a member of the negotiating team, and so completely free of any suggestion that I had been affected by the "London atmosphere".'

Those negotiating would inevitably have to compromise, but even this might not be good enough in the last analysis.

Consequently, by staying at home, he would be in a position to rally both moderates and radicals to fight for an absolute claim, instead of a less appealing compromise. 'Were there to be a "break" with any substantial section of our people discontented and restless, the national position would be dangerously weakened when the war resumed. I was providing for this contingency much better by remaining at home than by leading the delegation.'

Throughout the struggle his primary role within the movement at home was as a unifying figure. He had tried to be all things – a moderate among moderates and a radical among militants. He wished to maintain that role, so it made good sense not to get too involved in the nitty-gritty of the negotiations. Moreover, if the negotiations collapsed, de Valera would also be in a better position to initiate further contacts with the British if he had not been involved in the conference. In the last analysis his decision to stay in Dublin was based on sound, though selfish, political grounds. He knew that those who went were likely to become scapegoats – with the radicals if they compromised and with the moderates if they did not.

'We must have scapegoats,' de Valera told his cabinet.

Later in trying to justify his decision, he sought to rationalise his selfish considerations by cloaking them in the national interest. In the process he seemed to protest the merits of his own position a little too much. He contended, for instance, that by staying at home he could play his part 'in keeping public opinion firm' and also 'in doing everything possible to have the Army well organised and strong'.

'Feeling ran pretty high here, the Black and Tans and Auxiliaries were still amongst us,' Barton noted. 'The Republicans forces had to be kept together and consolidated, someone had to stay and keep the home fires burning and yet prevent them blazing up the chimneys. We felt de Valera was best fitted to do this.' That may have convinced Barton, who had been in jail throughout the worst of the troubles, but it sounded rather hollow to Collins, seeing that de Valera had spent most of the Black and Tan period in the United States.

'Collins was determined that Dev should go,' according to Barton. 'A vote was eventually taken with each of the members of the cabinet being asked whether the president should go to London. Griffith said, "Yes", Brugha "No", Stack "No", Cosgrave "Yes", Collins "Yes", and Barton "No". The vote was therefore tied at three for going and three for staying, leaving de Valera to exclude himself with his own vote.'

Thus it was Barton who provided the crucial vote that allowed de Valera to remain at home. 'I voted against Dev going for purely tactical reasons,' Barton later explained. 'He was undoubtedly our best negotiator and the most difficult antagonist the British had to meet but he was also our President and the National pivot. If Dev went on the delegation and the negotiations failed we had a reserve. We could never discuss and return to Ireland except to commence war. If Dev remained in Ireland we could always break off negotiations and threaten war and still have Dev in the background to come in at the last and find some way of carrying on if the Army was not ready. If Dev went on the delegation then our last word must be said in London. If he remained in Dublin the scene of negotiations must return there before the final rupture.' It should be remembered that Barton had helped to negotiate the Truce 'mainly to enable the volunteers to rearm and equip'. Hence he felt that this aim could be furthered by de Valera staying in Dublin.

Chapter Four

'BETTER BAIT FOR LLOYD GEORGE'

The president proposed that Griffith should be chairman of the delegation. 'All agreed that Arthur Griffith must act as chairman,' Barton noted. De Valera then proposed Collins as vice-chairman, even though he knew that Griffith and Collins were more amenable to the British terms than any other members of the cabinet. He was using them. Three months later, for instance, he wrote to Joe McGarrity in the United States that he selected them because he thought they would be 'better bait for Lloyd George – leading him on and on, further in our direction'.

'That Griffith would accept the Crown under pressure I had no doubt,' he explained. 'From the preliminary work which M.C. [Collins] was doing with the IRB, of which I had heard something, and from my own weighing up of him, I felt certain that he too was contemplating accepting the Crown.'

Stack made 'a weak kind of objection', according to himself. He complained that 'both gentlemen had been in favour of the July proposals'.

'Collins then took up my objections to himself, and denied that he would accept the proposals,' Stack noted. 'I reminded him of what he had said at Blackrock. He protested he said nothing of the kind.'

Well, Stack explained, he got the impression that Griffith only wanted some modifications.

'Yes,' said Griffith, 'some modifications.'

'Cathal and the President then assured me I had misunderstood Mick at Blackrock,' Stack noted. 'I accepted this and said no more.'

Collins still protested his reluctance. 'We all realised that the delegation would not be representative if he was not included,' Barton noted. The Big Fellow's reluctance to go was prompted by a number of reasons, some selfish. 'Of course,' he later wrote, 'we all knew that whatever the outcome of the negotiations, we could never hope to bring back all that Ireland wanted and deserved to have, and we therefore knew that more or less opprobrium would be the best we could hope to win.' Nobody could be expected willingly to court such infamy, and Collins was no exception. 'I had got a certain name, whether I deserved it or not,' he later told the Dáil, 'and I knew when I was going over there that I was being placed in a position that I could not reconcile, and that could not in the public mind be reconciled with what they thought I stood for, no matter what we brought back.'

'For my own part,' Collins explained on another occasion, 'I anticipated the loss of the position I held in the hearts of the Irish people as a result of my share in what was bound to be an unsatisfactory bargain. And to have and to hold the regard of one's fellow countrymen is surely a boon not to be lost, while there is a way to avoid it.'

Instead of arguing on those lines in cabinet, however, Collins actually made many of the same points in favour of his own exclusion that de Valera had already made for not going. He could be of use to the delegation if he were 'kept in the background (against all eventualities) to be offered in a crisis as a final sacrifice with which to win our way to freedom'.

'It is not a question of individuals now,' the president told Collins in an obvious appeal to his vanity. 'It is a question of the nation and you and I and the cabinet know that the British will not make their best offer in your absence.'

'I had no choice,' Collins explained afterwards. 'I had to go.' But he made it clear to everyone that he was going against his better judgment.

'Brugha was next proposed and flatly refused to have his

name considered,' according to Barton. 'His business he said was Minister of Defence, and with the Army he would stay. As far as I remember none urged him to change his mind for all realised that negotiations were not likely to last more than a first session if Cathal was present.'

'Cathal is the honestest and finest soul in the world, but he is a bit slow at seeing fine differences and rather stubborn, and the others would not seek to convince him, but would rather try to outmanoeuvre him, and there would be trouble,' de Valera explained afterwards. 'If I were going myself,' he added, 'I would certainly have taken him with me.'

Collins suggested Stack, 'but he too definitely refused saying he was not fitted for such work and would not consent to go in any circumstances,' Barton recalled. 'I then proposed that Gavan Duffy should go as the inclusion of a man with knowledge of law and legal terms was essential. Collins proposed [Eamonn] Duggan as a more suitable legal man. Duggan was approved. I then suggested Mulcahy, but Brugha refused his consent. Collins proposed "either Barton or Childers or preferably both should go." Dev stated that he was anxious that Childers should be secretary, and this was agreed to without demur. Stack supported my selection and it was agreed. Personally I was opposed to going, feeling I had not the necessary knowledge or ability, but after so many had made objections I felt diffident about refusing, especially as I had made a strong appeal to Collins to sink his objections in the national interest. Dev finally proposed Gavan Duffy and the team was complete.' It was significant that nobody suggested the one remaining member of the cabinet, W. T. Cosgrave.

The final three were selected 'to work in well' with Griffith and Collins, according to de Valera, who described Duggan and Gavan Duffy as 'mere legal padding'. Although born in Cheshire, England, George Gavan Duffy had a sound nationalist pedigree. He was the fourteenth of seventeen children of Sir Charles Gavan

Duffy, one of the founders of the Young Ireland movement in 1840s. Charles Gavan Duffy emigrated to Australia in the 1850s and became prime minister of Victoria in the 1870s. George was born after his father returned to Europe in 1882. Brought up in Nice, George spoke French and Italian fluently. He returned to England in his teens to study at Stonyhurst, and he was a member of Roger Casement's legal team at his trial in 1916. Elected to the First Dáil in 1918 Gavan Duffy was sent as an envoy of the Irish Republic to Paris and later to Rome.

Gavan Duffy, Barton, and a young, rather volatile, Collins had served together on a delegation that went to London in December 1918 to try to enlist the help of President Woodrow Wilson, who was in Britain on his way to the Paris Peace Conference. Gavan Duffy drew up the petition, but it was ignored by Wilson, much to the annoyance of Collins, who suggested they kidnap the president to make him listen to them. Now the three of them were selected to go back to London under very different circumstances.

Throughout the remainder of his life, de Valera went to great pains to justify his decision to exclude himself from the delegation. While the reasons he gave to the cabinet were undoubtedly factors, there were other reasons that he was only prepared to elaborate on privately. In December 1921 he explained these in some detail in a letter to Joe McGarrity, and again to Lord Longford more than forty years later.

He admitted that he was using Griffith and Collins as mere bait. 'I felt convinced on the other hand that as matters came to a close we would be able to hold them from this side from crossing the line.'

Following the selection by the cabinet, the Dáil met in private session on 14 September to ratify the delegation. W. T. Cosgrave moved that the president should head the delegation. But his own assistant, Kevin O'Higgins, promptly undermined Cosgrave by endorsing de Valera's decision. 'It was a matter of tactics,' O'Higgins argued, according to the official report. 'They had to safeguard the Republic and the symbol of the Republic and to face the unpleasant fact that the plenipotentiaries might have to discuss other proposals than the sovereign independence of Ireland and it was not right the President should discuss such proposals.'

Griffith was then ratified as chairman, but when Collins' name was submitted for formal ratification, he explained that he 'would very much prefer not to be chosen'. He said that he believed de Valera should head the delegation.

If he was not president and, as such a symbol of the republic, de Valera said, he would go himself. As this was out of the question, he argued, 'It was absolutely necessary that the Minister for Finance should be a member' because he 'was absolutely vital to the delegation'.

'To me the task is a loathsome one,' Collins told colleagues. 'If I go, I go in the spirit of a soldier who acts against his better judgment at the orders of a superior officer.'

After Collins relented, the Dáil promptly approved his nomination, and the other names were approved without any discussion. But Gavan Duffy did object to members of the delegation being categorised as plenipotentiaries. He thought they were being given too much power. De Valera – who had twice previously threatened to resign if full and unfettered plenipotentiary powers were denied to the delegation – was insistent. He wished to use the term plenipotentiaries 'to give to the world the impression that they are sent over with full powers – to do the best they could to reconcile the Irish position with the British position. They should have full powers because if they go over they needed to have the moral feeling of support of the position to do the best they could for Ireland.

'Remember what you are asking them to do,' the president said. 'You are asking them to secure by negotiations what we are totally unable to secure by force of arms.'

Afterwards Collins was still uneasy about his appointment.

'I should not have been asked to go,' he told his friend Batt O'Connor afterwards as he paced about the room. 'I pleaded strongly against my selection.'

'You will get betters terms for us than anyone else,' O'Connor argued.

'It is a mistake to send me. De Valera should go. Who ever heard of the soldiers who fought the enemy in the field being sent to negotiate the peace,' he said. 'I am being put in an impossible position.'

'Sit down man,' O'Connor pleaded. 'He did not seem to hear me, but continued to stride up and down the floor.'

'I fought hard against my selection,' he blurted out again. 'De Valera pressed me. For no other man living would I have consented.'

He should have been allowed to remain a hidden force behind the scene, and his name used during the negotiations to extract the maximum terms from the other side, he argued. 'Peace must mean of necessity some adjustment of the extreme demands on both sides – on our side as well as theirs,' he said. 'It is not the soldiers who fought on either side who should settle the adjustment. Who is to direct the fight if we have to go back to war, which is only too likely?'

For months Collins had an uneasy feeling about the hostility mounting towards him within the movement. Having been the most wanted man in Ireland over the past couple of years, it would have been understandable if he was becoming somewhat paranoid, but there were some people out to get him. He was being warned not to trust de Valera, and while he clearly had reservations, he still had not come down on the side of distrust. But the hostility of Brugha and Stack were something else.

Collins admired Brugha's bravery and respected his sincerity but this respect was not mutual. Brugha was not among the brightest people. De Valera considered him dull-witted, while

Richard Mulcahy considered him 'as brave and as brainless as a bull'. Brugha had been mercilessly questioning the manner in which Collins had handled some of the finances. Collins had not been able to explain all the money used for arms purchases. He had used money as if it had been his own to pay some of the men working for him, much to the annoyance of Brugha, a dedicated and selfless fanatic. There was no question of Collins misappropriating money for his own use, but he was prepared to be generous with those he thought deserved the few extra pounds. Brugha resented this and needled Collins to account for every pound spent, if not every penny.

Another matter began to surface when it became apparent that a young man connected with the Yost typewriter firm had been ordered to leave the country on insufficient information in the course of hostilities. Brugha and Mulcahy agreed that the young man should be allowed to return, but the intelligence branch under Collins, which had been involved in the original mistake, was slow to act. Brugha was incensed and he wrote a stinging letter to the adjutant general on 30 July.

Mulcahy believed that Brugha really wished to break the hold that Collins had on the army, and that he was trying to insert Stack as deputy chief of staff as a means to that end. Mulcahy appointed Eoin O'Duffy as his deputy chief of staff on 1 August, and he took particular exception to the tone of Brugha's letter to the adjutant general. It was not conducive to discipline to have the minister for defence undercutting the chief of staff by going behind his back and dealing directly with one of his officers, especially in an abusive manner. 'Unless something can be done to eliminate the tendency to revert to this tone when differences arise,' Mulcahy wrote on 2 September, 'I cannot be responsible for retaining harmony and discipline among the Staff.'

'Before you are very much older, my friend,' Brugha wrote four days later, 'I shall show you that I have as little intention of taking dictation from you as to how I should reprove inefficiency or negligence on the part of yourself or the D/I* as I have of allowing you to appoint a deputy chief of staff of you own choosing.

'In regard to your inability to maintain harmony and discipline among the Staff, it was scarcely necessary to remind me of the fact, as your shortcoming in that respect – so far at least as controlling the particular member already mentioned is concerned – have been quite apparent for a considerable time.'

The following week Brugha gave Mulcahy an ultimatum to furnish him with details of the Yost case within twenty-four hours, and when this was not done, he suspended the chief of staff and ordered him to 'hand over to the Deputy Chief of Staff all monies, papers, and books, and other property of the Department in your possession.' In short, Mulcahy was being ordered to hand over his command to Stack.

Brugha's real grievance was that Mulcahy had not been 'controlling' Collins. He was, therefore, anxious to insert Stack in order to control the Big Fellow.

The IRA headquarters staff had reservations not only about Stack's bungling in relation to the arrest of Casement, but also his poor performance in relation to republican courts, and his failure to attend any staff meetings while he was officially the deputy chief of staff during the Black and Tan conflict. As a result the staff backed Mulcahy, who also got the support of influential divisional commanders for his replacement of Stack. Even people like Liam Lynch, Frank Aiken and Seán Russell, who would all later break with Mulcahy and Collins, strongly supported the chief of staff in the Stack controversy.

De Valera therefore overruled Mulcahy's suspension. But talk of reorganising the IRA roused serious suspicions that sending Collins to London was part of a wider scheme to undermine his influence within the IRA. In the midst of what

* *Director of intelligence, Michael Collins*

was going on many people urged Collins to stay in Dublin.

'I had warned Collins not to go unless de Valera also went,' Tim Healy wrote, 'but he was too unselfish and unsuspecting to refuse.' Whatever about being unselfish, he was far from unsuspecting, though he did try to give a contrary impression afterwards. 'Before the negotiations began,' he later contended, 'no doubt of de Valera's sincerity had a place in my mind.' That was patently untrue, but he did give the president the benefit of his doubts.

The proposed conference at Inverness hit a snag over de Valera's reply accepting the invitation. 'In this final note,' he wrote, 'we deem it our duty to reaffirm that our position is and can only be as we have defined it throughout this correspondence. Our nation has formally declared its independence and recognises itself as a sovereign State. It is only as the representatives of that State and as its chosen guardians that we have any authority or power to act on behalf of our people.'

'Lloyd George was aiming to treat with us as if we were simply another "Irish Parliamentary Party",' de Valera later explained to Joe McGarrity. 'It was necessary for us to make quite explicit that we regarded ourselves in no such light. We were the Government of a nation that had declared its independence and we were prepared to face a renewal of the war rather than abandon that position. If there were members of the cabinet who felt otherwise they certainly did not express it. They approved the reply as I sent it, and a day or two after, in secret session, despite the threats which Lloyd George conveyed to us, Dáil Éireann endorsed it unanimously, and this after I had gone out of my way to make certain that every Member of the Assembly should realise to the full what the consequence of our standing firmly by that paragraph might involve.'

Maybe Collins openly supported it in cabinet and in the Dáil, but he certainly had reservations. Harry Boland and Joe McGrath were to deliver de Valera's reply to Lloyd George at Gairloch,

Scotland. Collins realised the letter accepting the invitation would scupper the talks.

'You might as well stay where you are,' he told McGrath.

Lloyd George cancelled the conference, insisting that there could be no question of recognising Irish independence. De Valera replied that he did not necessarily expect the British to recognise that independence but merely to realise that the Irish recognised it themselves. There followed a protracted exchange of letters and telegrams as Lloyd George and de Valera sought an agreeable basis for the conference.

'De Valera always drafted these letters,' according to Barton. 'We sometimes suggested amendments.' There were essentially two points at issue in their correspondence. Initially de Valera stated that the conference should consider Ireland's right to self-determination, while Lloyd George insisted that it could only consider the detailed application of his July offer.

De Valera promptly modified his demand to a request for unconditional discussions, but Lloyd George held his ground. In six of his seven communications he stressed that only the July proposals could be considered, but in his final telegram he backed down and agreed that the conference could 'explore every possibility' of settlement 'with a view to ascertaining how the association of Ireland with the community of nations known as the British Empire may best be reconciled with Irish national aspirations'. This formula was essentially a compromise on their original positions, but de Valera seemed to get the better of the argument because he had taken the more flexible stand.

The second point at issue involved recognition of Irish sovereignty. Although de Valera contended he was only stating that the Irish representatives recognised their own government, Lloyd George wanted no confusion on the point. There would be no question of his government affording recognition to the Dáil regime or even acknowledging that the Irish recognised their own regime. He stressed this point in his telegram on 29 September when he extended another invitation for the Irish side to send representatives to a conference, this time in London.

De Valera's acceptance of this invitation involved dropping the self-recognition stand, though he did try to confuse the issue by stating that 'our respective positions have been stated and are understood'. This was an attempt to give the impression he was still holding to his earlier position, but his remarks were not a condition. They were a statement, which could only be logically interpreted as an admission that he understood and accepted Britain's insistence that there could be no conference, if he persisted with his claim of self-recognition.

'In these preliminaries the English refused to recognise us as acting on behalf of the Irish Republic and the fact that we agreed to negotiate at all on any other basis was possibly the primary cause of our downfall,' Barton later argued. 'Certainly it was the first milestone on the road to disaster. It is important that you must remember that every member of the Cabinet was party to and equally responsible for this decision. Many and long were the Cabinet meetings we held. The final decision to meet the English was a unanimous one.'

'The communication of September 29th from Lloyd George made it clear that they were going into a conference not on the recognition of the Irish Republic, and I say if we all stood on the recognition of the Irish Republic as a prelude to any conference we could very easily have said so, and there would be no conference,' Collins noted. 'What I want to make clear is that it was the acceptance of the invitation that formed the compromise. I was sent there to form that adaptation, to bear the brunt of it.'

Chapter Five

'THE SAME CONSTITUTIONAL
RIGHTS THAT CANADA AND
AUSTRALIA CLAIMED'

De Valera had indicated in the Dáil that he intended to appoint
Harry Boland as one of the secretaries to the delegation, along
with Erskine Childers and somebody with a good command of
the Irish language. But then he decided to send Boland to the
United States instead, to prepare people there for a settlement
incorporating less than the desired Republic. 'I have a nice job
now to prepare Irish-America for a compromise,' Boland said.
He told Joe McGrath that he 'was going back to America on
the President's instructions to prepare the American people for
something short of a Republic'.

Collins and Boland, who had been the best of friends for
years, were involved in a classic love triangle, as both were in
love with Kitty Kiernan. Before leaving for America Harry told
Collins that he had proposed to Kitty and she had accepted. 'Of
course, he was upset and assured me that it did not follow if
you did not marry me that you would marry him,' Harry wrote
to Kitty.

Next day Harry sent Kitty a further letter. 'Mick and I spent
the last night together. He saw me home at 2 a.m., as I had to
catch the 7.35 a.m. I bade him goodbye – only to find him at
Kingsbridge as fresh as a daisy to see me off. I need not say to
you how much I love him, and I know he has a warm spot in

his heart for me, and I feel sure in no matter what manner our Triangle may work out, he and I shall always be friends.'

Before the plenipotentiaries left for London they were furnished with credentials on 7 October 1921. President de Valera signed those credentials authorising each of the plenipotentiaries 'to negotiate and conclude on behalf of Ireland with the representatives of his Britannic Majesty, George V, a Treaty or Treaties of settlement, Association between Ireland and the community of nations known as the British commonwealth'. The cabinet also issued them with the following secret instructions:

(1) The Plenipotentiaries have full powers as defined in their credentials.
(2) It is understood however that before decisions are finally reached on the main questions that a dispatch notifying the intention of making these decisions will be sent to the Members of the Cabinet in Dublin and that a reply will be awaited by the Plenipotentiaries before the final decision is made.
(3) It is also understood that the complete text of the draft treaty about to be signed will be similarly submitted to Dublin and reply awaited.
(4) In case of break the text of final proposals from our side will be similarly submitted.
(5) It is understood that the Cabinet in Dublin will be kept regularly informed of the progress of the negotiations.

Since the Dáil had already conferred full plenipotentiary powers, the instructions from the cabinet, an inferior body, were not legally binding in any instance in which they limited the powers of the delegation. Indeed, from the instructions themselves, it would seem that they were not intended to limit those powers, because the first of the instructions basically reaffirmed that the delegation had the full authority 'to negotiate and conclude' a treaty. The word 'understood', which was used in each of the three clauses that seemed to limit the delegation's authority, indicated that the instructions were really an informal understanding that the plenipotentiaries were morally obliged to try to uphold.

The instructions were designed by de Valera to ensure that he would ultimately have a kind of control over the delegation. 'I expected to be in the closest touch with it,' he wrote. 'In fact, it was my intention to be as close almost as if I were in London.' In short, de Valera wanted ultimate control of the negotiations, while he was putting all of the responsibility for whatever happened on the members of the delegation.

Erskine Childers was named principal secretary to the delegation, and there were three other secretaries – John Chartres, Diarmuid O'Hegarty and Fionán Lynch. Chartres was included as a kind of constitutional adviser, while O'Hegarty took charge of the typing staff and Lynch was included to fulfil de Valera's desire for a fluent Irish speaker on the staff. 'We never saw anything of Lynch and I do not know what became of him,' Barton noted.

Childers was expected to have a strong influence over Barton, who was like a younger brother. They were double first cousins. Childers' father and Barton's mother were brother and sister, as were Barton's father and Childers' mother. Childers' parents died when he was quite young and the Bartons assumed responsibility for rearing him and he spent his holidays with them. As a result Barton and Childers were as close to brothers as any two cousins could be. They even shared two names each, as their full names were Robert Erskine Childers and Robert Childers Barton.

The president believed that Childers and Barton 'would be strong and stubborn enough as a retarding force to any precipitate giving away by the delegation'. If de Valera really suspected that Griffith and Collins were weak, why did he not include Childers in the delegation proper? It was naive to think that a secretary would be able to control the delegation through his influence with Barton, especially when de Valera had questions about Barton's ability to cope with pressure. In April 1921 he actually wrote to Collins that he thought that Barton was 'on the verge of a breakdown'. Yet a few months later he was relying on him to restrain Griffith and Collins.

Childers was to keep de Valera informed on the activities of Griffith and Collins. Now in his early fifties, he was born and educated in Britain, but of course, he spent his holidays with the Bartons in Glendalough, County Wicklow. Having graduated from Cambridge University, he joined the staff at Westminster and served for fifteen years (1895–1910) as a clerk in the House of Commons. He was a distant relative to Hugh Childers, who had served over thirty years in parliament and had been a member of various Gladstone administrations and had served as chairman of the royal commission which famously found in 1895 that Ireland had been grossly overtaxed throughout most of the nineteenth century.

Erskine Childers took a leave of absence to serve in the Boer War, and afterwards returned to work as a parliamentary clerk. In his spare time he wrote the bestseller *Riddle of the Sands*. Published in 1905, it has been generally considered the first of the modern spy novels. It was widely credited with alerting the British to their naval weakness to a possible German attack. Erskine became deeply committed to Home Rule and resigned as a parliamentary clerk in 1910. Two years later he published *The Framework of Home Rule*, which was a detailed, exhaustively researched study of home rule and the involvement of Irish people in the various colonies. Childers landed the arms at Howth from his yacht, the *Asgard*, in 1914, but he then joined up and served with distinction in the Royal Navy during the First World War, and he served in the secretariat of the Irish Convention of 1917–1918. He was therefore particularly well qualified to serve as chief secretary of the delegation sent to

London in 1921. Indeed, one might even suggest that he was over-qualified and should have been a member of the delegation proper, but there was always a strain between Griffith and him. Both had spent time in South Africa, where Griffith sided with the Boers. There was a deep unbridgeable gulf between them, for which Griffith was largely responsible.

Childers, whose recreational passion was sailing, was a dedicated individual who tended to become fanatical about his interests. He was a tireless secretary who would work deep into the night without taking time off to relax.

De Valera assumed he could control the delegation himself, even though he had saddled the plenipotentiaries with the full responsibility of negotiating a settlement by insisting that the Dáil give them unfettered negotiating powers. He met Gavan Duffy, Childers and Chartres at 11 o'clock on the night of 7 October and gave them partially completed copies of a couple of draft treaties.

Draft Treaty A was an incomplete document in which External Association was outlined in treaty form. It envisaged Britain recognising Ireland as 'a sovereign independent state' and renouncing 'all claims to govern or to legislate' for the island. In return, Ireland would become externally associated with the British commonwealth, enjoying equal status with the dominions and being separately represented at imperial conferences. Instead of the common citizenship of the dominions, External Association would substitute reciprocal citizenship – the subtle difference being that Irish people would be Irish citizens rather than British subjects, but they would enjoy the same rights and privileges as British subjects while residing within the British commonwealth, and British subjects would enjoy reciprocal rights with Irish citizens while resident in Ireland.

The president had thought it necessary to seek reciprocal rights because he was afraid of losing the sympathy of Irish people throughout the British empire if the Dáil looked for a settlement that would make Irish immigrants aliens within the commonwealth. In many respects the distinction between reciprocal and common citizenship represented on a personal level the distinction between External Association and dominion status at the national level. External Association was designed to ensure that Ireland would legally have 'a guarantee of the same constitutional rights that Canada and Australia claimed', according to de Valera.

His controversial *Westminster Gazette* interview was the inspiration for another aspect of Draft Treaty A, which called for the British commonwealth to guarantee 'the perpetual neutrality of Ireland and the integrity and inviolability of Irish territory'. In return Ireland would commit 'itself to enter into no pact, and take no action, nor permit any action to be taken, inconsistent with the obligation of preserving its own neutrality and inviolability and to repel with force any attempt to violate its territory or to use its territorial waters for warlike purposes'. Once ratified by the respective parliaments the Treaty would be registered with the League of Nations at Geneva and the dominions would try to get 'the formal recognition of Ireland's neutrality, integrity and inviolability by the League of Nations in conformity with the similar guarantee in favour of Switzerland'.

In spite of its title, Draft Treaty A was not a serious effort to draw up a draft treaty, as has often been suggested. It was strictly a negotiating document, which the Irish delegation would present in response to the British proposals of 20 July. De Valera proposed a series of contingency documents be drafted. Draft Treaty B would be the document the delegation would publish as the Irish alternative in the event the negotiations collapsed, while Draft Treaty S would be the document the plenipotentiaries would sign as a treaty. The president made no effort to draw up Draft Treaty S. In fact, he actually suggested a series of ancillary treaties on the constitution, finance, trade and joint commission. His suggestion sounded liked some kind of complicated mathematical formula, as he proposed that these should be called Draft Treaty C, Draft Treaty F, Draft Treaty T, and Draft Treaty J respectively. As those were being updated from day to day they should be called, Draft Treaty Aa, Ab, Ac, or the Break Treaty should be Draft Treaty Ba, Bb, Bc, etc., consecutively and dated.

'We must depend on your side for the initiative after this,' he wrote to Griffith. The choice of the term 'your side' was possibly an unconscious reflection of the division within the cabinet even at that early stage. As far as negotiating tactics went, de Valera's advice was that the most difficult issue, the question of the crown, should be left until last.

'Supposing they refuse to do this?' Griffith asked.

'Well, you can put it to them that we ought first of all discuss the things there will be no great dispute about.'

'But supposing they insist on considering the question of the Crown first?'

'You can only use your powers of persuasion. After all, they cannot want to have a break on the first day.'

Griffith pressed for further advice. 'Well,' said de Valera, 'there you have the situation. You'll have to make the best of it.'

'Oh, wait now,' cried Griffith. 'That won't do!'

'Why?'

'It's not enough to say, "make the best of it".'

'I'm not talking about a settlement,' de Valera explained. 'I'm talking about the method of handling the negotiations. You see, if we get them to concede this and this and this and this, and then come to a stumbling-block, like the question of the Crown, which they say is a formula, then we can put the question before the world and point out that they want to renew the war on us for a formula.'

'We all realised that to secure the position of an isolated Republic was now impossible unless we drove England's military forces out of the country,' Barton wrote. 'In the Dáil members understood that our objective was External Association. The definition of that term was vague and even the delegates had but a hazy conception of what was to be its final form. This however was clear to us, External Association meant that no vestige of British authority was to remain within Ireland. The compromise was to be as regarded our foreign relations.'

Joe McGrath and Dan McCarthy were sent ahead to obtain two houses for the delegation and a fleet of Rolls Royce cars for their use. The headquarters were at 22 Hans Place and the other house was at 15 Cadogan Gardens about ten minutes' walk away. They employed a head cook, assistant cooks, cleaners and house maids, some from the Irish community in London, but Collins selected three waiters and six house maids as a kind of reward for their past services, and the delegation brought its own typists and clerks, as well some waiters.

Emmet Dalton was detailed to arrange for the purchase of an aeroplane to be on standby to whisk Collins back to Ireland if the negotiations collapsed precipitately. Contact was made with two Irishmen who had served as pilots in the Royal Air Force. One of them, Charlie Russell, had spent some time in Canada, so he purchased the Martinsyde aircraft posing as a Canadian requiring it for a Canadian project. The aircraft was reportedly capable of carrying at least five passengers with a range of five hundred miles at a speed of one hundred miles per hour. Both pilots had a number of practice flights to familiarise themselves with the plane, which was maintained in readiness at Croyden aerodrome.

The two pilots were on standby to fly Collins home. The plan was to cross the Bristol Channel to the Wexford coast and then fly north to Dublin. They would land on Leopardstown Racecourse, where a landing strip would be marked out while the aircraft was in flight. None of this became necessary, so the aircraft later became part of the nucleus of the Irish Army Air Corps and was named 'the Big Fella'.

Most of the Irish delegation arrived in London on the evening of 8 October. The first party consisted of all of the plenipotentiaries with the exception of Collins. There were also the four secretaries and four typists – Lily O'Brennan, who was a confidential typist for Childers, and the other three were Kathleen McKenna and the sisters Ellie and Alice Lyons. In addition there was propaganda minister Desmond Fitzgerald, journalist Mike Knightley, and David Robinson, whose duties were never quite clear, along with the wives of Eamonn Duggan and Fionán Lynch, who acted as chaperones. The women stayed at Hans Place, though some of them worked in the house in Cadogan Gardens.

Collins was behind the selection of a Miss O'Donoghue as housekeeper along with Tom as head waiter in Hans Place, and Eddie the head waiter at Cadogan Gardens. All three were from the Gresham Hotel. It was his way of replaying their loyalty. He also brought along a veritable entourage of bodyguards, whose functions were never quite clear. But it was obvious that some British people were deeply resentful of the Irish republicans. On the Sunday night the word 'MURDERERS' was painted on the footpath outside 22 Hans Place in large one-foot-square letters in red.

Collins set out the following day. 'Goodness knows I have a heavy heart this moment,' he wrote to Kitty Kiernan, 'but there is work to be done and I must not complain.' His entourage – which included Liam Tobin, Emmet Dalton, Tom Cullen, Joe Guilfoyle, Joe Dolan, Ned Broy and Seán MacBride – left Dun Laoghaire quietly on the Sunday. They 'were there really in order to supervise safety and intelligence arrangements for Collins', according to MacBride. He was particularly critical of the amount of drinking by those in Cadogan Gardens, including Collins. Although he liked to depict himself as some kind of confidant of Collins, there was a big age gap between him and the seventeen-year-old MacBride, who was brought essentially as a messenger boy. He did not know what they were actually doing. 'They may have been drinking when they went out,' he admitted, 'but I didn't go out with them.'

'I wouldn't say there was much justification for the charge that members of the staff of the Irish Delegation were having too good a time,' Robert Barton said. 'We worked very hard. There were occasional evenings of relaxation when we went to the theatre, but I don't think there was anything to give rise to any suggestion that we were in any way dissipated.'

Collins contributed to the rumours by going to Wormwood Scrubs prison with two colleagues to visit Neil Kerr, who had been his agent in Liverpool for spiriting people across the Atlantic and across the Irish Sea. 'He had evidently been drinking heavily,' the prison governor wrote to Lloyd George. 'He said his two companions would also be present. I replied that I had only instructions to admit him, Michael Collins. He then assumed a bullying demeanour.'

'Mr Lloyd George won't thank you for being discourteous to me,' Collins said. 'He had become truculent and announced his intention of seeing all the prisoners.' When he met Kerr he was caught trying to slip him some tobacco.

'You go sit down, you did not ought to be here at all,' Collins told the warder.

'I consider Mr Michael Collins was not in a fit condition to visit prisoners, as in my opinion he appeared to be under the influence of drink,' the warder reported.

The Big Fellow reportedly spent over three hours in the prison, making himself thoroughly obnoxious in the eyes of the prison authorities by 'boasting about all the loyal people he has shot'. Eventually he was persuaded to go.

'There might have been a certain amount of reason for criticism in some ways but, on the whole, I should say it was a very quiet and respectable and well-behaved delegation,' Barton continued. 'There was a lot of visiting by people who had not seen the leaders and wanted to see them.' An important American banker invited them to dinner at the Savoy Hotel. 'We could not accept as we had little spare time but, since he was an influential USA citizen and sympathetic, we did not like to refuse,' Barton said. 'We all went to breakfast with him.'

'Most of my time was taken up running dispatches from London to Dublin,' MacBride recalled. 'Many of these I delivered directly to de Valera or Kathleen O'Connell,' he added. 'I knew that a lot of the dispatches were written by Erskine Childers who was secretary of the delegation. Collins wrote private letters to people such as Seán Ó Muirthile who was the IRB man. My function was to bring all letters backwards and forward.'

Collins invited various people to join him in London, some as a kind reward for past services, and others to advise him, such as Joseph Brennan, a civil servant involved in finance, and J. J. O'Connell of IRA headquarters staff to advise on military matters. Collins did not do Brugha the courtesy of even informing, much less consulting him, about the selection of defence advisers, much to Brugha's indignation.

Collins, Desmond Fitzgerald and Diarmuid O'Hegarty had their offices in Cadogan Gardens, and Kathleen McKenna and Alice Lyons worked there during the day. Collins was first spotted in London by the media on 10 October. 'Coming swiftly from Cadogan Gardens, he sprang nimbly into a waiting car in an attempt to evade the ambush of reporters and photographers lying in wait,' Kathleen McKenna recalled. 'He was in splendid form – smiling, active, boyish, restless. He gave me the impression of a young colt set free in a field of lush grass.'

Next morning the *Daily Express* had a purported interview with him in which he was asked how he got to Hans Place without being seen by the press. 'Why it was the easiest thing in the world,' Collins reportedly replied. 'I adopted the same principle that enabled me to conceal my whereabouts so long in

Ireland. I always watch the other fellow instead of letting him watch me. I made a point of keeping the other fellow on the run, instead of being on the run myself.'

He said he travelled to Euston under an assumed name and slipped into a taxi unnoticed with a friend. He was good humoured but his face became stern as he said the *Daily Express* had called him a murderer.

'We had neither the desire not the intention to be unfair either to you or the Irish cause,' the reporter explained.

'Well, perhaps not,' Collins supposedly said as the cloud passed from his face. 'I don't think that the *Daily Express* was more unfair than others, but you know, none of your English newspapers really understands us. You don't see things from our point of view.'

'I never said any such thing,' Collins wrote to Kitty Kiernan next day. 'Newspaper men are inventions of the devil.'

'We held a long conference that night and decided that we should let the English do the talking and make proposals before we attempted to explain to them our scheme for External Association,' Barton recalled. Childers and Chartres met the secretaries of the English delegation and made the final arrangements for the conference to start next morning.

Chapter Six

'I HAVE COME TO CALL

A SPADE A SPADE'

The conference was due to begin at 11 a.m. on 11 October 1921. The Irish delegation set out from Hans Place in their fleet of Rolls Royce cars. The bulk of the delegation was in the first car, with Collins in the second car, along with Liam Tobin, Emmet Dalton, Tom Cullen, Joe Guilfoyle and Joe Dolan.

The precincts of Downing Street presented an extraordinary spectacle. 'Men, women and children knelt in prayer across the thoroughfares; paths lined with our supporters, including nuns and clergymen, reciting the rosary, singing hymns, crying words of encouragement, pouring blessings on the undertaking,' Kathleen McKenna noted. 'There were tricolours, banners, flags, lengths of cloth and cardboard on which slogans and wishes in Gaelic and English appeared.'

Collins bolted from the car into 10 Downing Street, as if trying to avoid the cameras. There was a certain amount of resentment that the government was negotiating with Irish rebels who had killed many British servicemen. A wreath was specially placed at the nearby cenotaph that day: 'In memory of the 586 members of his Majesty's naval, military and police forces murdered in Ireland.'

There was an ugly incident in Downing Street involving an artist named Harry Chance. He was arrested for causing a scene. He snatched a tricolour from a London-based Irish woman, spat on the flag and wiped his feet on it.

'When I spat on the flag,' Chance told the court next day, 'I did not do so out of disrespect for the Irish people, but because I have the utmost contempt for Michael Collins and the other people who were being tolerated in Downing Street. I have had friends and relatives killed by those people in Ireland in a most cowardly manner. By tolerating these people in England it is throwing mud in the faces of all decent people, including the men who served in the war. All this occurred right under the memorial to the men who fell in the war. Michael Collins ought to have been hung, drawn, and quartered years ago.'

Chance promised not to re-offend and he was just bound to the peace. But Kathleen McKenna noted that 'threatening letters to Michael Collins poured in daily'. Some of the men were worried about the Big Fellow's safety.

'One morning, I opened an envelop addressed to him containing a piece of cloth, and a letter enclosed stated that the cloth contained disease germs which the writer hoped would kill Collins and everyone near him,' Broy recalled. 'I immediately threw the lot into the nearest fire and suffered no ill effects from handling the missive. I did not know if there were really germs in the enclosure and considered its immediate destruction more prudent than investigation. Collins was not present when this letter arrived and when I told him about it he started pulling my leg, saying that all letters received by a good secretary should be carefully filed and indexed and asked me what precedent I had for destroying official correspondence. He said he would have to ask the Dáil to add an analyst to the team of experts attached to the Delegation.'

Collins was somewhat morose about the talks from the outset. 'Either way it will be wrong. Wrong because of what has come to pass. You might say the trap is sprung,' he wrote to his friend and aide, Joe O'Reilly, on the first day of the conference. 'I have come to call a spade a spade,' he added. 'It is the only name I know it by.'

Art O'Brien, the designated Irish ambassador to Britain

asked to be introduced to the British delegation, so that he could introduce their Irish counterparts, but Tom Jones was instructed to lead the Irish delegation to the cabinet room. Jones led the way, followed by O'Brien, Griffith, Collins and the others in single file.

'Lloyd George received us,' Barton recalled. 'He shook each of us warmly by the hand and introduced us to his colleagues who were standing behind him.' Only Lloyd George shook hands with the Irish delegates. The others just acknowledged each other across the table. This procedure had been followed to avoid a possible scene, as the prime minister was afraid the Irish might balk at shaking hands with Hamar Greenwood, the chief secretary for Ireland, and some of the British were obviously not enamoured with the possibility of shaking hands with Collins, the man they considered the head of the murder gang.

Greenwood was seated at the end of the British side of the table with Laming Worthington-Evans, the secretary of war, next to him. At the other end of the same side sat Gordon Hewart, the attorney-general, with colonial secretary Winston Churchill next to him, followed by Lord Birkenhead, the lord chancellor. Lloyd George took up his place in the centre on Birkenhead's right, and two secretaries, Tom Jones and Lionel Curtis, sat on either side of the prime minister in chairs that were slightly withdrawn from the table. Sir Austen Chamberlain, the Conservative leader, would normally sit on his right, but he was absent from the opening conference due to a backache.

'It was clear from the start that English interest was centred on Michael Collins,' according to Barton. 'We Irishmen were nervous and ill at ease, it was our first introduction to diplomacy. The English were at home and confident in surroundings where they had met and outmanoeuvred or intimidated their opponents in a hundred similar struggles.' Of course, the British were not nearly so experienced, but Barton's account was indicative of his tendency to be overawed not only by the British but even by his own colleagues. 'As it was Griffith and Collins were far more influential than the other members,' Barton wrote. 'Duggan was a cipher being an echo to Collins. Gavan Duffy had been away since early in 1919 as ambassador in France and Rome. I was quite a newcomer and had spent the last seventeen months in English Gaols entirely cut off from all communication.'

In all there were seven plenary sessions during the next two weeks of the conference. Collins said very little at any of the four sessions during the first week, which was taken up with general discussions on the July proposals.

From the outset the British took the offensive by insisting that those proposals would have to form the basis of any agreement. The Irish representatives, on the other hand, were trying to get External Association, even though they had not worked it out in any detail. Initially therefore they tried to follow de Valera's line in trying 'to hold back on the question of the Crown', until they knew what they were 'going to get in exchange for some accommodation regarding it'.

Collins was clearly ill-suited to this type of negotiating. He had little time for the endless beating around the bush. But, of course he soon found it impolitic to be as candid as he would have liked. As a result the first day with its two plenary sessions was particularly trying. 'I never felt so relieved at the end of any day, and I need hardly say I am not looking forward with any pleasure to resumption,' he wrote to de Valera. 'Such a crowd I never met.'

He was obviously deeply troubled. He had a reputation for being anti-clerical ever since his emigrant days in London when he called for the extermination of the Roman Catholic clergy, or in the GPO during the Easter Rebellion when he mocked Volunteers who sought a priest to make what they feared might be their last confession. It may well have been indicative of the weight upon his mind that he actually went to early morning mass and communion each day of the negotiations.

One parish priest, Fr T. Maguire, wrote advising Collins to avoid all British hospitality, to stay indoors, and to go to daily mass and communion. 'I know full the English methods in these matters,' Collins replied. 'The other part of your advice is being attended to also – though not – for essential reasons – quite fully.'

Broy was in the next room to Collins at Cadogan Gardens, and heard him get up around seven o'clock a few mornings. One morning Broy got up, expecting to find Collins having breakfast, but one of the orderlies told him that the Big Fellow went out alone each morning. 'I was alarmed at this, as there was still very strong anti-Irish feeling in London, particularly against Collins,' Broy explained. 'Next morning when Collins left Cadogan Gardens, I decided to follow him at some distance in case some enemy had noticed his habit of going out early and planned some hostile action. I kept a good distance behind and saw him enter the Church of St Mary (Cadogan Place). I entered and stayed at the back of the church and saw Michael at Mass in a most devout manner. When Mass had ended he remained on his knees, then got up and lit a candle, knelt again, and then lit another candle. When he moved to leave the Church, he saw me and at first frowned and then laughed.'

Broy was making no apologies for following him, because of the real danger that somebody might attack him. 'I said that unless somebody else accompanied him to early Mass, I would do so, and to do anything else would be gross neglect on my part,' Broy added. 'He agreed that I was right and that I could come with him each morning to Mass, if I desired. So from then on we went together. Sometimes we went to St Mary's and sometimes to Brompton Oratory.'

'On his return from morning Mass his surplus energy was

expanded at the expense of sluggards and late-risers,' according to Kathleen McKenna. 'The least they received from Mick on their pleasant dreams was a jug of cold water.'

'From the moment of Collins' arrival at 15 Cadogan Gardens until the end of the negotiations, he was occupied night, noon and morning in one form of activity or another and at night pressure all the time dealing with the most various problems and everything was dealt with with the utmost precision and efficiency, whether a military question arising in Ireland, or a complicated financial or economic subject,' Ned Broy recalled. 'The result was that he hardly ever got to bed before 1 a.m. and yet always arose about seven in the morning and always looked as fresh as if he had just taken a cold plunge.

'He duly pulled us all out of bed in the morning whether we complained of fatigue or not, and repeated the process when going to bed in the small hours, unless one had taken the precaution of locking the bedroom door,' Broy added. The feet of some of the beds were hinged and Collins would bend those back during the night so that some of the men awoke to find themselves sleeping at an angle to the floor.

'I remember looking into Emmet Dalton's bedroom one night and seeing him in his bed with the bed making an angle of thirty degrees with the floor,' Broy noted. 'As Collins had not yet come in I asked Emmet what happened to his bed. He said Collins would come in to bend the legs later on, and to save him the bother, Emmet had bent them up himself.'

Collins 'was brusque, violent, boisterous, fond of good-humoured horse-play, and quick-tempered,' according to Kathleen McKenna. One night when they were having a banquet at Hans Place, Collins arrived during the meal with Liam Tobin, Tom Cullen, Emmet Dalton, Joe Guilfoyle and Joe Dolan. 'They were a happy, boisterous group who preferred horse-play to formalities,' she recalled. 'I do not know how it came about but first of all they began throwing cushions at one another, then the tangerine oranges, apples and nuts from the table. We all knew Collins' exuberant character.'

On another night he took a central part in a battle on the top floor at Cadogan Place, where some furniture was broken. Joe McGrath, in his capacity as the delegation's accountant, came from Hans Place to inspect the damage.

'Well, the pack of dirty idiots! Look what all that will cost now for repairs!' McGrath exclaimed.

As minister for finance, Collins authorised payment for the damage done.

The task confronting the relatively inexperienced Irish negotiators was a formidable one, especially for Collins. At thirty he was by far the youngest of the delegates on either side of the conference table. All the others were in their forties or fifties.

Nevertheless he was soon to find himself in the unenviable position of sharing much of the leadership responsibility over a divided delegation that obviously lacked the full confidence of the cabinet at home. Yet he had to face a determined British delegation consisting of an experienced and seasoned team of negotiators, headed by Lloyd George, backed up by the most powerful men in the Conservative Party as well as his own wing of the Liberal Party.

Collins was uneasy with the British representatives because he disliked most of them with a varying intensity. Of course all of them were professional politicians, and most were lawyers – two types of people for whom Collins had a distinct aversion. He was convinced the genial Lloyd George – whom he found 'particularly obnoxious' – and Winston Churchill, the prime minister's erstwhile Liberal colleague, were both unprincipled individuals who would do anything for political gain.

'Churchill was a rude as could be,' according to Barton, who noted that the future British leader sat through the conference making paper boats and looking quite hostile. 'He always looked at us as if he would be glad to cut our throats, a very different attitude from Lloyd George, who was so affable.'

Collins considered Lloyd George, who was a trained lawyer, crafty and shrewd, because he behaved in a paternalistic way, apparently trusting that his benevolent air would surmount all obstacles. 'Lloyd George's attitude I find particular obnoxious,' Collins wrote during the second week of the conference. 'He is all comradely – all craft and wiliness – all arm around the shoulder – all the old friends act. Not long ago he would joyfully have had me at the rope end. He thinks that the past is all washed out now – but that's to my face. What he thinks behind my back makes me sick.' Collins believed the aptly nicknamed 'Welsh Wizard' desperately needed to boost to his flagging reputation and that he 'would sell his nearest and dearest for political prestige'.

'I hate demonstrative indications of feeling,' he would later write to Kitty Kiernan during the talks. 'They stand somehow in my mind for a kind of insincerity.' He added that 'it really means that I'm on the side of people who do things, not on the side of people who say things.'

Five of the seven members of the British delegation were lawyers, as were George Gavan Duffy and Eamonn Duggan on the Irish delegation. Collins got on with Duggan, who was totally in his control. The one lawyer with whom Collins would develop a surprising rapport was Lord Birkenhead, the lord chancellor, who had the reputation of being the staunchest unionist on the British side. As Frederick E. Smith, he had been one of Sir Edward Carson's staunchest unionist supporters. If there was to be a settlement, they would be seen as the people who compromised most. Hence they understood each other.

'When Michael Collins found that the hated Birkenhead was a human being and an adventurous spirit like himself, suspicion and hatred gave way to confidence and trust,' according to Geoffrey Shakespeare. 'Thereafter Birkenhead played an increasingly important part.'

'If all the British delegation had his capacity for clear thinking, capacity for work and getting ahead, things would be much easier,' Collins wrote. Describing the lord chancellor as 'a good man', he summed him up as a 'lawyer, but with a great difference. Concise.'

Austen Chamberlain, an older half-brother of future prime minister Neville Chamberlain, was the leader of the Conservative Party. He was a political heavyweight who was in his thirtieth year in parliament and had been chancellor of the exchequer as early as 1903. Collins did not like him because he considered him a difficult person. He was too formal, the kind of politician who played safe, staying in the middle of the road rather than standing by any convictions. Time would prove Collins unfair. Chamberlain sacrificed his own chances of becoming prime minister in the coming months by loyally supporting Lloyd George while his party revolted and brought down the coalition government and Andrew Bonar Law became prime minister. But all that was to happen the following year. As of the autumn of 1921 Collins thought Chamberlain was the type of person who 'says one thing and apparently means another'. He compared him with Gavan Duffy on the Irish side. The big difference was that Chamberlain had real clout within the British delegation.

Chamberlain, on the other hand, has his own reservations about Collins. 'He had his own code of honour, and to it he was true, but it was not mine, and between him and me there could be no real sympathy and perhaps only partial understanding,' Chamberlain explained.

Winston Churchill, the secretary for the colonies, was first elected to parliament as a Conservative more than twenty years earlier, but he then bolted the party that his father had once led. He joined the Liberal Party and supported David Lloyd

George in the heave to oust Herbert H. Asquith as prime minister in 1916. Lloyd George included Churchill in the British negotiating delegation because he was too dangerous to leave out. In the eyes of many people Churchill was coming to the end of his political career because he had backed the wrong political horse in deserting the Conservative Party. Nobody on his own side really trusted him, so it was hardly surprising that Collins should have reservations. He believed Churchill's only goal was political advancement. 'Will sacrifice all for political gain,' Collins wrote. 'Inclined to be bombastic. Full of ex-officer jingo or similar outlook. Don't actually trust him.'

There could be little rapport between Collins and the chief secretary for Ireland, Sir Hamar Greenwood, who was seen as the chief defender of the Black and Tans. He was a Canadian lawyer in his early fifties. Collins considered him a bombastic and over-riding individual. 'A man who earns my personal detestation,' he wrote, adding that these feelings were reciprocated.

The attorney-general, Sir Gordon Hewart, was another lawyer in his fifties. Collins described him as 'a difficult man to deal with', because he 'never relaxes'. The final member of the British delegation was the new secretary of war, Sir Laming Worthington-Evans, who had only been appointed to the position earlier in the year.

'This is a real nest of singing birds,' Collins wrote of the British delegation during the second week of the conference. 'They chirrup mightily one to another – and there's the falseness of it all, because not one trusts the other.'

From the outset the British were insisting on their July proposals, which offered a form of dominion status that was limited by trade and defence restrictions. The Irish delegation was effectively seeking the *de facto* independence of the dominions. In countering the British proposal, the Irish delegation argued that even though they were looking for more, the British offer did not even amount to dominion status, because unprecedented defence and trade concessions were being demanded of Ireland.

Collins argued, for instance, that the dominions were free to withdraw from the British commonwealth, but the right was being denied to Ireland. 'Bonar Law said that the Dominions could vote themselves out of the British Empire,' Collins said.

'All that means is that we might not undertake military operations against the Dominions which did so,' Lloyd George replied. In other words, British could undertake measures against Ireland that they would not employ against the other dominions because they were so far away. This was precisely why de Valera believed that Ireland needed something more than dominion status to ensure the country enjoyed the same freedom as Canada or the other dominions.

'Unprecedented naval concessions were being demanded from Ireland,' Collins argued. 'You are asking more from us than from them in this naval business.'

Lloyd George suggested the conference set up a subcommittee to examine the defence question.

'We would like that very much,' Collins replied.

Chapter Seven

'LIKE A LONDON POLICEMAN BEING AFRAID OF A CHILD'

Three different subcommittees were established to consider defence, finance and issues relating to violations of the Truce. Collins was the only Irish plenipotentiary on all three sub-committees. He attended all eight meetings of the three sub-committees, as did Childers, while Barton and Duggan joined them at the five meetings of the Committee for the Observance of the Truce.

The first of the Truce subcommittee meetings on 12 October brought Collins, Barton and Duggan face to face with Secretary of War Sir Laming Worthington-Evans and Chief Secretary for Ireland Sir Hamar Greenwood, as well as Under-Secretary of State Sir John Anderson and assistant Under-Secretary Andy Cope, along with Major General Henry Tudor, head of the Black and Tans and crown police in Ireland, and General Sir Neville Macready, the general office in charge of British forces in Ireland.

'As it was the first time I had come face to face with Collins,' Macready wrote, 'I naturally was interested in a man who was in fact the principal figure in the rebellion.' He found the Big Fellow a very interesting character. 'Tall, dark, strongly though loosely built, with an apparent indifference to personal appearance,' Macready wrote, 'he exhibited the Irish characteristics in a marked degree, being when the occasion offered, a *bon vivant*, an admirer of the other sex, and from all accounts a cheery companion when free from the cares of office. Fearless he certainly was, to which he added a degree of cunning which stood him in good stead in many a tight corner.'

'Among the various Sinn Féiners with whom from time to time I came in touch,' Macready continued, 'Michael Collins struck me as being the easiest to deal with. Of a type common in Ireland, his like can be seen by the score on any Irish race-course, but he had what few of his countrymen possess, a sense of humour, and, above all, the gift during a conversation of sticking to essentials.' When colleagues drifted off the subject under the discussion, he would call them back to order, 'and complete the business with the least possible waste of time'.

The high-powered team that the British assembled to discuss the Truce may have temporarily intimidated Collins. Macready privately explained, for example, that Collins initially came across badly because he sought to get out of difficult positions by making 'poor jokes in bad taste'. Collins wrote next day that it looked for a time that the conference might collapse over Truce violations. He explained that he 'never felt so ashamed' as when the British produced a photograph of some IRA volunteers with a machine gun and handkerchiefs over their faces. This was 'cheap bravado,' and he felt 'let down'. They could continue drilling at the camp if they just discontinued the publicity, which was 'the real grievance', because they had not been seeking such publicity before the Truce.

Another issue of contention was the publicity being given to republican courts. Those had been given practically no publicity prior to the Truce, so Childers wrote to de Valera that 'it would be absurd that the negotiations should break on such an issue when serious issues were at stake'. De Valera responded that the British should be told that 'the publicity given in Dublin and some other places was not authorised by our Headquarters, and we shall continue to discourage publicity. We cannot go beyond that.'

'We cannot give way an inch on this question of civil functioning, but it is certainly too bad that the other side should have got the opportunity which the blaze of publicity gave them,' de Valera wrote to Griffith on 14 October. 'I would advise if the discussion is continued, that you call over the Minister of Home Affairs.'

Stack had refused to go to London as one of the plenipotentiaries, yet de Valera was now suggesting that he should be allowed to deal with matters relating to his own department. Before this letter reached London, however, the issue had been resolved by agreeing to stop the publicity. 'It is agreed on both sides that no courts shall be held in Ireland otherwise than as before the Truce,' Childers informed de Valera, who concurred but stressed 'the courts would go on in secret'. If there was any publicity, he contended, this would be the result of 'the increased freedom of the newspapers during the Truce and not from any deliberate act of ours'.

Many of the Truce violations were minor matters. With the British raising issues like the republican courts and IRA training camp, Collins complained that a British agent had followed him to mass at Maiden Lane on 16 October, and that a British officer name Tully was circulating photographs of him in the Athlone area, while a British colonel had issued instructions on 1 October for the British army to be ready to hunt down the rebels once the peace collapsed, when they should be given 'no peace' until 'all important leaders have been arrested or satisfactorily accounted for'. Collins added that he had seen many other similar orders since the Truce. 'Such documents were bound to lead not merely to individual breaches of the Truce but to a general disregard of it,' he warned.

'For the moment I don't know that it was issued,' Worthington-Evans replied.

'We know,' the Big Fellow insisted. 'You can't issue these documents without my knowledge.'

On the third day of the conference there was a report that Collins spotted a rifle in the hallway of 10 Downing Street. 'What is the meaning of this provocative display?' he asked in a jocose manner.

The prime minister laughed and picked up the rifle, explaining that it was the first American rifle made for the First World War. Collins thereupon suggested that he should sit in a chair with the rifle in his hands and Lloyd George should call the *Morning Post* to send over a photographer. Everybody reportedly laughed.

Next day Collins celebrated his thirty-first birthday with a small private party. 'It was a lovely party,' he wrote to Kitty, 'but it was unpleasant as I have too many things to carry at the present moment. It is not right for me to inflict myself on people.' The pressure of the negotiations was obviously wearing on him. 'I don't like gramophone effects,' he continued. 'I like the people to say what they themselves think and mean.'

The finance subcommittee only met once and its deliberations were inconclusive, while the other two subcommittees were more important. On those Collins was helped by some of his own men like Emmet Dalton, J. J. O'Connell, Eoin O'Duffy and Diarmuid O'Hegarty, together with Erskine Childers, who soon proved to be a particularly unhappy choice, because he was 'altogether too radical and impractical' in the estimation of Collins.

Childers was not shy about pushing his own strong views. On the third day of the conference, he was with Collins when they met Churchill and the first sea lord, Admiral David Beatty, who was about to leave for the Washington naval conference.

'Ireland, an island with a maritime frontier, is to be denied responsibility for her own naval defence' just because she happened to be sixty-one miles from Britain, Childers argued.

'Now, gentlemen, I mean to demonstrate that Ireland is not only no source of danger to England, but from the military standpoint, is virtually useless.'

'This announcement staggered me probably more than it did the other two,' Collins recalled. 'It was ridiculous balderdash. I felt like wanting to get out of the room, but I naturally realised that I must make the pretence of standing by my colleague. Churchill and Beatty exchanged a glance, and then gave Childers their attention again.'

'Take the matter of Irish bases for English submarine chasers,' Childers continued. 'From the viewpoint of naval expediency Plymouth is a far better base than any port on the Irish coast.'

'You really think so?' Beatty asked.

Childers insisted this was the case. 'For instance,' he added, 'supposing Ireland were not there at all?'

'Ah,' said the admiral with a smile, 'but Ireland is there.'

'And how many times have we wished she were not!' interjected Churchill.

While the hypothetical approach adopted by Childers would have been appreciated by the more theoretical mind of a mathematician like de Valera, it had no appeal for the practically-minded Collins, who did not even bother to relate the details of the hypothetical argument.

Using a map marking the locations of ships sunk by U-boats during the Great War, Beatty argued that in some situations certain Irish ports would obviously be more strategic than Plymouth for anti-submarine warfare. Childers had no real answer, much to the chagrin of Collins, who noted that he 'never felt more a fool' in his life.

'I had an idea,' Collins continued. Pointing to the French coast, he suggested that Le Havre would make 'an excellent base for British forces engaged in hunting submarines'.

'Quite so,' replied the admiral with another smile, 'but we can't take the French port!'

'If that constitutes duress,' Collins later explained, 'I'll admit that we were under duress. But to my way of thinking it is plain talk, right talk, and the kind of talk I prefer my opponents to use.'

Of course, Collins could not have known that Beatty did not attach a great deal of importance to Irish bases. It was Churchill who thought the bases were important, and he was thinking of air bases, naval bases and recruiting stations.

Beatty and the other admirals thought naval bases in Ireland were of 'little importance' when Churchill discussed the matter with them before the sub-conference meeting. 'Our position is,' he insisted on behalf of the government, 'we must have free use of the Irish coasts in peace or war for Imperial defence.'

After the meeting Collins again wrote to Kitty Kiernan that he preferred people to be open. 'I would like people to say what they themselves think and mean,' he wrote. Yet even at that early stage of the conference he had found himself having to support arguments in which he did not really believe.

The meeting with Admiral Beatty was considered an informal one to facilitate Admiral Beatty before he left for the Washington naval conference. The first subcommittee meeting on defence was four days later. Some of the arguments would later be of particular historical interest during the Second World War, especially when Churchill as first lord of the admiralty would dispute Ireland's right to remain neutral. 'Legally,' he wrote in 1939, 'I believe they are "at war but skulking".' Some of the arguments of 17 October 1921 would be tested under real conditions, so in view of the subsequent historical import, it is worth considering the subcommittee deliberations between Churchill and Collins in particular depth.

'At the outset,' Churchill explained, 'I want to make it quite clear that the British government do not want any facilities, naval, air or military, from Ireland for the purpose of interfering with the internal forces of Ireland. The only facilities we want are those necessary to enable us to discharge our responsibilities of self-guarding the British Empire in peace and war, of protecting our commerce and maintaining our food supplies.' He then read a formula covering Britain's needs from the naval perspective:

The Irish government confides the responsibility for the naval defence of Irish interests on the high seas to the Royal Navy and for this purpose as well as for those of general Imperial defence places its posts, harbours, and inlets unreservedly at the disposal of the Imperial Government in peace or war.

'The suggestion that we should bind ourselves to place ports and inlets at your disposal puts us in the position of servants,' Collins argued.

On considering the number of facilities that Admiral Beatty had requested, Churchill said he was surprised there were so few. The Royal Navy desired Berehaven 'so that they might have a station from which they could convoy their food ships, attack hostile submarines and generally protect them in case of war'.

Collins said that he could see no necessity for such demands. 'You have force and therefore you have security,' he said.

'You cannot realise that in England there would be a certain feeling against handing over at once these fortified ports to Ireland,' Churchill contended. 'We cannot object of course to your having full dominion development and we would be glad when the opportunity came to enable you to take responsibility for these defences.'

'Where were the facilities they desired?' Childers asked.

'What we want is naval places of strategic importance,' Worthington-Evans said.

'This document appears to mean that you are at liberty to take over any site in any part of Ireland,' said Collins.

'Certainly, if these sites were necessary for the defence of the Empire,' Vice-Admiral Osmond Brock interjected.

'Of course we can do this in Australia,' Churchill added.

'As a practical man,' Collins asked Churchill, 'do you think that we are going to build a big navy?'

'Honestly, I do not,' replied Churchill, 'and why then should we get into these depths? Why should these questions be raised?'

'It is we really who are dealing with this in a practical manner,' said Collins.

'We must deal with realities,' Churchill insisted.

'Quite so,' Collins agreed. 'Why then put in references to matters which are not real, and which are offensive to our susceptibilities? Take for example the proposal of taking over any of our property. That looks very much like free-booting.'

'At present it is our undoubted right to take over these places,' Churchill insisted.

'That is not conceded. You take them by force,' Collins argued.

'But we want to substitute law for force,' Churchill said.

'Why not let these matters rest upon the basis of common interest?' asked Collins.

'I am afraid we could not do that,' Churchill replied. 'We could not justify ourselves before Parliament. No British Government could afford to take such a course.'

'Could not neutralisation of Ireland be your best safeguard?' Childers asked.

'We could not agree to that at all,' Churchill insisted.

'But is it not true that the Dominions can remain neutral in time of war?' J. J. O'Connell asked.

''Tis not so,' Churchill argued. 'In theory when the King declares war, constitutionally all his subjects are at war. In practice, I admit that there has been some differences of opinion. The claim has been advanced in certain cases that the Dominions may remain neutral, but the responsible authorities of these Dominions do not hold this opinion and it is not shared by the British Government. If a dominion declared its own neutrality at the outbreak of a war it would be equivalent to declaring its intention to leave the British commonwealth – it would in fact be a revolution. I do not know how we would deal with it or whether we would take any action. That would depend on the circumstances of the case.'

Collins and Childers argued that various leading politicians had asserted that the dominions had the right to remain neutral, and Childers noted that the dominions had signed the Versailles Treaty separately. If they had the right to make peace, then 'it surely followed they would have a voice in the making of war'.

'The position is really this,' Churchill explained. 'If we set about a war of aggrandisement, or an unjust war, there would undoubtedly be considerable divergence of opinion amongst some of the Dominions. The British Empire can only go to war when a strong and united feeling in favour of war exists.'

'That is all in favour of our arguments,' Collins insisted. 'Assume the neutrality of Ireland. In a just war Ireland would in her own interest unite with you.'

'The constitutional position is that war is made on the advice of the Dominion Ministers,' Childers argued.

'Not quite,' said Churchill.

'But it is developing to that,' said Collins.

'Yes.'

'If you engage in an unjust war would not all your safeguards regarding the Dominion go?' Collins asked.

'I think that is so,' Churchill admitted

'That is just the point,' Collins said. 'Good feelings are much better than good clauses.'

But Churchill insisted that the defence situation had to be clarified. 'Even if you were a Republic we would have to have a treaty covering this matter.'

'I take it that you would agree that our coming into a war as a free associate would be preferable to our being forced to come in. But so long as our position does not interfere with your safety that should be sufficient. I think we could agree on that basis,' Collins said.

The issue of bases was about more than naval ports. The British also wanted air facilities, but they showed little interest in military bases though Worthington-Evans noted 'the Curragh had always been a camp and was always a source of income to Ireland. Perhaps Ireland would not like the Curragh to go.'

'But we will want it to train our territorial force,' Collins insisted.

'It is really only a question of the defended ports,' Worthington-Evans replied.

'I cannot see what you people are afraid of,' Collins added. 'It is like a London policeman being afraid of a child.'

'Yes,' said Churchill, 'but there are dangerous children who play with matches and fireworks.'

On the issue of air bases, Collins noted that Irish territory was of no significance in the air war with Germany. Therefore he tried to manoeuvre Churchill into the position of arguing that such facilities would be necessary in the event of war between Britain and the United States.

'What we want really is that we may have Irish ports from which our destroyers can leave to protect and convoy our food supplies at those places where trade routes converge and where the submarines operate most effectively. We want our aeroplanes to start from flat places in connection with these naval ports to scour for submarines. I want to be quite frank – we do not want you to think that we want these ports as facilities for war with the United States. You are forcing me into a position, and I do not want you to say that you are prepared to agree to everything but that you broke because we wanted facilities for war with the States.'

'The fact that you are taking over certain concessions from Ireland would give the impression that you are at present securing facilities for such a war,' Collins argued.

They ended the day's discussion arguing about British recruiting stations in Ireland. Collins contended that Britain would not be able to recruit because Irish people would no longer join the British services. But Churchill argued that his government were only seeking that recruiting should not be proscribed. 'We will be satisfied if there is no ban,' Churchill concluded.

The spotlight was very much on Collins at the talks. 'Collins seems to have attracted everybody,' Austen Chamberlain noted. Health minister Alfred Mond said at a military dinner on 17 October that Collins was a better general than any of the English generals, much to the irritation of Field Marshal Sir Henry Wilson.

'He had certainly done a thing that none of us had done yet – that was that he had taken the Prime Minister and the Cabinet by the throat and cowed them,' Wilson said.

'It was the British Army he cowed,' Mond replied.

'That's a lie, and you know it is a lie and you will apologise,' the field marshal insisted.

Mond apologised. 'The matters amicably settled, Mond went to work and cursed Lloyd George in a way that did me good to hear,' Wilson continued in his diary. 'Mond said that Lloyd George knew nothing, cared nothing except for himself, interfered with everybody, and made chaos of everything he touched!'

The same day Collins submitted a memorandum, written by Childers, and the subcommittee held a further meeting shortly after noon. 'This able memorandum will shorten the task of this committee, in fact will bring it to an end. It amounts to a reasoned, measured, uncompromising refusal to meet us at any point,' Churchill began. 'The right to build an Irish navy is claimed. I regard this as a mortal blow.'

Childers argued that Ireland, 'an island with a maritime frontier, is to be denied responsibility for her own naval defence'. This was, in essence, a denial of Ireland's 'existence as a nation'. But in the memorandum submitted to the British before the meeting, Childers conceded that the use of the requested facilities would be a convenience to the admiralty, but it would have 'the grave disadvantage of curtailing the status of Ireland'. The memorandum added 'an offensive fighting navy is not of course feasible or dreamed of', with the result that British apprehensions were not understandable, 'for no Irish naval forces could be a menace to England'.

'Ireland would be very unlikely to plan the building of submarines which are eminently an offensive weapon out of harmony with her purely defensive policy,' the memorandum continued. As far as Collins was concerned, however, this concession made nonsense of the Irish arguments. The right to have a navy was useless if Ireland could not have submarines, seeing that the Irish people simply could not afford to build and sustain a navy of surface ships. Believing that attack was the best method of defence, Collins thought that submarines, which were comparatively inexpensive to build and cheap to run, were the country's only hope of defending herself properly.

In a speech in Ballinamuck on 17 February 1918, he had said that within three years of independence Ireland would be able to run ten submarines and 'they would make England keep her Dreadnoughts and Super-Dreadnoughts in their own ports'. If Churchill had been aware of that speech he would, no doubt, have made use of it, but being a practical individual Collins must have appreciated the British thinking on the issue, in the light of his own arguments in Ballinamuck.

By renouncing the right to have submarines, Childers effectively undermined the Irish case by conceding 'a point that really mattered. This cannot be stated too emphatically,' Collins later contended.

He realised, of course, that concessions would have to be made on defence, or he would hardly have submitted the memorandum drawn up by Childers to the British in the first place. The difference between himself and Childers was that once Collins recognised the necessity to concede a point, he was prepared to carry the concession to its logical, or practical, conclusion. Yet, like one of those politicians he so despised, he now went through the motions of arguing the case.

Collins afterwards told Childers that he thought the British might yet acknowledge Ireland's right to neutrality. 'I am more doubtful,' Childers noted in letters to both de Valera and Brugha.

Childers thought the British demands were motivated by political considerations, rather than strategic interests. 'They took the line of evading the strategical argument as much as they could by harping on the political impossibility of neutrality, but we got them down to a certain amount of detail,' Childers wrote to Brugha. 'They have a poor strategical case.'

Chapter Eight

'THERE MIGHT BE A PLAN FOR A BOUNDARY COMMISSION'

Lloyd George and his colleagues were exploiting their own political difficulties. Griffith recognised that they were doing this 'for negotiating purposes, but it would be a mistake for the people at home to think there are none'.

'There is no doubt whatever that Lloyd George has the diehard crowd to fight,' de Valera acknowledged, 'but it is well that he should realise there are people in this country who are just as determined.' Some Irish groups had actually been petitioning the delegation, much to the annoyance of Griffith.

'I received a resolution from the Mayo Co. Council to the effect that we should break off negotiations unless the prisoners were released,' he complained to de Valera. 'So the whole national fight of the past five years is sought now to be put on the basis of an amnesty movement. I suppose there is nothing more behind these resolutions but stupidity and mawkishness, but it is bad to see any section of our people back to resolution-mongering and seeking unwittingly to regard us as a political party whose policy they control rather than an established Government whose policy they uphold.'

In the midst of all this Collins was deeply uneasy. 'Trouble everywhere,' he wrote to Kitty next day. 'Last night I escaped all my own people and went for a drive alone.' He was feeling lonely and made arrangements for her to spend some time in London with him.

The negotiations were especially trying for Collins as he felt he had to act as a politician. 'To be a politician,' he wrote to a friend, 'one needs to have the ability to say one thing and mean another; one needs to be abnormally successful at the "art" of twisting the truth. Can you wonder that I think and think yet never manage to achieve peace of mind?' He was afraid that anything he might say would be twisted and used against him. 'I do not in the least care for the false atmosphere of these discussions,' he wrote.

In this frame of mind he tended to become undiplomatically irritable. During one subcommittee meeting, Emmet Dalton recalled that Churchill was making a forceful case about Irish violations of the Truce.

'Have we any answer to these?' Collins scribbled in a note to Dalton.

'No.'

Collins then listened for a while longer before suddenly becoming exasperated and slamming his fist on the table. 'For Christ sake,' he said, 'come to the point.'

The loquacious Churchill was momentarily stunned speechless. He sat there with an astonished expression on his face. At that point Collins erupted with an infectious laugh. Even Churchill joined in the laughter, thereby dissipating much of the force from his carefully prepared argument.

Yet this was only a moment of light relief for Collins, who was otherwise deeply agitated. He was finding it necessary to hide his true feelings, not only from the British but also from some of his own colleagues, especially Childers, who was critical of the Irish delegation for conceding too much. Chiders was sending his own secret reports to the members of the cabinet in Dublin. It would not long before Collins would come to the conclusion that those in Dublin were the 'real problem' in the search for a settlement.

The trade issue was discussed at the third plenary session of the conference on 13 October. Barton did most of the talking for the Irish side. He noted that the Dominions had complete control of their trade, and Ireland was therefore being put in an inferior position by the British demand for free trade between the two countries. 'Why do you put us in this unfair position?' he asked.

'We propose a mutually binding and reciprocal treaty,' Lloyd George explained.

'I hear that Resolutions are on the way from the Dublin Chamber of Commerce contending that Ireland should have complete fiscal control,' Barton said.

'How can we protect ourselves against the danger of dumping?' Collins asked.

'You can produce more cheaply,' Lloyd George replied. 'If there is no Treaty there may be a demand here for protection against Irish cheap labour.'

'We do not want to impose a tariff on Britain but we want the free development of our industrial life,' Collins insisted.

'I propose we shall both be bound,' Lloyd George said.

'I want most favoured nation treatment,' Barton argued. 'We won't penalise you as regards other nations.'

But Lloyd George wanted more. If Ireland was going to be free to impose a tariff, then Britain should also be free to do so also, even to introduce one first. 'We bind ourselves to receive your stuff without tariffs,' he said, 'and you bind yourselves to receive our stuff without tariffs.'

'It is not unreasonable to give us safeguards for our development?' Collins asked. 'I mentioned the case of dumping.'

'Perhaps the Attorney-General can find a formula for that,' the prime minister said.

'Take the trade for 1921 between Ireland and England as a basis and allow for fair increase,' Collins argued.

'I think we can go into the question of meeting the case of the crushing of an infant industry in its cradle,' Chamberlain replied.

There was no Ulster clause in Draft Treaty A, and the Irish delegation had to deal with the question at the fourth plenary session of the conference on 14 October, before the clause had arrived from Dublin. Griffith did most of the talking for the Irish side, with Collins and the others merely interjecting, while Lloyd George did most of the talking for the British.

'If the British government stands aside and does not throw its force behind Ulster we will come to an agreement,' Griffith argued, 'but so long as they feel the British behind them there is *non possumus*. Northern Ireland is but a portion of Ulster. What you have done is as if some few counties in England had been separated from the rest. In the six county area there is a population of 1,200,000 of whom 800,000 are Protestant, 400,000 Catholics. In the whole of Ulster the population is 1,600,000, with Protestant 850,000, Catholics 750,000.'

'You and Northern Ireland are faced with the coercion of one-third of its area,' Collins told the British delegation. 'Tyrone and Fermanagh, more than half Armagh, a great deal of Derry and a strip of Antrim will go with the authority they prefer and can put this N.E. corner into the position of Vienna. As to the use of force: if our people are attacked they will have to defend themselves.'

The Ulster question had undermined Gladstone and it would have defeated his own government if he had not introduced partition, the prime minister contended. 'Ulster was arming and would fight,' he said. 'We were powerless. It is no use ignoring facts however unpleasant they may be. The politician who thinks he can deal out abstract justice without reference to forces around him cannot govern.' He had tried to persuade Craig and Carson to accept a united Ireland in 1916 but they refused.

'They said their followers would desert them if they did,' Lloyd George added. 'It is a mistake to assume that the population of Ulster for the time being is opposed to partition. It is not. I am glad that de Valera has come to the conclusion we favoured that force is not a weapon you can use. It would break in your hands. We should have a terrible civil war and you would draw men from all parts into the vortex of the whirlpool. Mr Collins shakes his head. He knows Ireland. I know Great Britain and the Empire. It would resolve itself into a religious war. You do not want to begin your new life with a civil war which would leave you with despoliation in its train. Therefore I am glad that we are agreed that force is impossible.

'Take the case of the Dominions,' Lloyd George continued. 'They all began with partition except New Zealand.' Australia, Canada and South Africa were all partitioned. 'Use persuasion and we will stand on one side.' The prime minister repeatedly referred to de Valera's assurance ruling out the use of force. He was content to allow Dublin to induce Belfast to agree to unity by any peaceful means.

'It is not intended to use force, not because Ulster would not be defeated in a fight,' Collins said, 'but because defeat would not settle the matter.' He made it clear, however, that some provisions would have to be made for many of the nationalists who had been included in Northern Ireland against their will.

The historical province of Ulster consisted of nine counties, but the unionists might not have been able to rule the whole province, so it was partitioned, with Counties Donegal, Monaghan and Cavan being hived off to join the rest of the island. But the Catholic minority in the six counties was still much greater than the Protestant minority was in the island as a whole. Thus if the Protestants were entitled to partition, the Catholic minority in Northern Ireland had an even better case for further partition. The two largest counties in Northern Ireland – Fermanagh and Tyrone – actually had Roman Catholic majorities that wished to go with the rest of the island. In addition, the adjacent areas of south Down, south Armagh and the city of Derry (or Londonderry) had Catholic majorities. All of those had been included in Northern Ireland to give unionists the maximum area that they could safely control. Collins quoted Edward Carson as having said that 'a strong Ulster of six counties could do far more than a weak tottering fabric of the whole nine counties'.

'In order to persuade Ulster to come in,' Lloyd George argued, 'there is an advantage in her having a Catholic population. I think you will get Ulster into an Irish unit on agreed terms. We promise to stand aside and you will have not only our neutrality but our benevolent neutrality.'

'We do not want to coerce them,' Collins explained, 'but we cannot allow a solid block who are against partition in the north of Antrim, through a part of Derry and parts of Armagh and Strangford Lough. If we are not going to coerce the N.E. corner, the N.E. corner must not be allowed to coerce.' At this point he made what was, in the light of subsequent events, a particularly significant addition. 'There might,' he added, 'be a plan for a boundary commission or for a local option, or whatever you may call it.' This was the first time anyone mentioned a boundary commission.

'You speak of Great Britain stepping out, but you are not stepping out, because you have set up a boundary already. That is not letting us have a fair go,' Collins argued when they discussed the Ulster question at the fifth plenary session of the conference on 17 October. 'The present six counties implies coercion; South and East Down, South Armagh, Fermanagh and Tyrone will not come in Northern Ireland and it is not fair to ask them to come in it. We are prepared to face the problem itself – not your definition of it.'

'We do not care in the slightest degree where Irishmen put Tyrone and Fermanagh,' Lloyd George replied, 'but it is no use making peace with you if we are going to have civil war with Ulster.'

'But you will have civil war because nearly half the area will come into the Southern Parliament,' Collins insisted.

Somebody mentioned that there were 50,000 Protestants in Dublin. If the Catholics in Northern Ireland were to be allowed to transfer, what about the Protestants in Dublin?

'I have yet to meet the Dublin Protestant who wants to come into the Northern Parliament,' Griffith replied.

'What about "scattered non-contiguous areas" comprising nationalists pockets deep in unionist hinterland?' Lloyd George asked.

'There we would have to do a deal in exchange,' Griffith replied, pointing to north-east Antrim.

'That is not self-determination, but a deal,' the prime minister said. 'That is what we had to do. I do not see how you are to get out of that except by dealing yourselves with north-east Ulster. We will stand aside. Whatever agreement you come to we will give whatever sanction is required.'

'But you give an unfair advantage to Ulster,' Collins argued.

'You are putting a premium on the present status,' Gavan Duffy interjected.

'That means that Irishmen cannot agree among themselves and we must come in,' Austen Chamberlain explained.

The British made a mess of what they did, as far as Collins was concerned. The country was already partitioned before the Truce, but it had hardly gone into effect. 'You will be faced with the necessity of coercing large districts into allegiance to this new Northern Ireland Parliament,' he insisted. 'They have made no arrangements to function.'

'That is because of this conference,' Lloyd George replied. 'They would go ahead tomorrow.'

'It will never function,' Griffith argued. 'Four hundred thousand people when dragged in will not obey it.'

The discussions dragged on with Griffith insisting, 'We cannot agree to the Six County basis.'

'Not as a basis of reason, but for practical action?' Birkhenhead interjected.

'If Ulster knew the six county area was not to be retained, we could discuss then with her various solutions of the problem,' Gavan Duffy argued.

'If we are to reach a settlement we cannot leave this in doubt,' Lloyd George concluded, and they adjourned for the day.

Immediately afterward the prime minister passed a note to Tom Jones about the situation in Fermanagh and Tyrone. 'This is going to wreck settlement,' he wrote.

As part of the proposed financial settlement, Britain was demanding that Ireland should contribute to her war debt, but this issue never really posed a serious problem during the London conference. It was eventually entrusted to separate negotiations. Of course, the manner in which Collins dealt with the issue – when the subcommittee on finance met for the only time on 19 October 1921 – provided a classic example of his style of negotiation.

Instead of countering the British demand by building a case to show that Britain owed Ireland money, so that the British might of their own accord suggest an acceptable compromise, Collins began by suggesting a compromise. He contended that, as Ireland had been grossly overtaxed during the nineteenth century, she should now start out with a clean slate.

As the British were to receive reparations from Germany, Collins demanded that Ireland should get a share of those re-parations. Moreover, citing the 1895 report of a famous royal commission chaired by Hugh Childers, a distant cousin of Barton and Erskine Childers, Collins noted that Ireland had been over-taxed to the extent of £350 million. 'You say "let bygones be bygones" but still you start with your War Debt, and want us to take over a portion of the liability.' The British were still over-taxing Ireland by about £21 million a year and they were expecting the Irish now to be grateful because they were going to reduce that to £14.5 million a year.

'We are quite willing to consider any proposal you put forward,' Worthington-Evans said.

'If we go into all past details, you will find that you owe us money,' Collins argued. 'I say, let us get rid of these details and let us treat the past as the past.' But the British persisted.

'I will put some arguments that may surprise you,' Collins said.

'Mr Collins will never surprise me again,' Worthington-Evans replied. 'We would like to have a statement of your counter-claims. Could you put these in now? It need not wait for our memorandum.'

'According to my figures our counter-claim works out at £3,940,000,000,' Collins replied.

'I suppose that dates from the time of Brian Boru!' Chancellor of the exchequer Robert Horne interjected. 'How much did we owe you then?'

'Oh, no,' Collins said, 'it is the capital sum since the Act of Union. Of course I have included in my calculations your restrictions on our capital development.'

'It is really damages for bad treatment then,' said Horne.

'Perhaps you do not know, but at the time of the Union we had a flourishing tobacco industry,' Collins explained. 'The Joint Exchequer board placed a tax on manufactured tobacco and destroyed the industry. In this case I have only put down the capital value of the industry at the time.

'We are making a claim for reparation,' Collins continued. 'You may not think we have a claim, but we have.'

Afterwards John Chartres was furious at Horne's remark about Brian Boru. 'Did you see how they laughed at us?' he asked. 'It was infamous.'

The two sides exchanged a number of detailed memoranda arguing the case. Collins enlisted the services of Joseph Brennan, who had been serving with the British administration in Ireland. Even though Brennan was technically on the crown side,

Collins was always prepared to enlist the help of such Irishmen, regardless of past political affiliation. Indeed such people had made a vital contribution to his intelligence system.

'Never mind what the record of these people was in the past,' Collins told Childers, 'let us assume now that they are in the Irish cause up to their necks.'

Examining the further financial aspects of the negotiations would be both tedious and somewhat pointless, because the two sides ultimately concluded that a financial settlement should be left to separate negotiations later. But it should be mentioned that the choice of advisers was causing resentment with some of those in Dublin. De Valera wrote that Brugha felt that as he was minister of defence, the defence advisers – who included Eoin O'Duffy, J. J. 'Ginger' O'Connell and Emmet Dalton – 'should have been summoned through him'. The president added that Brugha 'would like to know why that course was not followed'. Likewise, constitutional advisers should have been summoned through Stack, according to de Valera.

Griffith accepted the principle, but by then the advisers had already been chosen, so it did not matter. Yet it was another instance in which the delegation did not challenge an apparent infringement of its powers. The plenipotentiaries were only answerable to the Dáil, which appointed them, and certainly not to any individual members of the cabinet, especially those who had refused to be part of the delegation.

If Collins saw ominous implications in the president's letter, these were only minor to the sense of foreboding he must have felt next day when the delegation learned from the morning press that de Valera had sent an open telegram to Pope Benedict XV in response to an exchange of messages between the pope and King George V.

'Isn't this grand?' Gavan Duffy said, producing the morning newspaper with a report about the president's telegram.

In responding to a message from the pope, the British king

had expressed the hope that the negotiations would 'achieve a permanent settlement of the trouble in Ireland and may initiate a new era of peace and happiness for my people'. De Valera complained that this implied the Irish strife was an internal British problem and the Irish people owed allegiance to the king, whereas Ireland had already declared her independence.

Although de Valera's inference was not unreasonable, the king's message was vague enough to be interpreted differently. His use of the term 'my people' could be interpreted as just the British people, seeing that the Irish Republic had already been declared.

The whole matter was ambiguous, as the president himself admitted in his own telegram to the Vatican. De Valera had backed off on the self-recognition issue in accepting the final invitation to the conference, but he was exploiting the pope's telegram to raise the issue again. He actually used the king's message as an excuse to reproach the pope, whose telegram was the offensive one from the Irish standpoint. If the pope had been evenhanded, he should have sent a similar telegram to the president in Dublin. But de Valera was not about to insult the pope publicly, so he complained about the king's message instead.

'I am sure this was somewhat disconcerting but it could not be helped,' de Valera explained to Griffith. 'They must be taught that propaganda stunts, such as the exchange of messages between themselves and the Vatican, will not be allowed to pass unchallenged by us. Though it might be explained on the Vatican's part, the balance of the probabilities to my mind is that the inspiration of the Vatican's message came from British sources. We cannot expect the Vatican to recognise us, but we have a right to expect that it will not go out of its way to proclaim its denial of recognition as it did by addressing King George alone as if he were the common father, so to speak, of both disputant nations.

'By this message,' de Valera continued, 'the Vatican recognised the struggle between Ireland and England as a purely domestic one for King George, and by implication pronounced judgment against us.'

Griffith and Collins were understandably annoyed that, while they were involved in tense and delicate negotiations, the president had – without even notifying them – revived the self-recognition issue by insulting the British king in an attempt to chide the pope. The British press, which was particularly critical of de Valera's actions, variously accused him of churlishness, childishness, clumsiness, impertinence, truculence, wounded vanity and a desire to wreck the talks by 'insulting the King'.

The telegram was not an attack on King George V, according to the *Irish Bulletin*. It was aimed at the 'statement drafted by the British cabinet', which had tried to secure a momentary political advantage by essentially suggesting that the Irish negotiators had not got 'their authority to speak in the name of the nation'.

'We knew nothing about it until it appeared in the press,' Griffith complained. 'In the negotiations we had been trying to hold back on the question of the crown until we knew what we were going to get in exchange for some accommodation regarding it. The telegram projected the crown right into the forefront of the negotiations.' It also fuelled Collins' suspicions that de Valera was preparing to blame the delegation for any compromises by covering up the fact that he had compromised on the self-recognition issue by agreeing to the conference.

Chapter Nine

'HAVING WALKED IN I HAD TO STAY'

At the sixth plenary session of the London negotiations on 21 October, Lloyd George cited the seizure of an Irish arms shipment by German police in Hamburg as evidence of a Truce violation. He added that there were other provocative acts – the worst of which was de Valera's telegram to the pope. 'This situation cannot be prolonged,' the prime minister insisted. 'We must know where we are. We have discussed in the best spirit on both sides various proposals but we have not really come to the question on which settlement depends.'

Collins had, that morning, submitted a document on defence drawn up by Childers. Lloyd George described it as 'a formidable document' that 'challenged the whole position with regard to what is vital to our security against attack'.

Members of the British delegation had risked their political futures by negotiating and they had to know where the Irish stood on some of the more vital issues. 'We must know your attitude on certain vital questions,' he said. 'Is allegiance to the King to be finally repudiated? Can you under no condition accept the sovereignty of the King in the sense that Canada and Australia accept it? Is the communicating link of the Crown to be snapped forever? Are you prepared to be associated with the fraternity of Nations known as the British Empire? Do you accept in principle that we must take necessary measures to give us facilities for our security not as a treaty which can be cancelled, but as a fundamental part of an arrangement?'

He did not expect immediate answers, as he knew that Irish would have to consult among themselves. 'I suggest an adjournment until this afternoon or longer,' Lloyd George said. 'You are entitled to ask that. At any rate there should be an answer to these questions given early.'

Griffith, who had deliberately been delaying consideration of External Association and the country's relations with the crown, bought some more time by promising to put forward counter proposals the following week. The conference then turned to the defence document submitted in the name of Collins that morning.

'Dominion status is not our claim,' Griffith explained, 'but the British offer falls short of it in every way.' The British offer was being exaggerated. The July proposals would not accord Ireland the same freedom as the dominions. Ireland's status was being demeaned by the demand for unprecedented defence concessions.

'All the dominions can have an army and a navy if they wish,' Griffith noted, but this right was being denied to Ireland and the British were demanding unprecedented bases in Ireland. The British had not demanded bases from Canada, Australia or New Zealand. They did have a base for a time at Simonstown, near Cape Town, in South Africa but this 'has been handed over to the South African Government, and there is no naval station or dockyard in the hands of the Imperial Government in South Africa,' Griffith stated, quoting from an official British document. The demand for unprecedented concessions was an affront to Ireland.

'We began with each Dominion in this way,' Lloyd George argued. 'We ask you to go through the same process as the Dominions. The memory of recent events will pass away but you must allow a few years to pass. We cannot take risks for 40,000,000 people.'

'It is not a question of building a navy – it is a question of our having the right to build it,' Griffith insisted. 'In this you are putting us in an inferior position to the Dominions.'

Collins defended the document drafted by Childers. 'How does it interfere with your security?' he asked. An internationally guaranteed neutrality would provide better protection for Britain.

'We cannot be sure that the Irish would have power to keep an effective neutrality,' Churchill replied. 'We could not guarantee the confluence of trade in an area where submarines were lurking unless we had Queenstown and other ports. I pointed out how mines could be laid as has been done in the case of the *Audacious*.' It had been sunk off the north coast of Ireland by a German mine in October 1914. Churchill insisted that no British government could entertain Irish neutrality. 'I urged Collins to consider what possible safeguards he could give us and reiterated that our demand could not be minimised in any important respect, but that if they could be clothed in some form more acceptable to the Irish people I should offer no objections,' Churchill noted.

'Do you not agree that if neutrality were a greater safeguard to you than anything else it would be a greater value to you than your proposals?' Collins asked.

'I do not accept that,' Churchill replied. 'A completely honest neutrality by Ireland in the last war would have been worse for us. Ireland's control of her neutrality might be ineffective.' Even assuming good will on the part of the Irish, Britain's security would be endangered. 'But there may be ill will and bitterness,' Churchill continued. 'If Ireland were equipped with craft she could deny her ports to the British and afford a nesting place for our enemies.'

'All your argument depends on your security,' Collins said. 'We propose a condition which I contend is a better guarantee of security.' He went on to explain neutrality in the context of External Association, which was the first time that External Association had been mentioned during the negotiations.

Lloyd George asked that the promised Irish counter proposals clarify the situation. 'It is essential,' he said, 'that they contain the clear and definite attitude of the Irish Delegation on three points, namely, (1) Allegiance to the Crown. (2) The question whether Ireland is prepared to come freely of her own accord within the fraternity of nations known as the British Empire. (3) Whether Ireland is prepared to accept in principle our claim that we must have necessary facilities to ensure the security of our shores from attack by sea.'

Before tackling the issue, the Irish delegation had Childers write to de Valera for advice on the best way of approaching the allegiance issue. The plenipotentiaries felt they could respond with an outright refusal to consider allegiance, he explained, or they could 'obtain a field of manoeuvre and delay the crucial question' by saying that 'they would be prepared to consider the question of the Crown', if agreement were reached on all other issues. But the cabinet never responded.

Although there was no mention of the crown in any of the partial draft treaties that de Valera gave to Childers and Chartres on 7 October, Chartres began working on a relationship consistent with External Association. During the first two weeks of the conference he drew up a couple of memoranda suggesting that the 'The King could be recognised as the official head of the whole combination.' The Irish would recognise the crown as head of the External Association. 'Freedom must be technical as well as substantial,' Chartres argued. 'There will be no Veto, no Viceroy, no Union flag. The King will have no concern, however technical, in Irish legislation, [and] not be the head, however shadowy, of the Irish Army.

'As an external act of recognition Ireland should vote a modest annual amount to the Civil List,' Chartres added. 'It would be a sum voted annually by the Irish to the King, not as King of Ireland, or as any factor in the Government of Ireland, but by way of contribution in respect of those "affairs of agreed common concern" outside Ireland in which Ireland would be associated with the partnership of States over which the King reigns.'

That weekend Collins returned to Dublin and pleaded with de Valera to go back to London with him, but the president refused on the grounds that there was no necessity at the time. He added, however, that he would go later if it could be shown that his presence was really required. In an undated letter written to a friend during the negotiations, Collins alluded to his growing distrust of de Valera. 'I was warned more times than I can recall about the ONE,' he wrote. 'And when I was caught for this delegation my immediate thought was of how easily I walked into the preparations. But having walked in I had to stay.'

Childers sending reports to the members of the cabinet at home compounded his uneasiness. He was not just reporting but commenting on what was happening and even suggesting what he thought should happen, as well as consulting people outside the delegation. 'Neutrality was brushed aside at the 1st session of the main conference. It was argued more reasonably at the informal Defence Conference,' Childers wrote to de Valera. 'We must put up a strong fight for neutrality.'

What the plenipotentiaries should or should not do was not his call, though in fairness, it was essentially the role that de Valera envisaged for him. He was making observations that conflicted with the views of the leaders of the delegation. Collins described his reports as 'masterpieces of half-statement, painting a picture far from the true state of things'. For instance, he was reporting separately to Brugha on defence matters. Brugha had refused to be part of the delegation and Childers had no right to consult him off his own bat, even if it was only about defence over which Brugha was the responsible minister. Following the meeting with Admiral Beatty, Childers wrote to Brugha: 'They claim the occupation of three ports but it looks as if they might propose that these should be under Irish maintenance and control in peace time, subject to an agreement for facilities in them,' he wrote. 'In war they want access to all our coast. They also want coastal Air Station for anti-submarine work, but we have no details till Monday. This, of course, would mean their occupation of the soil in peacetime. We are contesting every point and keep the Neutrality solution in the foreground.'

'Personally,' Brugha replied next day, 'if it were a case of war or peace over the leasing of even one port I would deliberate very deeply before I came to a decision.'

Childers noted that his memorandum on defence submitted by Collins was initially treated as if it would lead to the break-up of the conference, 'but two hours of warm argument followed! At the end they asked us to bring up a formula which would meet our views and theirs,' Childers wrote to Brugha on 18 October. 'They evidently do not stand by theirs of the 17th which was sprung on us and was explained today to mean, among other things, that we were to be allowed no naval forces at all.'

'There is nothing to be pessimistic about anyway as you people over there, no more than ourselves, are not likely at the finish to accept anything that would put us in an inferior position,' Brugha responded. 'Your memo means there is not going to be a settlement.'

Collins understandably saw such correspondence as intolerable. He also surmised – correctly as it turned out – that Childers was also sending messages to de Valera, though a series of telegrams through third parties were little more than suggestions that an official report was on the way, or a request for an acknowledgement that a report been received by then.

Griffith had detested Childers for years, and now Collins came to look on him as a kind of spy within the delegation. They therefore decided to eliminate him from the actual discussions by secretly having Eamonn Duggan suggest to Andy Cope that Lloyd George should invite the two Irish leaders to a private discussion after one of the plenary sessions of the conference. Cope and the assistant cabinet secretary Tom Jones were working in the background to help Lloyd George achieve an Irish settlement.

The prime minister jumped at the opportunity of cutting

out Childers, whom he considered a retarding influence. During the seventh plenary session of the conference, the Irish counter proposals, presented on 24 October, were discussed in a general way. Childers only recorded two brief interjections by Collins, totalling a mere twenty-three words. The Big Fellow clearly felt inhibited in the presence of Childers and the others, so he let Griffith do most of the talking for him. There was no significant progress that day, except in the area of defence.

The counter proposals reiterated that the British offer did not even amount to dominion status, because of the unprecedented defence concessions being demanded, as well as fiscal demands that were not being made on the dominions. 'We are to bear a financial responsibility for your Imperial debt which they do not bear,' the Irish delegation asserted.

They called on Britain 'to renounce all claims to authority over Ireland and Irish affairs' and in return, 'Ireland will consent to adhere for all purposes of agreed common concern, to the League of Sovereign States associated and known as the British commonwealth of Nations'. In relation to defence, Ireland would solemnly 'bind herself to enter into no compact and to take no action nor permit any action to be taken inconsistent with the obligation of preserving her freedom and integrity'. The British commonwealth, League of Nations and the United States of America 'would be invited to join that guarantee'. If they declined, 'we propose that the question of our naval defence should be discussed and adjusted between the Imperial Conference and the representatives of Ireland'.

'Now as to "agreed common concern", what do you mean by that?' Lloyd George asked.

'War and peace, trade, all the large issues,' Griffith explained. 'It is a matter of drafting.'

'More or less, the same matter as we have of common concern with the Empire,' the prime minister observed. 'What do you exclude?'

'I would not like to say at this moment,' Griffith replied.

'Great Britain and the dominions discuss defence of the empire at Imperial Conferences,' the prime minister said. 'Would you regard that a matter of common concern?'

'Yes,' replied Griffith. But he added that if 'Canada had trouble with another country we might not consider it our concern'.

The Irish document did not mention neutrality, but the proposals amounted to seeking an international guarantee of Ireland's permanent neutrality, if possible. There was no mention either of the common citizenship of Britain and the dominions. Instead, the Irish proposed 'mutual agreements in regard to reciprocity of civil rights'.

'Would you be British subjects or foreigners?' the prime minister asked.

'We would be Irish subjects,' Griffith said. 'We would assume that Irishmen in England and Englishmen in Ireland would have the same rights. The position would be the same as at present. We would make no change and expect you not to make a change. Actually it would be status quo.'

'Our experts think it impossible to defend the main stream of commerce unless we can defend ourselves against submarines, and for that end have certain facilities in your harbours,' Birkenhead said. If these facilities were provided, neutrality would be 'reduced to a shadow – a meaningless trophy which would give you nothing'.

'In principle we make no objection to taking those safeguards which are necessary to your security,' Griffith explained. 'We accept the principle that your security should be looked after, though the working out of the details might be very difficult.'

'Britain had won on defence,' Frank Pakenham (later Lord Longford) declared in *Peace by Ordeal*. If this was so, they really won before the negotiations began, because de Valera had long ago acknowledged that Ireland would accommodate Britain's legitimate security needs. That had been at the very heart of his controversial *Westminster Gazette* interview in February 1920, and he had reaffirmed it just before his arrest in June in a twenty-minute interview with Chris O'Sullivan for an Australian syndicate headed by Keith Murdoch, the father of Rupert Murdoch. O'Sullivan asked what attitude the Irish would adopt, if there were a settlement and Britain subsequently became involved in a war.

'In that event Britain would have the right to throw her troops across Ireland' to repel an attack, de Valera replied.

As a courtesy O'Sullivan showed his report to Childers, who had arranged the interview. Childers was appalled at the report.

What was wrong with it? O'Sullivan had asked.

'Sometimes de Valera doesn't appreciate fully what "Republic" means,' Childers replied. 'No Republic could agree in advance to another power throwing troops across its territory. This commits us to something that could not be tolerated. I cannot let it go,' he said. 'Cancel it.'

Childers may have been able to block the president in June, but he had very little influence following Griffith's acceptance of the principle that Ireland would provide Britain with defence facilities. Of course, it did not mean that the right to neutrality was being abandoned; it still remained to work out the details of the necessary defence concessions.

Affording facilities to Britain 'would entitle other nations with whom we were at war to make you an enemy,' Birkenhead argued.

Collins admitted this. 'A country refusing to recognise Ireland's neutrality would make Ireland an enemy,' he said. Hence the British should not worry about Irish neutrality.

'They contemplate a situation where they would not automatically be at war,' Chamberlain observed when the British delegates withdrew to talk among themselves in Frances Stevenson's office.

'They will give way on that,' Birkenhead predicted.

Members of the British delegation generally believed that Griffith's answers marked an important advance in the negotiations. But Birkenhead said that the answers 'have shaken me'. He thought Lloyd George and Chamberlain should make it plain to Griffith and Collins that the crown had to be accepted as 'we cannot possibly have agreement without that'.

'They have some idea of a president,' Churchill noted.

Before going to Downing Street on 24 October the Irish delegation was informed that Lloyd George and Chamberlain wished to meet with Griffith and Collins for about ten minutes after that day's conference meeting. Thereafter the conference never met again in full session. Instead there were twenty-three informal sub-conference meetings before the signing of the Treaty.

Barton was given to believe by Griffith that 'Lloyd George was conscious of what he thought must be obvious to us also, namely that the negotiations were making no material progress. He explained that their cabinet was a coalition and that its members represented different parties with divergent political views. He held that the conferences with our delegation were too large for the interchange of views and the discussion of matters vital to a final settlement. The impression conveyed was that Lloyd George's difficulty was rather with his own colleagues than with us and that if we wanted to make any progress at all we must assist him to get rid of his recalcitrants by agreeing to a reduction of members during two or three sub-conferences.'

'We discussed this proposition among ourselves,' Barton continued. 'Griffith was very anxious to agree to it and none of us had any reasons for opposing him. It was a temporary expedient. It was not suggested that these meetings should become stereotyped. So Duffy and I agreed.'

There were no secretaries to take notes at those meetings. Childers and Chartres attended one meeting each, but that was in their capacity as advisors. Griffith attended twenty meetings.

Collins was at nineteen; three of the four meetings that he missed were held during his frequent visits to Dublin. Barton attended four sub-conference meetings, and Gavan Duffy and Duggan two each.

Barton and Gavan Duffy quickly became disillusioned at their virtual exclusion from the conference talks. 'We were led to understand that the difficult people were Hamar Greenwood and Worthington-Evans,' Barton noted. Although Collins despised Greenwood, the latter was the most sympathetic of the British delegates towards External Association. As a Canadian he understood the Irish desire to ensure that they had the full freedoms enjoyed by Canada.

Barton quickly concluded that the British argument for the rationalisation of the conference was specious. He did not suspect his colleagues were behind the whole thing at first. 'We all thought more progress might be made in this way,' he explained. 'Gavan Duffy and I had not at that stage lost confidence in our colleagues!'

'That the reasons given for the smaller conference were false is now obvious to me,' Barton later wrote, 'and I have grave doubts as to whether the suggestion emanated from the English in the first place at all.' Of course, he was right. Duggan said he had been told by Cope that the prime minister wished to arrange the meeting, but it was Duggan who suggested to Cope, on behalf of Collins, that Lloyd George should ask for this meeting with Griffith and Collins. Technically Duggan was telling the truth when he said that the British requested the meeting. He just did not bother to mention that he had asked them to request it.

As the British delegates were conferring amongst themselves Barton, Duggan, Gavan Duffy, and the two secretaries – Childers and Chartres – were led to another room while Griffith and Collins were asked to remain in the cabinet room for the private meeting with the prime minister and Chamberlain. In his account of the day's discussions Griffith merely reported that Collins and himself 'were asked to see Lloyd George and Chamberlain this evening'. It was actually Griffith and Collins who conspired to bring about the rationalisation of the conference, mainly in order to exclude Childers. But Barton thought it was a ploy to cut out Duffy and himself. 'I believe that this suggestion was the thin end of the wedge to get rid of us both,' he wrote. Of the four sub-conferences to which he was invited, three were in the final thirty-six hours of the conference. In the following days they would become increasingly suspicious, especially of Duggan's meetings with Cope.

'Duggan was practically a cipher throughout the negotiations and acted as an echo to Collins, but there was a constant correspondence by meetings between Cope and Duggan,' Barton explained. 'Duffy and I soon became suspicious that our leaders were giving away more than we were willing to give away and the delegation took sides against itself.'

'From the moment Griffith and Collins met Lloyd George and Chamberlain alone their power to resist was weakened,' Barton wrote in 1924. 'They became almost pro-British in their arguments with us and Duffy and I often felt that we had to fight them first and the English afterwards. We grew personally anti-pathetic to one another and the cleavage showed itself in numerous ways. Duffy and I felt that we were kept deliberately in the dark and that another channel of communications over which we had no control was opening up by clandestine meetings between Duggan and Alfred Cope.'

Of course, at the same time Griffith and Collins felt that they had gone to London to negotiate and compromise, not make a hopeless stand. They likewise felt that they had to struggle with their own colleagues within the delegation first before confronting the British. It was all part of the tug-of-war that de Valera envisaged.

Chapter Ten

'THE OATH –

THAT'S A PRETTY BIG PILL'

The first sub-conference meeting was supposed to be for only ten minutes but it lasted about an hour and a half and that was longer than the last plenary session which preceded it. The prime minister and Chamberlain briefed their colleagues afterwards.

'Griffith is better than Collins,' Lloyd George said. As representatives of a republic Griffith had said they could not accept the crown, but if everything else was satisfactory, he would undertake to recommend it.

'If we came to an agreement on all other points,' Griffith wrote to de Valera that evening, 'I could recommend some form of association with the Crown.'

Collins was not sure what acceptance of the crown entailed. 'What does it involve?' he asked.

'The oath of allegiance,' Lloyd George replied.

'That's a pretty big pill,' said Collins. 'Cannot we have an oath to the constitution?'

Lloyd George believed at this stage that the Irish would accept the crown, if they were satisfied on other matters, but Chamberlain thought the crown would be the real difficulty, because the Irish seemed to be thinking of 'a republic within the Empire'.

Next afternoon, when he and Collins met Chamberlain and Attorney-General Gordon Hewart, Griffith emphasised that he could only recommend acceptance of the crown, if unity were assured. Chamberlain asked if it would be easier to accept the six county set-up, if Stormont agreed to come under the Dublin Parliament. No, they replied. Why would the British not 'agree to a County Option?'

Chamberlain told his colleagues afterwards that he said that they 'could not put a more difficult question'. Birkenhead and Churchill realised that they were in a very difficult position on the Ulster question. 'We can't give way on six counties,' Churchill argued. 'We are not free agents; we can do our best to include Six in larger Parliament plus autonomy. We could press later to hold autonomy for Six from them instead of from us.'

'I rather agree with Winston,' Birkenhead said. 'Our position re Six Counties is an impossible one if these men want to settle, as they do.'

'I don't see how Ulster is damnified,' Churchill said. 'She gets her own protection, an effective share in the Southern Parliament and protection for the Southern Unionists.'

'If they accept all subject to unity we are in a position to go to Craig,' Lloyd George argued. 'If they don't, the break is not on Ulster. My proposal is to put Ulster on one side and to ask S[inn] F[éin] for their views in writing.'

'I think it conceivable that if they could agree with Craig on unity,' Chamberlain said, 'they would accept the Six Counties.'

When Griffith talked about 'some form of association with the Crown', he was not necessarily talking about allegiance, as Chamberlain clearly realised. Griffith was thinking on lines being advocated by John Chartres, but de Valera assumed he was referring to allegiance. When the Dublin-based members of the cabinet met to consider the report, the president asked whether anyone present would be willing to give allegiance to the British crown. All answered in the negative, including Kevin O'Higgins.

De Valera therefore warned the delegation that agreeing to allegiance was out of the question. 'If war is the alternative we can only face it,' he wrote, 'and I think that the sooner the other side is made to recognise it, the better.'

Griffith and Collins were furious. They considered the warning an unjustifiable interference with their powers. De Valera had been giving somewhat vacuous advice since the start of the conference, suggesting they do something without specifying what they should do. 'I note that LG is just covering again the ground he covered with me,' the president wrote to Griffith after just the first day of the conference, for instance. 'You will have to pick him up soon, I fear, on this "further than this we can't go" stunt.'

'The Ulster question should be pushed ahead at once,' he wrote to Griffith on 25 October, and in the same letter he suggested that 'the big question should be put to them at once'.

'The main thing now it seems to us is to clinch with them on the "Ulster" question without delay and get the basis for representation in an all-Ireland Parliament agreed upon definitely,' de Valera wrote next day. 'And after that, the "make or break" question.'

He had not provided the delegation with the Ulster clause for Draft Treaty A until after the issue had been first discussed at the conference, and when the delegation asked for advice on the crown, none was forthcoming. Yet when they took one of the courses outlined by Childers, he admonished them.

Griffith drafted a strong letter of protest and insisted that the whole delegation sign it. Barton, who considered the fuss a mere 'storm in a tea cup', initially refused to sign, as did Duffy. Collins complained that those in Dublin were attempting to put him in the wrong by trying to 'get me to do the dirty work for them'.

'Unless the Cabinet at home left our hands free,' Griffith said, according to Barton, 'he would go home, and it was largely to gain time and learn something more about the matter that Duffy and I signed it.'

'Collins was still very angry and said he would not sign the letter, but return home,' Barton continued. 'Duffy and I said that if Collins was not going to sign it, certainly we would not, for it would then look as tho' we were all willing to give allegiance while Collins refused.'

Eventually Griffith persuaded Collins to make his protest by signing the letter, instead of returning home. Barton, puzzled at 'what was the cause of Collins' extraordinary outburst', noted in the light of what he learned later that 'Collins feared he was being led into a trap by Brugha and Stack. That he was in some way to be committed to a compromise and discredited.'

'We strongly resent, in the position in which we are placed,' Griffith wrote in the letter signed by the delegation, which protested against 'this interference with our powers'. Although the instructions committed the delegation to refer back to the cabinet before signing any agreement, the powers given to the delegates imposed no limits on the fullest form of discussion, 'Obviously,' the delegation continued, 'any form of association necessitates discussion of recognition in some form or another of the head of the association.'

De Valera was stunned by the tone of the letter. 'There is obviously a misunderstanding,' he replied. 'There can be no question of tying the hands of the plenipotentiaries beyond the extent to which they are tied by their original instructions. These memos of mine, except I explicitly state otherwise, are nothing more than an attempt to keep you in touch with the views of the cabinet here on the various points as they arise. I think it most important that you should be kept aware of these views.'

The president soon came to appreciate that a form of recognition of the crown advocated by Chartres was compatible with External Association. He enthusiastically endorsed the idea and eventually persuaded Brugha and Stack to agree to recognise the king as head of an association to which Ireland would be externally linked.

Before allowing his name to go forward for re-election as president in August de Valera had stressed that no road to a peace settlement was being barred. But in an address to the Sinn Féin Árd Fheis (Convention) on 28 October he announced before his re-election as president of the party, that one road was barred and there were barriers on others. Ireland's representatives would never call upon the people to swear allegiance to the English king, he said, and they might therefore have to call upon them to face the 'abomination of persecution' if a settlement could not be agreed in London.

'The problem is to devise a scheme that will not detract from Irish freedom,' he told the Árd Fheis. 'They may come back having found what seems to them a way and recommend it to us. When they come we in the Cabinet will have to decide our policy with respect to the scheme, Dáil Éireann will then have to consider it. What may happen I am not able to judge, but I am anxious that you should realise the difficulties that are in the way, and the fact that the best people might legitimately differ on such a scheme. The worst thing that could happen would be that we should not be tolerant of honest differences of opinion. I believe that if such difference of opinion arose and were carried to the country it would mean disaster for our hopes.

'One question, the allegiance question, is closed from our point of view,' he said, winding up his address. 'The question of some form of association with the States of the British Empire is open. There is no reason why this nation should not associate itself with other nations provided the association was one a self-respecting nation might enter, and that it was not against our interests to do so. The question of defence is partially open. We have never denied that, if the rights of other people should conflict with ours, it was a question of adjusting our respective rights. We will not, however, ever take the view that English interest may override our rights.'

Some of those in Dublin were tending to underestimate the

weakness of Lloyd George's political position. His government had presided over victory in the First World War, and the coalition enjoyed the largest parliamentary majority in history, but his own party had been hammered in the 1918 general election and was a distinct minority within the coalition, while his Unionist coalition partners enjoyed a comfortable overall majority. In the coming days there would be two separate challenges to the government – one, a backbench revolt in the House of Commons, and the other at the Unionist Party Conference in Liverpool.

Many Conservatives, or Unionists as they were more commonly called at the time, were anxious to withdraw their party's support of the coalition and set up a government of their own. Unionist diehards, led by Colonel John Gretton and Captain Charles C. Craig, a brother of prime minister Sir James Craig of Northern Ireland, tabled a motion of censure against the government over its Irish policy. The challenges were not something that could be dismissed lightly, especially as there was an obvious alternative leader waiting in the wings. In March 1921 Andrew Bonar Law had stepped down as leader of the Conservative Party after ten years, and he resigned from the cabinet for health reasons, but his health had since improved. He was ready to take up where he had left off. He had always been a particularly strong supporter of Irish unionists. He could have challenged Lloyd George for the position of prime minister in 1916, but chose to support the Welshman instead. Born in 1858 in New Brunswick in what would later become Canada, he was the son of a Coleraine-born Presbyterian preacher. Bonar Law moved to Glasgow as a twelve-year-old to complete his education. He was elected to parliament in 1900 and became leader of the Conservative Party in 1911. One of the strongest opponents of Home Rule, he described 'fair play' for Ulster unionists as one of his two great political passions, with the result that the Conservative dissidents had an obvious candidate for the leadership in him. He had the experience and political stature to form a government. Indeed, within twelve months he and the Conservatives would oust Lloyd George.

With the censure vote due to be taken on 31 October 1921, Lloyd George was anxious for a distinct indication from the Irish delegation that a settlement was possible to keep most of the Conservatives in line. Cope suggested to Duggan that he call Tom Jones to arrange a meeting with the prime minister for Griffith and Collins. The meeting was duly arranged for Churchill's home, where the prime minister was due to dine on the eve of the censure motion.

Many people have exaggerated Churchill's role in the negotiations. He did not play a major part, other than in matters related to defence, which were essentially resolved during the plenary sessions. He only attended four of the sub-conference meetings – the one at his home and the other three in the last thirty-six hours before the Treaty was signed. None of his own team really trusted him. Even his Liberal colleague, Lloyd George, only included him in the delegation because he was too dangerous to leave out.

Churchill stated that there was always 'a certain gulf' between himself and Collins, who looked on him as a political animal who would 'sacrifice all for political gain'. Describing Churchill as 'inclined to be bombastic' and 'full of ex-officer jingo', Collins had his reservations. 'Don't actually trust him,' he wrote. Had he got on very well with Collins, Churchill would undoubtedly have played a much greater role in the actual negotiations.

While Griffith was upstairs with Lloyd George, Churchill and Birkenhead remained downstairs with Collins. 'He was in his most difficult mood, full of reproach and defiance,' according to Churchill. 'It was very easy for everyone to lose his temper.'

'You hunted me night and day,' Collins exclaimed. 'You put a price on my head!'

'Wait a minute, you are not the only one,' said Churchill, who took down a framed copy of a reward notice for his recapture after he had escaped from the Boers during the Boer War some twenty years earlier. 'At any rate it was a good price – £5,000. Look at me – £25 dead or alive. How would you like that?'

'He read the paper, and as he took it in he broke into a hearty laugh,' Churchill continued. 'All his irritation vanished. We had a really serviceable conversation, and thereafter – though I must admit that deep in my heart there was a certain gulf between us – we never to the best of my belief lost the basis of a common understanding.'

Upstairs, Griffith was holding out the possibility of accommodating the British on association, the crown and defence, if the British could assure 'the essential unity' of Ireland. This was the kind of talk Lloyd George had wanted to hear. 'If I would give him personal assurances on these matters,' Griffith reported, 'he would go down and smite the diehards and fight on the Ulster matter to secure essential unity.'

Lloyd George was 'in an expansive and optimistic mood' that night as one of his secretaries, Geoffrey Shakespeare, drove him back to Downing Street. 'We have really made progress tonight for the first time,' the prime minister said. 'I really feel there is a chance of pulling something off.' Next day the diehard censure motion was routed by 439 votes to 43.

The prime minister was apparently lulled into a false sense of security. He told friends he would resign if the Ulster crowd proved recalcitrant, but this was just a temporary thing. Some of the same diehards tabled a motion calling for the break-up of the coalition at the Unionist Party Conference that was due to begin in Liverpool on 17 November. Lloyd George was again in political difficulty.

He, Chamberlain and Birkenhead met with Griffith and Collins the following morning to get further assurances on the crown and empire. After the meeting Collins told Tom Jones that he was disappointed with the meeting, especially after the way things went at Churchill's home.

'I told him that unless a reasonable compromise was reached on Ulster,' Jones noted, 'I felt certain the P.M. would rather resign than start a war of reconquest.'

Griffith had agreed to provide the prime minister with a personal letter of assurance, which could be used to bolster wavering Conservative support. 'Provided I was satisfied on every point,' Griffith wrote, 'I was prepared to recommend recognition of the Crown, the formula in which this recognition was to be couched to be arrived at a later stage. I similarly agreed to recommend free partnership with the British commonwealth, the formula defining the partnership to be arrived at a later discussion.'

Next day, 1 November, Griffith presented the Irish delegation with the draft of a letter that he planned to send to Lloyd George to assure opponents within the Conservative Party that there was a real chance of a settlement. If Irish unity were assured, Griffith would be prepared to 'recommend recognition of the Crown' and 'free partnership with the British commonwealth'. This provoked a storm in the delegation.

'Duffy and I strenuously opposed the sending of a personal letter, and objected vehemently to its tone,' Barton noted. 'Childers, who being Secretary, and not a delegate, was diffident about taking a prominent part in such discussions, supported us. Collins and Duggan took very little part. We dispersed without having reached any agreement, and after Griffith had made use of some very abusive language to Duffy.'

'I felt very strongly the appeal that Dev had made to work as a team and made every effort to smooth our difficulties,' Barton explained. 'Griffith was very insulting to both Duffy and Childers.'

'Griffith was very anxious to sign that letter as from himself alone claiming that he wished to shield Collins from attacks that might be made upon him at home as a result of it,' Barton added. 'Duffy, Childers and I met afterwards, and decided that in no circumstances would we permit this letter to be sent as a personal letter, or in the form submitted to us.'

Collins was too busy hiding his own views to take an active part in the wrangling within the delegation, but his behaviour at a formal banquet in the Hans Place headquarters that night could hardly have endeared him to all of his colleagues. 'When the feast was at its height, Michael Collins with Liam Tobin, Tom Cullen, Emmet Dalton, Joe Guilfoyle and Joe Dolan came in,' according to Kathleen McKenna. 'They were a happy, boisterous group who preferred horse-play to formalities. I do not know how it came about but first of all they began throwing cushions at one another, then the tangerine oranges, apples and nuts from the table. We all know Collins' exuberant character.' This was the Big Fellow letting off steam.

Next morning Gavan Duffy was up early to put his views in writing against Griffith's plans to provide Lloyd George with a personal letter. At 9.45 a.m. Childers asked Griffith what time he wished the delegation to meet.

'What meeting?' Griffith asked. 'No meeting is required.'

There were others present in the room so Childers just whispered that the other delegates wished to make some suggestions. 'He was much put out, but consented to come to my room,' Childers noted. Barton, Gavan Duffy and Chartres were already there. Gavan Duffy read out the letter he had prepared protesting against the letter Griffith planned to send to Lloyd George.

'The main effect of the letter must be to undermine the stand we have taken,' he explained. 'We had in our last Memorandum very carefully limited the recognition of the British Crown that we would recommend; your letter abandons that for a form of words which by its very omissions will be used by Mr Lloyd George as indicating your willingness to sponsor allegiance by the Irish people to the British Crown.

'I want to see a settlement, which I am persuaded we can get on non-allegiance lines, explored to the utmost, before our Chairman even suggests that he is prepared to go further,' Gavan Duffy continued. 'Until such a settlement has been discussed, and our proposals criticised in writing by the other side, we cannot say that we have explored that avenue.' The British had not responded in writing to two Irish memoranda and Gavan Duffy argued that there should be a response to those before the Irish delegation furnished anything else in writing. 'We are entitled to have in writing from the arch-trickster of the Universe a reply on each matter we have put up.'

Griffith was determined to go ahead and he refused to countenance changes 'first with violent emphasis', according to Childers. But then he relented and agreed to modifications. 'After considerable debate our party won its points,' Barton explained. 'The letter was re-drafted, and was signed by Griffith as Chairman.'

Collins and Duggan had joined the meeting by this stage, but again they said very little. It is difficult to determine the extent to which Collins' willingness to compromise was influenced during the protracted discussions. He undoubtedly gave different impressions to different people. When a nationalist deputation from Northern Ireland called on him during the negotiations, for instance, he indicated that partition would not be acceptable in any form.

There was 'no principles whatever to justify' the cutting off of the six counties, he explained. 'In operation it would be a manifestation of the tribalistic interpretation of the principle of self-determination reducing it to an absurdity unless as originally enunciated the nation was understood as the unit – no other unit is possible in practice.' Yet he had already indicated a readiness to the British to recognise the separation of the area in the north-east in which the unionists had a majority. Tom Jones noted in his diary that on 1 November Collins 'remarked that they must be satisfied at present with the nominal unity of the whole of Ireland and that it would take time to make it real'.

The Big Fellow was obviously misleading somebody – but whom? Was he fooling the British by feigning a readiness to accept re-partition, if no other agreement could be reached, or was he deceiving the nationalist deputation by pretending to be unwilling to accept any form of partition? It is not possible to answer these questions with any degree of assurance. Indeed, in the light of subsequent events, it is not beyond the bounds of possibility that he was deceiving both, and himself as well.

Collins was playing a complicated and devious game in deliberately giving different impressions to different people. On the allegiance question, for example, he obviously tried to give the idea that he was prepared to take a firmer stand against the British than was apparently the case. 'They'll give us anything practically but say they must preserve the link of the Crown,' he explained in a letter home at the beginning of the third week of the conference. 'A very nominal thing is all they want.'

'Go to the devil says I in effect,' he wrote. Yet he was not the kind of man to be bothered about nominal things, and it was unlikely that he would have felt differently at this stage. There can be little doubt from his private correspondence that he had come to the conclusion that dominion status was the most they could expect to get for the time being. He wanted to accept it, but dared not admit this openly, because neither he nor Griffith really knew how far they could go with those in Dublin.

'What do we accept?' Griffith asked him privately.

'Indeed what do we accept?' Collins wondered. If they accepted any British terms, he was afraid it would be considered 'a gross betrayal or a similar act of treachery'. He was already in favour of a settlement on the dominion lines. 'Dominion status will be to a large extent beneficial to us,' he wrote to a friend on 2 November. 'I do not look on the above as being anywhere near a finalised solution. It is the first step. More than this could not be expected.'

But he did not say this at the meeting of the delegation that morning. 'Griffith and Collins insisted that we had undertaken to explore all avenues of settlement,' Barton noted. 'If we expected the English to explore our aims we must also be prepared to explore theirs.' Gavan Duffy, Barton and Childers insisted that Griffith tone down his approach. In return for Irish unity, Griffith wrote that he was 'prepared to recommend that Ireland should consent to a recognition of the Crown as head of the proposed Association of Free States'.

'After this discussion Duffy and I seriously considered the advisability of going back to Dublin,' Barton noted. Griffith and Collins delivered the revised letter to Birkenhead at the House of Lords around noon and they discussed it with Lloyd George, Birkenhead and Chamberlain that evening. The British tried to get them to drop 'a' from the phrase 'a recognition of the Crown', but Griffith refused. He also rejected an amendment stipulating that he would recommend that Ireland agree to be associated within the British commonwealth, but he assented when the British suggested 'free partnership with the other States associated within the British commonwealth'.

'I was prepared,' the final version of Griffith's letter to Lloyd George read, 'to recommend a free partnership with the other States associated within the British commonwealth, the formula defining the partnership to be arrived at in later discussion. I was, on the same condition, prepared to recommend that Ireland should assent to a recognition of the Crown as head of the proposed Association of free States.' All of this, of course, 'was conditional on the recognition of the essential unity of Ireland'.

'The tactical course I have followed,' Griffith explained to de Valera, 'has been to throw the question of Ulster against the question of association and the Crown. This is now the position: the British Government is up against Ulster and we, for the moment, are standing aside. If they secure Ulster's consent we shall have gained "essential unity" and the difficulty we shall be up against will be the formula of association and recognition.

'You will observe my words, which they accept, are consistent with External Association and external recognition.'

Chapter Eleven

'What about Bonar?'

A distinct fission quickly developed within the Irish delegation, with Griffith and Collins more amenable to the British proposals than Childers, Barton and Duffy. But de Valera had essentially anticipated this situation. He had selected Griffith and Collins in the hope that they could entice the British to compromise, while he hoped that Childers could use his influence to prevent the two Irish leaders giving away too much.

Griffith sought to get Lloyd George to pressure the Belfast regime into agreeing to a united Ireland by providing the prime minister with documentary evidence to deceive the unionists into thinking that the Irish delegation would accept dominion status and provide allegiance to the crown. The final version of Griffith's letter was not inconsistent with External Association, but in the different drafts he showed his hand, and the British were confident that he would ultimately agree to their terms. 'What they really meant to Griffith himself is a matter of speculation,' Barton wrote. 'It was my opinion at the time that he was sailing too close to falsehood and his diplomacy was really attempted deception, I told him so frankly; he bitterly resented it and henceforward I was in just as bad odour as Duffy and Childers. Like some of other determined leaders Griffith was autocratic and when thwarted, a tyrant.

'From that day on Childers, Duffy and I were recipients of more insults from our colleagues than I like now to remember,' Barton explained. 'You may wonder that we did not resign. We discussed doing so but it had been so impressed upon us that we were to act as a team that we considered that we should be wrong in permitting personal relationships to interfere with our outward solidarity.' He later wrote, 'In my opinion these Conferences between the English and Griffith and Collins on October 30th, November 1st, and November 2nd, sealed the doom of the Republic.'

Lloyd George was probably more hopeful than convinced that Griffith and Collins would accept the crown, empire, and British naval demands when he talked to the newspaper tycoon Lord Riddell on 30 October, but he believed they would demand Fermanagh and Tyrone. The prime minister described Griffith 'a pretty considerable man' and Collins as a different sort of person with 'a simple sort of mind such as is often found in great military commanders'. He noted that the two of them were 'very angry about de Valera's message to the pope'.

'Do you think the delegates want to settle?' Riddell asked.

'Yes, I am sure they do,' the prime minister replied. 'But I doubt whether they will be prepared to give way on the three points mentioned.'

Lloyd George had hoped to attend the Washington naval conference, but cancelled his plans due to the Irish negotiations. 'Things look very awkward,' he told Riddell on 3 November. 'Bonar Law has come out as an advocate of Ulster. Whether he thinks he sees his opportunity to become prime minister or whether he is solely actuated by a conscientious desire to champion the cause of Ulster I don't know but I can hardly bring myself to believe that he would desire to supplant me. However, as I have often told you, "there are no friendships at the top".

'I am not going to continue the Irish war if a settlement is possible,' Lloyd George continued. 'I shall resign and the king will have to send for someone else.' As a result of the talks with Griffith and Collins over the past few days Lloyd George had come to the conclusion that 'Sinn Féin are prepared to accept allegiance to the Crown and to agree that Ireland shall remain part of the Empire, subject to Tyrone and Fermanagh being joined to Southern Ireland,' he explained. 'If the matter can be settled on those lines I am not prepared to continue civil war.'

Childers was deeply upset about the defence situation, feeling that Griffith and Collins had given away too much. 'They had weakened badly on Defence and I protested at length, but in vain,' he wrote in his diary on 2 November. 'No one supported me.' De Valera had clearly overestimated Childers' influence. He was almost preoccupied with defensive matters, but nobody else shared that preoccupation.

'I think the position is bad,' Childers added having discussed matters with Gavan Duffy and Chartres. Barton shared the same view, but he was reluctant to express it outside the delegation.

'Duffy and I had cause for apprehension that our case was not being sufficiently pressed,' Barton explained. 'We decided that we must make some protest other than personal remonstrations with our colleagues,' he added. 'The cabinet in Dublin must be made aware that in our opinion the negotiations were not being properly conducted and that much more was being given away than they were aware. We felt that we were not fighting our case. We were instead giving it away and giving it away piecemeal to an extent that would make it difficult if not impossible to retrace the admissions made. One of us must therefore go to Dublin and inform our colleagues of the present state of affairs and ask that our hands be strengthened or at least the responsibility for the present policy and tactics in the negotiations to be shared by the Cabinet as a whole and not left to us alone.'

Having discussed it together, 'it was decided that Duffy should go as he was better acquainted with de Valera, Brugha, Stack and Cosgrave than I was and because his family traditions and longer connection with politics would cause his statement to carry more weight with the Cabinet than it would if it came from me'. This was further evidence of Barton's lack of self-confidence. After all he was a member of the cabinet. He may not have known his cabinet colleagues very well, but neither did Gavan Duffy, who was only included in the delegation, along with Duggan, as 'mere legal padding', according to de Valera.

Gavan Duffy went to Dublin on 4 November and the next day pleaded with de Valera to intervene and insist the conference go back into plenary session, but he received no support. 'Those to whom he spoke appeared to take very little interest in our apprehensions,' Barton wrote. 'They affirmed that they were fully acquainted with the situation from the correspondence received from Griffith and on Duffy's return he reported that our colleagues were completely satisfied. I gathered that he had been rather snubbed than welcomed.

'Had we been more experienced politicians we should there and then have resigned our posts,' Barton noted, 'but even Erskine Childers did not advocate this course.'

De Valera was content that things were going according to his plan. Griffith and Collins were acting as bait for Lloyd George, while Childers and Barton were preventing them from going too far. In fact, the president warmly endorsed the way the delegation had been handling things.

'I have been of the opinion from the very beginning of the negotiations that if the conference has to break the best issue to break on would be "Ulster," provided we could so manage it that "Ulster" could not go out with the cry "attachment to the Empire and loyalty to the Throne",' de Valera wrote to Griffith on 9 November. 'There can be no doubt whatever that the Delegation has managed to do this admirably. The danger now is that we shall be tempted, in order to put them more hopelessly in the wrong, to make further advances on our side. I think, as far as the Crown–Empire connection is concerned, we should not budge a single inch from the point to which the negotiations have now led us.'

The spotlight moved from the Irish Conference to Ulster for most of the fortnight leading up to the Unionist/Conservative

Party Conference. There were no sub-conference meetings between 3 and 12 November, but there was plenty going on behind the scenes on the Irish sides.

Lloyd George was initially confident that he could persuade Craig to accept the principle of Irish unity. On Saturday, 5 November, Craig 'discussed conditions under which an all-Ireland would function,' according to Lloyd George. 'But when he came again on Monday afternoon he had changed. Under no circumstances could Ulster look at an all-Ireland parliament.' Craig, who had just come from a meeting with Field Marshal Sir Henry Wilson and Worthington-Evans, was utterly intransigent.

Lloyd George was despondent and talked about resigning. 'I had about half an hour with him alone during which he paced up and down the cabinet room, more depressed than I had seen him at all since the negotiations began,' Jones noted in his diary.

'Craig will not budge one inch,' the prime minister said. 'He is sending for his cabinet as he will not be responsible alone for turning our offer down. This means, therefore, a break on Thursday. I would like you to see Griffith and Collins and prepare them for it. I shall go out. I will not be a party to coercing the South.'

'What about Bonar?' Jones asked. 'Isn't he helping you?'

'No, he is not. He's had six months' rest and has come back and is busy.'

'I always knew he was fanatical on Ulster,' Jones said, 'but I thought with peace in sight he would take a statesman's view on the situation.'

When Lloyd George talked about resigning, he was not thinking in terms of retiring but of stepping down as a tactic to provoke a political crisis. He thought that Birkenhead and Chamberlain would continue to support him and that the Conservatives might not then be able to form a government without the support of their leader in either of the houses of parliament, but Churchill warned him that Bonar Law would take up the challenge.

'Why should he not do so?' Churchill asked. 'The delusion that an alternative Government cannot be formed is perennial.'

This advice merely emphasised the weakness of the prime minister's position. He felt that he could not even depend on Churchill, who was from his wing of the Liberal Party. 'I cannot rely on Winston in a crisis,' Lloyd George told Jones. 'I never could.'

Jones was convinced that the prime minister was serious about resigning. He therefore urged him to stall.

'There is just one other possible way out,' Lloyd George said. 'I want to find out from Griffith and Collins if they will support me on it; namely that the 26 Counties should take their own dominion parliament and have a Boundary Commission.' He asked Jones to sound them out on this.

Next day Jones talked with Griffith and Collins for about an hour and a half at the Grosvenor Hotel. 'Collins was obviously very much upset at the news but it is much harder to tell what Griffith feels about anything as he keeps himself well in hand,' wrote Jones, who now tried to enlist the two Irishman in a bid to save the British government and thus stave off the danger of Bonar Law taking over as prime minister.

'I then threw out the suggestion of the southern parliament plus Boundary Commission as my own and asked them what did they think of it,' Jones continued. 'Griffith said that they preferred a plebiscite. Collins did not like the suggestion at all because it sacrificed unity entirely. I agreed, but what was the alternative? Chaos, Crown Colony Government, Civil War. We were bound to try every device to avert that. Griffith was not alarmed at the proposal and I left promising to sound the P.M. upon it.'

Collins was actually the first person to mention a boundary commission at the third plenary session of the conference. No doubt he would have preferred Irish unity, but a boundary commission was obviously the next best thing if unity proved impossible.

Jones told Griffith and Duggan next day that Lloyd George 'was prepared to play the Boundary Commission as an absolutely last card if he felt sure that Sinn Féin would take it'.

'It is not our proposal,' Griffith replied, 'But if the P.M. cares to make it we would not make his position impossible. We cannot give him a pledge, but we will not turn him down on it. We are not going to queer his pitch. We would prefer a plebiscite, but in essentials a Boundary Commission is very much the same.'

Collins, Childers, Barton and Duggan returned to Dublin, while John Chartres had already gone to Germany to try to straighten out complications as a result of the seizure in Hamburg of arms bound for Ireland. John Smith Chartres was the mystery man of the Irish delegation. Born in England of Irish parents in October 1862 he was the son of a staff surgeon in the British army. John worked for the London *Times* for a period before joining the ministry of munitions in 1905, and he was called to the bar in 1908. He travelled to Ireland frequently during the First World War for his work with the ministry for munitions. He was incensed at the suppression of Easter rebellion and afterwards offered his services to Griffith and was engaged to write an article on the death of Thomas Ashe for *Nationality*. He was appointed Irish envoy to Germany, where he engaged in smuggling guns for Collins. At fifty-nine he was the oldest member of the Irish team. There was no question about his loyalty, except in the overheated imagination of those inclined to think that anybody who differed with them was a spy.

Joe McGarrity received a telegram in Philadelphia on 8 November that was apparently based on information supplied by Chartres:

ONLY GREAT PRESSURE ON TRUSTEES IN L BY
DIRECTORS AT HOME WILL SAVE SURRENDER
OF FREE TITLE TO OLD HOMESTEAD STOP ALL
TRUSTEES WEAKENING INCLUDING M STOP C
STOP TOP MAN STANDS FIRM AND STRONG STOP
CORRECT OFFICIAL INFORMATION FROM INSIDE
STOP.

The message was easy to decipher. The 'trustees in L' referred to the delegation in London, while the 'directors' were the cabinet in Dublin, 'M.C.' was Collins and the 'top man' was de Valera. In short, the telegram amounted to a warning that Michael Collins and the delegation was cracking and only great pressure from the cabinet in Dublin could prevent a surrender. McGarrity telephoned the warning to Harry Boland, who cabled de Valera.

Seán T. O'Kelly, who had worked with both Gavan Duffy and Chartres on the continent, wrote at the time to a cleric at the Vatican that Griffith and Collins 'have fallen as complete victims' to machinations of Lloyd George. 'I am told the history of the present conference has been a story of continued surrenders on the part of ours while they have nothing so far from the enemy but promises.'

That weekend Collins, Barton, Duggan and Childers returned to Dublin. Childers made another futile effort to persuade de Valera to intervene to stop the sub-conference set-up. The president again refused, as he has rejected the entreaties from Gavan Duffy earlier. Barton also tried to persuade him.

'I pressed de Valera to return with us to London on the score that it would be impossible for us to get the maximum terms without his being present and that it was unfair to expect us to get the best terms without his assistance,' Barton noted. 'He was, however, unwilling to move from his decision.

'If negotiations should break down when he was with us, that would be the end, but, if they broke down without him, there was always a last recourse to him.' Barton had accepted that argument initially but thought it should have been reversed as the conference went on.

Thus de Valera had already turned down private requests from Collins, Gavan Duffy, Childers and Barton to return with them to London. He was obviously content with the way things were going, and he basically got the cabinet to endorse this.

While Collins, Barton, Duggan and Childers were in Dublin, Griffith met Lloyd George at the home of Sir Philip Sassoon in Park Lane on the night of 12 November. The prime minister read him the letter he had written to Craig two days earlier. In it he explained that Northern Ireland had a choice of joining with the rest of Ireland as a dominion, with all the existing safeguards provided for the local autonomy and such other safeguards that might be agreed, or remaining within the United Kingdom subject to contributing to the country's war debt and the imposition of a customs barrier with the rest of Ireland. He invited Craig and his ministers to London to discuss the extra safeguards, but Craig replied that the people of Ulster had accepted the partition parliament as the 'supreme sacrifice in the interest of peace' and they would not consider or discuss the matter 'unless His Majesty's Ministers consent to the withdrawal of the proposal for an all-Ireland Parliament'. If the rest of the island were being offered dominion status, however, he suggested than Northern Ireland should be accorded the same rights.

Having read his letter to Craig, and the latter's reply, Lloyd George explained that he was sending a further letter 'refusing their dominion proposal, but offering to create an all-Ireland Parliament, Ulster to have the right to vote itself out within twelve months; but if it did, a Boundary Commission to be set up to delimit the area, and the part that remained after the Commission had acted to be subject to equal burdens with England'.

'Lloyd George intimated that this would be their last word to Ulster,' Griffith reported. 'If Ulster refused, as he believed she would, he would fight, summon Parliament, appeal to it against Ulster, dissolve, or pass an Act establishing the all-Ireland Parliament.

'I told him it was his proposal, not ours,' Griffith added. 'He agreed, but he said that when he was fighting next Thursday with the Diehards and "Ulster" in front, they were lost if we cut the ground away behind them by repudiating the proposal.

'I said we would not do that, if he meant that he thought we would come out in public decrying it. It was his own proposal. If the Ulstermen accept it, we would have to discuss with him in the privacy of the conference. I could not guarantee acceptance, as, of course, my colleagues knew nothing of it yet. But I would guarantee that while he was fighting the "Ulster" crowd we would not help them by repudiating him.

'This satisfied him. They are to send this letter on Monday. Birkenhead, Chamberlain, and Derby will go to the Liverpool unionist conference and if the Ulstermen refuse, start it on Ulster. Until after that there is not likely to be much development. Before I left I told him that as I was helping him over the "Ulster" difficulty, he should help us over the "Crown and Empire," when they arose.'

To make sure there was no confusion on the point, Lloyd George had Jones outline the Boundary Commission idea in a memorandum. When this was shown to Griffith at the Grosvenor Hotel on the Monday, he confirmed that it was what he had agreed.

Griffith had already reported fully on his private meeting with Lloyd George the previous day. In fact, it was his longest report of the whole conference, but he did not subsequently mention that he nonchalantly approved the memorandum shown to him by Jones. It only confirmed what he had already reported, so he possibly attached no significance to the document. He never even mentioned it to Collins, who had not yet returned from Dublin. In the light of subsequent events, it would seem that efforts to ensure that Griffith would not repudiate the whole thing were necessary, because Barton and Gavan Duffy wanted Griffith to denounced the prime minister's letter of 10 November to Craig.

'A rupture very nearly resulted,' according to Barton. They argued that that the letter 'should immediately be repudiated', because Lloyd George suggested that a settlement with the Irish delegation was attainable 'based upon the proposals' of 20 July. Moreover, he added that 'Ireland would give her allegiance to the Throne, and would take her place in the partnership of Free States comprised in the British Empire.'

Barton and Gavan Duffy objected strongly to Griffith's tactics. 'He was, as we considered, permitting the English to delude the Ulster men with the idea that there was a possibility of our agreeing to a settlement, which brought Ireland within the Empire, whilst he was really well aware that no such settlement was possible,' Barton wrote. 'I even went so far as to tell AG that his tactics were "dirty tactics" and must lead to failure. We were, however, always in a minority.'

Chapter Twelve

'BULLETS FOR THE UNMENTIONABLES'

'Whilst the utmost co-operation should exist between Dublin and London, the plenipotentiaries should have a perfectly free hand but should follow original instruction re important decisions,' de Valera told the cabinet on 13 November. After a lengthy discussion on the situation, he 'gave as his opinion that it would be advisable to come to concrete proposals as soon as possible'. He thought the delegation should present alternative proposals in the form of a draft treaty. If this looked like leading to the break-up of the conference, he suggested that 'Ulster would be the best question on which to break'.

Collins and Barton were present at that meeting, as were Duggan and Childers, who had been invited to sit in as observers. During the meeting Brugha asked who was responsible for bringing one of the defence advisers to London. This was part of his needling of Collins. Nobody had to ask that question, as everybody knew that Collins was responsible. Colm Ó Murchada, the acting cabinet secretary in the absence of Diarmuid O'Hegarty in London, noted that de Valera 'expressed the opinion that all business should be transacted regularly thro[ugh] responsible ministers'. This was a clear rebuke for Collins.

When questioned by Brugha at one point during the meeting, Collins made a firm statement 'that there could be no settlement on the lines of Dominion Home Rule'. Barton found this reassuring.

Next day Childers called on de Valera at the Mansion House,

but he did not get much chance to speak to him privately as Desmond Fitzgerald was present. Childers noted that he just got 'a bare five minutes alone with the President'. He complained about the sub-conference set-up and the dissension within the delegation, but de Valera refused to act. If he had been interested in doing anything, he would obviously have made more time for Childers. As a result those in London felt powerless to stop Griffith. 'We could do nothing except try our best to induce our colleagues to run a straight course and adopt a stronger attitude,' Barton added.

Although de Valera was refusing to interfere with what was happening in London, Collins was uneasy because he did not know exactly what was happening in Dublin. While he was away de Valera and Brugha were trying to reorganise the IRA to undermine his influence. At the time of the Truce the IRA was only about 3,000 strong, according to Chief of Staff Richard Mulcahy, but since then there had been a massive influx of what some derisively called Trucileers – the fair weather volunteers who joined after the fighting had ceased. As a result IRA numbers swelled to 72,363 by the beginning of November. Efforts were still being made to impose Stack as deputy chief of staff to undermine the stranglehold that Collins had with the general headquarters staff.

'Dublin is the real problem,' Collins wrote on 15 November. 'They know what we are doing, but I don't know exactly the state of their activities.'

Collins got together that day in Dublin with Mark Sturgis, an assistant under-secretary of state for Ireland. 'Meeting him for the first time there is certainly nothing impressive about him,' Sturgis noted. 'He is certainly as Macready says much too quick to make jokes of everything and often bad ones.' But in the course of their meeting, which lasted over two hours, Sturgis changed his opinion, because the Big Fellow's style of negotiating seemed so open.

De Valera in London to meet Lloyd George in July 1921.

De Valera and colleagues going to London in July 1921.
From left: Griffith, Barton, Lord Mayor Laurence O'Neill,
Count Plunkett and de Valera.

The Irish team setting off for London. From left: Mrs Fionán Lynch, David Robinson, Griffith, Duggan, Mrs Duggan, Barton and Gavan Duffy. Kathleen McKenna is behind Barton with Alice Lyons and Lily O'Brennan.

The plenipotentiaries leaving for London. From left to right: Barton, Griffith, Duggan and Gavan Duffy.

Griffith and Collins in London.

Duggan and Gavan Duffy leaving 10 Downing Street.

*Lloyd George, Birkenhead and Churchill leaving
a session of the negotiations.*

Lloyd George, Craig and Churchill.

Michael Collins in London.

Gavan Duffy with Collins and Griffith in Hans Place.

*Leaving London after signing the Treaty: Gavan Duffy, Barton and
Griffith, with Childers and Fionán Lynch in the background.*

The delegation at Hans Place. From left seated: Griffith, Duggan, Collins; standing: Childers, Gavan Duffy and John Charters.

Release of prisoners from Kilmainhan Jail after the Treaty was signed.

months from the date hereof.

18.   This instrument shall be submitted forthwith by His
Majesty's Government for the approval of Parliament and by
the Irish signatories to a meeting summoned for the
purpose of the members elected to sit in the House of
Commons of Southern Ireland, and if approved shall be
ratified by the necessary legislation.

Decr 6ᵗʰ 1921

On behalf of the
British Delegation

D Lloyd George

Austen Chamberlain

Birkenhead.

Winston S. Churchill

L Worthington Evans

Hamar Greenwood

Gordon Hewart

On behalf of the Irish
Delegation

Art Ó Gríobhtha Gavan Duffy

Miceál Ó Coileáin

Riobárd Bartún

E S O Dugan

Seoirse Gabháin Uí Dhubhthaigh

The signed Treaty.

'Collins certainly gave it to me as his own opinion that there was an element of bluff in the Ulster position and that a modus vivendi would be found. He was equally frank when he spoke of the stupid things sections of his people had done and were quite capable of doing now unless firmly handled, and it was at that stage that my opinion of him as a big force began to improve. I certainly thought more of him at the end of the interview than the beginning. He was quick to see and to admit the growing difficulties of a jerry-built truce and made no sort of attempt to score or make points against me.'

It was ironic that Collins was actually more open with the enemy than with the dissident element within the delegation. The latter were really stuck in the middle, being ignored by the cabinet in Dublin and their colleagues in London. Next day in London Childers tried to get the delegation to discuss a draft treaty in line with de Valera's suggestion. 'We point out we don't know enough of what is going on and ask for a delegates meeting tonight,' Childers noted in his diary. Griffith seemed resentful, he refused to discuss it that night and he reminded Barton about his complaint about 'dirty politics'. Barton replied that it was their fault, as they were not being told enough.

Barton's uneasiness was understandable. While Griffith was not responsible for what Lloyd George wrote to Craig, he effectively accepted it by not objecting when he was shown the letter. By not clarifying the situation, at least, he was to an extent endorsing Lloyd George's assertion that the Irish delegation would accept allegiance to the crown and membership of the British empire. Unable to interest the delegation in drawing up proposals in the form of a draft treaty, Childers began drafting one himself, while Collins exhibited his indifference by sitting for a portrait.

Although Griffith seemed to think that Lloyd George was about to confront Craig with the Boundary Commission proposal, it was never likely that he would play that card before the Unionist Party Conference, which was due to begin in Liverpool on 17 November. Such a threat would likely incite the already volatile diehard group. Even though Colonel John Gretton's censure motion was routed in the House of Commons at the end of October, he went ahead and proposed that the party conference call on the Unionists to withdraw their support from the coalition.

Birkenhead was so worried about the challenge that he had a private meeting with Sir Archibald Salvidge, whom Lloyd George considered 'the nearest to a Tammany boss we have in this country'. Salvidge was reputed to be wavering and his support was considered crucial. Birkhenhead urged him to support the coalition actively as there was a real chance of peace. He said that Collins and Churchill had become 'bosom friends', but this conversation should be viewed within the context in which it took place.

He exaggerated Churchill's role in suggesting that Winston was winning over Collins. Conservatives despised Churchill as a political adventurer. The son of a former Conservative leader, he had deserted the Tories to join the Liberals. That he would get on with Collins might not surprise a Unionist, but it would have been something altogether different if Birkenhead admitted that he himself was getting on so well with Collins. This might have alarmed Salvidge to the possibility that it was Collins who was winning over Birkenhead and not the other way around. Unionists were already deeply suspicious of Lloyd George and Churchill, so news that Birkenhead might be going soft on Irish nationalists would have further fuelled their uneasiness.

Birkenhead was the member of the delegation with whom Collins got on best. 'I prefer Birkenhead to anyone else,' Collins wrote during the conference. 'He understands and has real insight into our problems – the Dublin one as much as any other.'

It was a strange relationship, because Collins generally disliked lawyers. He felt that lawyers like Gavan Duffy were so enamoured with the sound of their own voices that they talked too much and over-elaborated just to hear themselves. Collins did not have the patience to listen to that kind of thing, with the result that he was pleasantly surprised to find that Birkenhead was a very different type of person.

Birkenhead had been one of Sir Edward Carson's staunchest backers in the fight against Home Rule and had led the prosecution team at the trial of Sir Roger Casement in 1916. The Casement case came up in conversation, and Birkenhead arranged for Collins and Duggan to see the notorious 'black diaries', in which Casement recorded details of some of his homosexual activities. When a public clamour was raised to save him from the gallows following his trial, the British leaked extracts of the diaries to discredit Casement and stop the humanitarian campaign on his behalf. Nationalists subsequently accused the British of forging the diaries, but Collins had no doubts about their authenticity after he saw them.

At the Liverpool conference Gretton proposed a resolution: 'That, in the opinion of this Conference, some features of the Coalition policy are unworthy of unionist support.' The spectre of Bonar Law's return seem to pervade the debate, while the spirit of Lloyd George seemed to haunt it. Bonar Law had written a letter to the editor of *The Scotsman* the previous weekend emphasising that Ulster was as much a part of Britain as Scotland and he would resist any attempt by the British government to coerce the area.

Lloyd George believed what was going on in Liverpool was really a play for the leadership by Bonar Law, but the prime minister was confident of winning because he thought Bonar Law lacked the political courage necessary to win. He had been afraid to move for it in 1916 when he could have had it, and even now he decided to attend a war commemoration instead of the Liverpool meeting. 'If you are going to lead a revolt you must go all out for it,' Lloyd George said.

The conference cheered the mere mention of Bonar Law and some of the government ministers, but there was a distinct lack of enthusiasm the one and only time that Lloyd George's name was mentioned. Salvidge came out strongly in favour of the coalition by proposing an amendment:

That the Conference expresses its earnest hope that consistently with the supremacy of the Crown, the security of the Empire, and the pledges given to Ulster, and the safeguards of the interests of the minority in the South of Ireland, a solution of the Irish difficulties may be found in the Conference now in progress, which will bring peace to Great Britain and Ireland, and strength to the Empire.

Worthington-Evans was among those who spoke strongly in favour of the amendment, giving an assurance that there would not be any settlement that conflicted with it. 'I will not agree to any settlement of the Irish question which does not preserve the supremacy of the Crown,' he told the conference. 'I will not agree to any settlement which does not keep Ireland within the Empire. I will not agree to any settlement which does not leave the British Navy the sole guardian of the shore and the sea of Great Britain and Ireland and I will not agree to any settlement which does not make Ireland pay a fair share of the debt and of the pensions. Nor will I agree to any settlement which requires the coercion of Ulster to assent to it.'

The overwhelming majority at the Unionist Conference carried Salvidge's amendment, much to the delight of Lloyd George, but Tom Jones noted that it quickly became apparent, even though the diehards had again been routed, that the result 'was far from being a vote of confidence in the Prime Minister'.

The Big Fellow had begun sitting for a portrait by the Irish painter Sir John Lavery. This led to speculation that he had an affair with the painter's wife, Lady Hazel Lavery, and that she somehow played a significant role in the negotiations. Hazel was a society flirt, a strikingly good-looking American woman who was much younger than her husband, but she was ten years older than Collins. She had become enchanted with the Irish cause some years earlier and had sought a meeting with Collins by persuading her husband to ask him to sit for a portrait.

Hazel passed on the invitation through Michael's sister Hannie, but it was not until 16 November that Collins went to Lavery's studio at Cromwell Place. 'He walked into my studio, a tall young Hercules with a pasty face, sparkling eyes and a fascinating smile,' Lavery wrote. 'I helped him off with a heavy coat to which he clung.'

'There is a gun in the pocket,' Collins said excusing himself casually.

Lavery noted that Collins sat uneasily, always facing the door. That night Michael described the sitting in a letter to Kitty Kiernan. It was 'absolute torture,' he wrote, 'as I was expected to sit still, and this, as you know, is a thing I cannot do.'

Hazel took a fancy to Collins and figuratively threw herself at him. It is not unreasonable to assume that, notwithstanding his denials, the virile thirty-one-year-old availed of her sexual favours, but this does not mean she influenced his views on the negotiations.

History is replete with peripheral figures who believed that they had a vital input in critical events in which their involvement was actually little more than token. Hazel's biographer, Sinéad McCoole, wrote that 'the Lavery's friends believed Hazel played a central diplomatic role during the Treaty negotiations, particularly as an influence on Collins', but Collins had already indicated the kind of settlement he was seeking and the most her influence could have done was merely reinforce his convictions.

In the video, *The Shadow of Béal na Blath*, Colm Connolly contended that Hazel Lavery played a vital role in getting Churchill and Collins together, but this is absurd because Collins and Churchill only attended three sub-conference meetings together. The first of those, at Churchill's home, was almost three weeks before Michael even met Hazel Lavery, and the other two were on the final day of the negotiations.

Sinéad McCoole contended that 'Collins was a welcome guest at the Laverys' and would often stay late into the night reading books from their shelves'. But there were in fact only eighteen nights from the time he first went to Cromwell Place and the signing of the Treaty and Collins spent each of the three weekends in Dublin and at least ten nights there or travelling to and from London. It seems much more likely therefore that while this friendship began towards the end of the negotiations, the relationship could have developed afterwards. If those Cromwell Place dinner parties that McCoole believed Collins attended actually took place, they were probably during the visits that Collins made to London after the signing of the Treaty.

Following the death of Collins great efforts were made to protect his reputation. It would not have done to portray such an iconic figure as a womaniser and even an adulterer. His first biographer, Piaras Beaslaí, who knew him during his immigrant days in London, stated that Collins showed little interest in the opposite sex. 'The society of girls had apparently no attraction for him,' Beaslaí wrote. 'He preferred the company of young men, and never paid any attention to the girls belonging to the Branch, not even to the sisters and friends of his male companions.' He also added, 'the usual philanderings and flirtations of young men of his age had little interest or attraction for him'. Instead he was deeply involved in Gaelic Football and was a very active member of the Geraldines Club in London, as well as being active in the IRB and the Irish Volunteers, which were exclusively male organisations.

The most readable of his biographies – Frank O'Connor's *Death in Dublin*, which was published in the 1930s and later re-issued under the title of *The Big Fellow* – portrayed Collins in a similar light, as a young man who was particularly fond of horseplay with other young men. He would burst into a room looking for 'a piece of ear', which was his practice of biting the other man's ear until he surrendered.

Having read those portrayals, a grandnephew suspected that Collins was homosexual. He mentioned this to his grandfather, Michael's eldest brother Johnny, who was highly amused. He said that if Michael had a problem, it certainly was not that he was not fond of women. By the 1960s a new image of the Big Fellow began to emerge as amorous links surfaced with a range of different women: Kitty Kiernan, Susan Killeen, Sinéad Mason, Moya O'Connor and even one Dilly Dicker, an ubiquitous piano player. There were absurd suggestions that he was exhausted during the negotiations trying to satisfy a number of different women. Peter Hart even suggested in his biography that Collins might have consorted with prostitutes in London. He produced no evidence whatever to support his sensationalist contention; he might just as well have written that any Irishman who ever visited London may have consorted with prostitutes.

In the same sense no evidence has ever been produced to suggest that the amorous activities of Collins, real or imagined, had any influence on the negotiations. But that has not stopped silly, sensational speculation.

The one person who unquestionably had most influence on Collins was Griffith. Collins had admired him as a youngster but did question Griffith's non-violent approach to the struggle in the aftermath of 1916. Yet the two of them got on well together while de Valera was in the United States, and Griffith was instrumental in having Collins take over as acting president after his arrest in November 1920. Now their relationship would be tempered by their shared experiences under the pressure of the negotiations. They had to confront not only the British but also the dissidents within their own delegation, and the cabinet members in Dublin.

Griffith was clearly feeling the strain of the talks. He was suffering from hypertension, which would kill him within a year. It probably explains his volatility and irritability with the dissidents. He asked Collins to play a greater role in the negotiations, but they both realised that they would have to keep this secret. 'He and I recognise,' Collins wrote, 'that if such a thing were official it would provide bullets for the un-mentionables.' The two of them discussed their apprehensions about those in Dublin.

'You realise what we have on our hands?' Griffith asked.

'I realised it long ago,' replied Collins.

'I reminded him when I was young I thought of him as Ireland,' Collins added.

'We stand or fall in this together,' Griffith said.

'It is the one bright hope of mine in all this welter of action and counter-action,' Collins continued. It was the one redeeming feature in the whole situation as far as he was concerned. He was becoming increasingly more critical of those in Dublin, the longer the conference went on. 'From Dublin,' he wrote, 'I don't know whether we're being instructed or confused. The latter I would say.

'I will not agree to anything which threatens to plunge the people of Ireland into a war, not without their authority,' the Big Fellow told Griffith. 'Still less do I agree to being dictated to by those not embroiled in these negotiations. If they are not in agreement with the steps we are taking, and hope to take, why then did they themselves not consider their own presence here in London.' This seemed a far cry from the night that Griffith presided at the meeting of the Sinn Féin Executive in March 1919 when Collins announced that 'the proper people' were going to provoke 'a state of general disorder' to force a confrontation with the British 'and they were not to be deterred by weaklings and cowards'. That brash young man had three months earlier advocated kidnapping president Woodrow Wilson to make him listen to Irish demands, but had obviously learned much since then, because he was the one who deliberately frustrated Cathal Brugha's plan to kill members of the British cabinet.

Now he was working hand-in-glove with Griffith, whom he had really come to appreciate. 'He is the kind that takes a lot of knowing,' Collins told the journalist Hayden Talbot some months later. 'If he will talk to you, you will learn things about Ireland that no other man could tell you. It may be that Irish people and the world in general may never appreciate Arthur Griffith until he is dead and gone, but mark my words, it will come.'

Griffith clearly despised Childers and their relationship tended to poison relations within the delegation. In later life Barton tended to be very critical of Griffith and, as the longest survivor of the negotiations, he had a much greater influence on the history of the talks than on the conference itself.

'It is difficult to realise how Arthur Griffith came to be so closely identified with the Republic party and its leaders,' Barton wrote in February 1969. 'So far as I know Griffith, while in Ireland, never confided to any of us that he was not a true blue Republican. He did state that he considered passive resistance to be the form of revolt most likely to bring us success. In the Mansion House he subscribed to the oath of allegiance to the Republic and did not publicly divulge any reservations.

'And yet,' Barton continued in the same note, in terms that showed that Griffith did speak out, 'I have the clearest recollection of him standing in front of the fireplace in the secretary's office in Hans Place, London, and declaring that he had always believed that the ideal relationship of Ireland to England was that framed in a Constitution of the King, Lords and Commons of Ireland – the King being the King of both

Ireland and England. How did Griffith come to be able to hide this inconsistency? It was not in his nature to lie. Was it just ineptitude on our part that failed to apprehend it?'

Griffith never did hide his views in relation to republicanism, as Barton's own writings indicated decades earlier in 1924. 'Arthur Griffith as a study of his writings and utterances before and since December 1921 shows he was never a Republican or an advocate of physical force. I think this was pretty generally known to all the leaders.'

Chapter Thirteen

'To go for a drink is one thing'

Once the Unionist Conference was out of the way, it became possible to concentrate on the Anglo-Irish negotiations again. 'I think we should now get down to definite business and send them, as far as possible, our firm word; that is a draft which would mark as closely as possible the exact line on the main question on which we propose to take our stand,' de Valera wrote to Griffith on the same day, 17 November 1921. 'In that case our draft should be signed and they should be asked to sign theirs before it is sent.' This was de Valera's twelfth letter to the delegation, but in it he acknowledged twenty-one messages from Childers. Although he stated that he included Childers in the delegation to keep an eye on Griffith and Collins, he was not giving any advice to Childers. In fact he was hardly even acknowledging his correspondence. Childers would write a week later complaining again that he had not received any acknowledgement of his further correspondence.

Despite all their reservations, Barton wrote that neither he nor his colleagues initially suspected that Griffith and Collins might be prepared to accept dominion status. 'What we felt was that they were very much easier going than we were and that the English were getting very much the best of it,' Barton wrote.

While he realised that Childers was inclined to be over officious, he would have been less than human not to have been offended by the contemptuous attitude that Griffith displayed towards his cousin. After Griffith refused to call a meeting of the delegation to discuss drawing up formal proposals on 16 November, Childers drew them up himself in consultation with Barton and Gavan Duffy.

Childers was already working on drafting proposals for a treaty on 17 November when de Valera advised such a course. Next day there was a brief meeting of the Irish delegation before Collins set out to Dublin for the weekend. Childers, Barton and Gavan Duffy accused Griffith of delaying the return of Chartres from Germany. 'You won't agree to any appeal to J.C.,' Barton complained.

Actually Chartres did not wish to return, because he had become disillusioned with the situation. 'On the subject of the Crown,' he wrote to Griffith on 8 November, 'I have put forward ideas which, I think, would deprive the English of any sufficient ground for the revival of hostilities and at the same time keep the monarchy out of Ireland and so preserve intact our republic and its freedom.'

In view of the attitude of the dissidents within the delegation, however, Griffith recalled Chartres urgently. By this stage Collins was trying to hide his own views from Childers and company, with the result that there was very little mention of his contributions in the later Irish reports of the negotiations.

The atmosphere within the Irish delegation was little short of poisonous when Chartres got back on 21 November. The delegation had met at 11.30 a.m. before he returned. Barton had presented the draft treaty drawn up by Childers as his own in the hope of avoiding a scene with Griffith. Of course, everybody would have realised that Childers was behind it. He was clearly over-reaching his authority as chief secretary to the delegation. He was supposed to be facilitating the delegation, not trying to take over, or lead it. But as a member of the cabinet Barton was in a position to introduce proposals as his own and demand that the delegation afford them full consideration. Collins had just returned from Dublin and he brought a rough draft of a treaty from de Valera that was 'much the same as our memo' according to Childers. Griffith raised strong objections to the defence and trade provisions of the draft document and he launched a vicious verbal assault on Childers. At one point he accused Childers of trying to start another war, and he even blamed him for being responsible for starting the First World War with his book *The Riddle of the Sands*. 'I said I stood on the strategical case in both instances,' Childers noted. The meeting adjourned until 5 p.m.

When Chartres arrived back at Hans Place that evening the delegation was in the middle of another bitter wrangle, which only adjourned when Tom Jones arrived to talk with Griffith. The defence and trade clauses were redrafted.

'It is exactly like arguing with the British,' Childers wrote. He added that Collins 'showed complete ignorance of the defence position'.

At 11 p.m. Chartres redrafted the document from a jumble of papers. The delegation met again after midnight by which time Collins had left. Barton argued about trade and Childers about defence. Griffith was 'insolent to me about Secretary altering Drafts', Childers noted. 'I protest and virtually threatened resignation. He climbs down and calls another meeting for 9.30 tomorrow. Document supposed to be ready by 11 tomorrow.'

When the delegation reconvened the following morning Griffith admitted that he had not read any of the many documents on defence drafted by Childers. Gavan Duffy suggested that Barton should accompany Griffith and Collins in presenting the draft terms to the British. Griffith objected, but they pointed out that the British had three members at a number of the sub-conference meetings. It was therefore agreed that Barton would go and Chartres was asked to write a memo about the crown.

Griffith blurted out that he was personally willing to give allegiance to the crown 'to save country from war'. He implied that he was going to tell Lloyd George this, but Barton challenged him on this and he agreed not to do so.

'Duffy, Childers and I realised at once that our colleagues were not pleased with these draft proposals, but after a long discussion and some alterations to the subsequent clauses' they agreed to send them to the British. The first three clauses of the Irish proposals of 22 November contained the essence of External Association:

1. Legislative and Executive authority in Ireland shall be derived exclusively from the elected Representatives of the Irish people.

2. Ireland agreed to be associated with the British commonwealth for the purposes of common concern and, in respect of those purposes, to recognise the crown as the symbol and accepted Head of the Association

3. In matters of common concern, which are declared to include Peace and War and Defence, the rights and status of Ireland shall be in no respect less than those enjoyed by and of the component States of the British commonwealth represented in the League of Nations. There shall be between Ireland and these States such concerted action, founded on consultation, as the several Governments may determine.

The defence clauses stipulated that Ireland should, 'as far as her resources permit', provide for her own defence and that her rights and status should 'be in no respect less than those' of any of the dominions. While Irish bases would be provided for Britain, these would be handed over to the Irish within five years and Ireland would agree that her forces would not be larger in relation to Ireland's population than the British forces were in relation to the population of Great Britain.

'One of the additions they insisted upon is worth mentioning,' Barton noted. 'Our draft proposals had made no reference to the exclusion or inclusion of Ulster. We were visualising a united

Ireland and it was not our purpose to consider dismemberment, but Griffith and Collins insisted that reference must be made to a settlement of this Ulster problem. We therefore were reluctantly compelled to preface the document with this note: "The following proposals are put forward upon the assumption that the essential unity of Ireland is maintained." And they added Clause 10: "In the event of the existing Legislature of N.E. Ireland accepting its position under the National Parliament, Ireland will confirm that legislature in its existing powers and will undertake to provide safeguards designed to secure the special interests of the area over which it functions." In the opinion of our side of the delegation these references were but a source of weakness.'

Griffith saw Childers as a tiresome obstacle, because he seemed to be forever producing documents, and he found his fussy civil service habits infuriating. Childers made multiple copies of reports all stamped 'SECRET' in large bold letters in bright red ink. The sight of the stamp infuriated Griffith. The British realised that Griffith was likely to accept membership of the British commonwealth, but Barton, Duffy and Childers still did not believe that External Association had been explored properly, and they insisted on its inclusion in the latest Irish proposals.

'The document in many respects marks a big advance on any previous document but is still so worded as to leave the position too ambiguous and uncertain,' Tom Jones wrote. But Lloyd George was unhappy.

'This is no good,' the prime minister said. 'They are back on their independent state again. These clauses about the Navy won't do. We must have complete control of naval defence.'

Jones noted that Churchill had indicated that the Irish could have Simonstown status. By this he was apparently suggesting that the Irish could take over their ports once they were strong enough to defend them.

'They cannot have Simonstown terms,' the prime minister

insisted. 'South Africa did not get them until fifteen years had passed during which they had put 70,000 troops into the field on the side of the Empire. When Ireland does that she can have Simonstown terms.' The prime minister was also disappointed that there was no reference to safeguards for Ulster Protestants. He told Jones to go back and tell the Irish leaders that he would break off the negotiations unless they withdrew the document.

'Are they in the Empire or are they out? Are we to control or are we not?' These were some of the questions he told Jones to put to them. 'What are the safeguards for Ulster?'

'All of my colleagues would share my view of this document,' the prime minister said. 'If they are not coming into the Empire, then we will make them.'

Griffith refused to withdraw the document. 'Owing to the Crux over the crown and empire, they feel their position weakened if not gone,' he wrote de Valera that night. 'In view of your letter of October 25th I cannot discuss the alternative with them.' He thought the conference was on the brink of collapse. 'I presume Lloyd George will send a letter terminating the negotiations and to this we shall reply, and then leave London for home, unless you think the time has come for you to cross over here.'

Next morning Childers presented the delegation with a document headed, 'Concessions Contained in our Proposals of 22 November'. He noted that eight of the ten clauses in latest proposals involved Irish concessions. 'Ireland's full claim is for a Republic, unfettered by any obligation or restrictions whatever,' Childers began. Neither Griffith nor Collins ever thought that they had come to London to make such a claim. They were sent to negotiate a compromise, but Childers seemed to be dangerously close to suggesting that the delegation was responsible for watering down the absolute claim. Griffith 'exploded', but this did not stop Childers, who compounded his insensitivity by arguing that the sub-conference meetings should be discontinued. He was clearly exceeding his authority. He was reflecting the views of Barton and Gavan Duffy, but they should have had the courage to insist on their own inclusion. They did, in fact, insist that Barton should accompany Griffith and Collins that afternoon.

'The presentation of the draft of our proposals was the first rude shock the English had received,' Barton noted. 'It was the first time they had come up against the united strength of the Delegation since the preliminary series of conferences early in October. Our draft was forwarded by a messenger without comment or explanation. It created a sensation in Downing Street. In it no quibbling or suggestion of recognition of private undertakings. It was a clear concise statement of Ireland's independence with conditional terms for a free alliance for specific purposes viz Peace, War and Defence.'

The prime minister accused Griffith of going back on their understanding about Northern Ireland. 'On Ulster Lloyd George declared that I had assured him I would not let him down if he put up the proposals subsequently embodied in their memorandum to Craig, and complained that we had not embodied them in our memorandum,' Griffith wrote to de Valera that night. 'I said I had given him that assurance and I now repeated it, but I told him at the time it was his proposal – not ours. Therefore, it did not appear in our document. Our proposal was, in our opinion, better, but it was different.'

Lloyd George was satisfied. 'He had misunderstood us in this instance and said as much,' Griffith continued. 'He would put his proposal to Craig from himself only.'

Members of the British government were sending mixed signals in relation to the Boundary Commission. On 23 November Austen Chamberlain led Bonar Law to believe that the Boundary Commission would only make minor adjustments. He was satisfied that Northern Ireland would not be forced under Dáil Éireann so he agreed to advise Craig and Carson that they could not expect the British government to fight to maintain the existing border.

Griffith intimated Sinn Féin would accept the Boundary Commission proposal if Craig accepted it, but he knew there was no possibility of this. The real problem was the crown and the empire.

Meanwhile Childers observed that Barton 'made notes which added much and showed AG[riffith]'s minutes of such Conferences cannot be relied on even if and when RCB[arton] is present'. Barton noted the next meeting was going to deal with constitutional matters. Lloyd George suggested that Birkenhead and Attorney-General Gordon Hewart should meet with Griffith and Collins. The latter suggested that the Irish side should have a constitutional lawyer with them, by which he meant Chartres, but the others felt it should be Gavan Duffy. Barton told Collins that Gavan Duffy must go and this was agreed. Barton and Gavan Duffy also argued that Childers should go as an authority on the whole subject. This was essentially left hanging overnight.

'Why did they bring that pip-squeak of a man Barton with them?' Lloyd George asked Jones afterwards. 'I would not make him a private secretary to an under-secretary.'

While Griffith could not hide his contempt for Childers, Collins was quietly critical of him. 'He is sharp to realise how things will have due effect in Dublin – and acts accordingly,' Collins wrote. 'To go for a drink is one thing. To be driven to it is another.'

The suggestion that Childers should be included as an expert in the Irish team for the constitutional discussions on 24 November had been left hanging overnight and Gavan Duffy called for a meeting of the delegation next morning. Griffith 'lost his temper', according to Childers. He said he had had enough of Gavan Duffy's intrigues and he accused him of letting him down on neutrality at an early conference. Barton and Gavan Duffy insisted that Childers should go to the meeting. Griffith got 'very angry', and Collins remarked with a smile that he did not know Childers knew anything about constitutional matters. Charters made a perfunctory offer to withdraw himself. 'I of course jumped on the idea of JC[harters] not going and effaced myself,' Childers wrote.

Gavan Duffy and Chartres accompanied Griffith and Collins to meet with Birkenhead and Hewart at the House of Lords. Childers also accompanied them but Griffith 'went in first and needless to say arranged that I would be left out!' Childers observed somewhat bitterly.

'We had Duffy with us today,' Collins wrote to a friend. 'It went fair, no more than that. If Duffy spent less time admiring his own voice we'd do better. Proof of it is when G[riffith] and I are together. You would appreciate the difference.'

The meeting achieved very little but it did have an extraordinary sequel when Hewart forwarded to the Irish delegation a synopsis contradicting an earlier account stating that the Irish should not suppose that war was the alternative. 'What the Attorney-General stated was "the Irish delegates must not suppose that the British Government was contemplating with equanimity the alternative was war".' This was, in effect, a threat to resume the war.

'There was war in the air,' Barton noted. 'I thought the negotiations had ended but there was to be one more conference before we returned to discuss the situation at home.'

While the British were able to function as a united delegation, the Irish were divided. Collins no longer trusted Childers, but, unlike Griffith, he hid his feelings. For instance, Collins offered to present a document that reflected his thinking on the crown and empire. There was no problem about submitting this memorandum, unlike at the start of the month when Griffith furnished Lloyd George with the letter of 3 November, but the lack of opposition this time was possibly because Childers was the main author of the memorandum, as it had his figurative fingerprints all over it. Collins essentially accepted the arguments of Childers who had studied in detail and written about the constitutional aspects of the dominions in his book *The Framework of Home Rule*.

Like Childers, Collins was now arguing for External Association as simply a means of ensuring that Ireland would have the same *de facto* status as Canada. 'The only association which it will be satisfactory to Ireland to Great Britain and the Dominions for Ireland to enter will be one based, not on the present technical legal status of the Dominions, but on the real position which they claim, and have in fact secured,' Collins contended. 'In the interest of all the associated states, in the interest above all of England herself, it is essential that the present *de facto* position should be recognised *de jure*, and that all its implications as regards sovereignty, allegiance, [and] constitutional independence of the governments, should be acknowledged.'

He went on to argue that such an association 'might form the nucleus of a real League of Nations of the world', which would be 'the best and only way' for England to ensure her permanent security. 'Into such a League might not America be willing to enter?' Collins asked. 'Without real and permanent co-operation between Britain and America world peace is an idle dream,' he continued. 'With such co-operation war would become impossible.

'The possibility of such a League, and the need for it, would be more clearly understood if it were more fully recognised how far the claim of the Dominions to independent statehood has matured, and the progress which has been made in finding ways in which independent nations may act in concert.'

Chamberlain described the memorandum as 'extraordinarily interesting though sometimes perverse and sometimes Utopian. Who (outside our six) would guess the name of the writer?' Chamberlain wrote to Birkenhead.

Chapter Fourteen

'BY TUESDAY NEXT'

Griffith, Collins and Barton returned to Dublin for a cabinet meeting on 25 November. While they were gone Jones had a thirty-minute conversation with Chartres when he delivered a memorandum offering to contribute to the King's Civil List.

> I pleaded with him on the subject of allegiance but found him utterly irreconcilable on allegiance to the King in Ireland. He had seen such things done in the King's name by the King's servants in the last two years that he would rather, as he put it, go underground tomorrow than consent to any intervention ever again by this country in the domestic affairs of Ireland. He spoke with great earnestness and there was no misunderstanding the dept of his conviction.

But Chartres was more moderate than some of the cabinet in Dublin. When Collins gave the cabinet the memorandum by Chartres proposing a voluntary contribution to the king, Brugha dissented. 'It is not going to settle the matter,' he complained. 'I don't believe we are going to settle on that.'

Collins said that the memorandum was already presented to the British.

'I pointed out that I had not agreed to that,' Brugha noted afterwards. He had refused to go to London as part of the delegation, yet he seemed to think that he should be consulted not just on defence matters, but on other matters, such as the crown, as well.

'Well,' de Valera asked, 'can we have unity or can we not?'

Brugha replied that it could be recorded as 'agreed to, with one dissenting'.

'This means now that we have not unanimity in the cabinet and the object all along in these negotiations was to have unanimity,' de Valera said.

'Very well,' Brugha responded, 'if it has been handed in I am agreed in order to preserve unity to the finish.'

They were far from united, however. Mulcahy attended the cabinet meeting as the controversy over the attempt to impose Austin Stack as deputy chief of staff was coming to a head. The headquarters' staff was balking, and Mulcahy asked that the cabinet clarify the situation for the staff. With Mulcahy objecting to Stack's appointment, de Valera tried to mollify him by suggesting that Eoin O'Duffy could remain as deputy chief of staff, but Stack would be 'Cathal's ghost on the Staff'. Mulcahy refused to accept this and others were invited into the meeting.

They sat around the perimeter of the drawing-room of the Mansion House, where the cabinet had been meeting. De Valera, who was sitting at one end of a small table at which his ministers were still seated, said that he wished to reform the headquarters staff. Having spoken briefly about the changes that he wished to make, he asked the men for their opinions. One after another they spoke against the changes, taking turns in the order in which they were sitting from the left-hand side of the room. J. J. O'Connell expressed the general tone when he said 'the General Headquarters Staff had been a band of brothers'. All spoke in the same vein until it came to O'Duffy who was sitting in the second-last position on the right-hand side. His voice became shrill and he became a touch hysterical as he characterised the effort to appoint Stack as a criticism of himself.

De Valera then became somewhat hysterical. He pushed the table in front of him as he rose and declared in a half-scream, 'Ye may mutiny, if ye like, but Ireland will give me another Army.'

Then, Mulcahy recalled, 'He dismissed the whole lot of us from his sight.'

As they were leaving Mulcahy walked down the steps of the Mansion House with Seán Russell, who was also a rather highly strung individual. He was very pale and incensed at the way de Valera had addressed Mulcahy. 'I didn't think that there was a man in Ireland that would speak like that to my Chief,' he said in a tense kind of whisper.

In his biography of Collins, Rex Taylor quoted from the record of undated exchanges between Griffith and Collins during the latter stages of the negotiations.

'I will not agree,' Collins declared, 'to anything which threatens to plunge the people of Ireland into a war – not without their authority. Still less do I agree to being dictated to by those not embroiled in these negotiations.' It was significant that he actually placed more emphasis on his objection to being 'dictated to', than to plunging the country into war. After all he, more than anybody else, was responsible for provoking the Black and Tan war. Now his ego had become involved.

'If they are not in agreement with the steps which we are taking, and hope to take, why then did they themselves not consider their own presence here in London?' asked Griffith. 'Brugha refused to be a member of this delegation.'

'Supposing,' Collins added, 'we were to go back to Dublin tomorrow with a document which gave us a Republic. Would such a document find favour with everyone? I doubt it.'

'So do I,' remarked Griffith. 'But sooner or later a decision will have to be made and we shall have to make it.'

The negotiations on the association question were coming to a head when the delegation got together again in London. De Valera noted that the latest British proposals had no address and no signature. 'You could in your reply, if you thought it desirable, follow the same course and send them an unsigned draft,' de Valera wrote on 27 November. 'But there has been so much "beating around the bush" already that I think we should now get down to definite business and send them, as far as possible, our final word.'

Childers had been preparing a whole series of documents on dominion status. 'The Dominion Status' contrasted the real status of the dominions with their legal, technical status. It noted that the British Government, or the Imperial Executive, could make treaties in the name of the dominions; but, in fact, the dominions had to be consulted. The British could commit the dominions to war and peace, but the dominions actually had to be consulted first. In it he contrasted the real status of the dominions with their inferior legal status. In theory the dominions were subject to the crown on all matters but in reality the king's representative acted on the advice of the dominion cabinets in all domestic matters. He summarised the situation by contrasting the technical *de jure* status of Canada with real, *de facto* status in separate columns.

Canada's legal status was that of 'a subordinate dependent of Britain holding her self-governing rights under a British Act of Parliament'. It could therefore be legally repealed or amended at Westminster without Canada's consent. But Canada's constitutional position under Britain's unwritten constitution was something quite different. She was an independent country in total control of her own affairs. Although Canadians swore allegiance directly to the British crown and were technically subject to the royal veto, Childers argued that in fact the crown has no authority in Canada. 'It signifies sentiment only' because 'the Canadian owes obedience to his own constitution only'. In short, he wrote, 'Canada is by the full admission of British statesmen equal in status to Great Britain and as free as Great Britain.'

In another memorandum – headed 'Notable Definitions of Dominion Status' – Childers quoted pronouncements by prominent people on the real status of the dominions. 'We have received a position of absolute equality and freedom not only among the other States of the Empire but among the other nations of the world,' Smuts had told the South African parliament on 10 September 1919. Bonar Law told the House of Commons on 30 March 1920 that the dominions 'have control of their whole destiny'. Lloyd George had actually written to General James Hertzog, 'The South African people control their own national destiny in the fullest sense.'

Childers contended that the British had no intention of giving Ireland the same status as Canada, seeing that they were demanding trade and defence concessions that were unprecedented in the case of Canada. Even if those demands were dropped, Ireland could not enjoy the same status, because the Canadians essentially enjoyed their freedom as a result of their distance from Britain. The British were simply too far away to enforce their legal edicts. If they tried to use force it would lead to complications with United States in view of the Monroe Doctrine. But Ireland was close enough that British laws 'could be enforced against Ireland so as to override the fullest constitutional freedom nominally conferred'.

Although Childers had prepared a memorandum for the British, at this point he believed the negotiations had reached an impasse, but he noted in his diary that night that 'it is pretty clear' that Griffith and Duggan 'took steps, possibly through Cope or C.[ope] may have taken the initiative to re-open the matter'. Griffith insisted on presenting his own document to the British. It included the first two clauses of the proposals of 22 November (see p. 174) with the added specification of the offer to vote an annual contribution to the king's personal revenue as a token recognition of the crown.

'Useless to criticise much,' Childers noted in his diary, 'I object to the Defence par[agraph] which gives away our case but only succeeded in getting it slightly altered. AG made the usual explosion about waste of time. Little help from anyone else.'

Other than the first three clauses, all the other points were covered in a note three paragraphs long. While the dominions considered the crown a symbol of external unity among the distant members states of the British commonwealth, Griffith argued, 'Ireland, on the contrary lies beside the shores of Great Britain, which has been accustomed for generations to interfere, in the name of the crown, in every detail of Ireland's life. The desire and temptation to continue interference will remain if the Crown remains, as it cannot be the symbolic Crown that the Dominions know, but will continue to possess the real power of repression and veto which Ireland knows.' The defence issue, to which Childers took exception, was not covered by a paragraph but a mere sentence: 'We acknowledge a reasonableness in the desire of the British Government for certain naval facilities in Ireland differing from those which they receive from Canada or the other Dominions.'

There was one curious development when the delegation met that evening before the sub-conference meeting. Griffith 'asked me, Charters, and GD [Gavan Duffy] to draft an alternative form of oath, saying I was an expert with words,' Childers noted in his diary. It was the 'first time he has ever asked me for advice of any kind!'

'We cannot make peace on these terms,' Chamberlain wrote to Lloyd George, 'but we must not break on this document.'

As Collins had not yet returned from Dublin, Duggan joined Griffith to discuss the latest document with Lloyd George, Birkenhead and Sir Robert Horne at Chequers on the evening of 28 November. 'We told them we had no authority to deal with them on any other basis than exclusion of the Crown from purely Irish affairs,' Griffith reported. 'We then entered into a general discussion in which they knocked out my argument in the document we sent in – that the Crown in the Dominions was merely a symbol but in Ireland a reality – by offering to put in any phrase in the Treaty we liked to ensure that the functions of the Crown in Ireland should be no more in practice than it is in Canada or any Dominion.' In short, the British trumped the Irish argument for External Association by offering to ensure that Ireland would have the actual freedom enjoyed by Canada and the dominion by inserting in the proposed Treaty any phrase desired by the Irish delegation to ensure that Ireland would have the same *de facto* status as Canada. The British guaranteed, for instance, that the representative of the king in Ireland would be 'merely a symbol, and that no one would ever be appointed to whom the Irish Ministry offered any objection'.

Griffith might just as well have written that the British undermined de Valera's argument, which the Irish delegation had been pressing. It also undermined Childers, who had been arguing that Canada was essentially independent. If the British were not going to honour the commitment to Ireland by not according the *de facto* status of Canada, they could just as easily violate External Association, because it was not going to move Ireland an inch further away from Britain. The negotiations were clearly coming to a conclusion. Indeed, Barton saw no point in remaining in London. He wished to return home the next day, 30 November, but the others thought this would be seen as an affront to Griffith.

On the afternoon of 30 November Collins joined with Griffith and Duggan for a further meeting at 10 Downing Street with the prime minister, Birkenhead and Chamberlain. Lloyd George informed them that he would present the Irish delegation with Britain's final terms in the form of a draft treaty on Tuesday, 6 December.

'They proposed to send their final proposals to Craig and ourselves on Tuesday,' Griffith reported. 'We objected. We should see them beforehand. They agreed to send us them on Thursday evening, but formally to hand them to us Tuesday.'

Craig told Stormont that he had been authorised by the prime minister to issue a statement. 'By Tuesday next,' he said, 'either the negotiations will have broken down or the prime minister will send me new proposals for consideration by the Cabinet.'

The British draft treaty – delivered to the Irish delegation late on the night of Wednesday, 30 November – offered the Irish Free State, as Ireland would be known, the same status as the Dominions in 'law and practice'. The exceptions, which really limited Irish freedom in relation to that of existing Dominions, were in matters of trade and defence. The British insisted on free trade and also stipulated that the coastal defence of Britain and Ireland would 'be undertaken exclusively' by the British, who would retain control of four specified ports and such other facilities as might be desired 'in times of war or of strained relations with a foreign Power'. The British and Irish armies were to be the same size in relation to each other as each was to its country's population. Another specific difference was the form of the oath to be taken by all members of the Free State parliament, who would swear 'allegiance to the Constitution of the Irish Free State; the Community of Nations known as the British Empire; and to the King as head of the State and of the Empire'.

On the Ulster question the draft treaty gave a fleeting re-cognition to Irish unity in that it applied to the whole island even though the representatives of Northern Ireland were not even consulted, but the proposals protected their interests by stipulating that the area could opt out of the Irish Free State and retain its existing status. In that event, however, a Boundary Commission would be established to adjust the boundary of Northern Ireland 'in accordance with the wishes of the inhabitants, so far as may be compatible with economic and geographic conditions'.

The previous day Lloyd George and Churchill met T. M. Healy. Churchill told him the British government would appoint a Boundary Commission that would 'ensure the transfer to the

Free State of the counties of Tyrone and Fermanagh, South Armagh, and (if I remember rightly) South Down'. Churchill continued that 'the inevitable result' would be that Craig would have to accept Irish unity.

'That,' said Healy, 'is a statement of supreme importance. Do you mind repeating it, so as to enable me to transmit it to those men. I cannot imagine anything better calculated to silence their objections.'

Healy took down Churchill's words in shorthand. 'Am I to understand,' he asked, 'that that assurance is endorsed by the Prime Minister?'

'It certainly is,' Lloyd George replied.

Collins and Griffith were already convinced the Boundary Commission would transfer extensive territory, but the main issues facing them at the time were the crown and empire. Many believed Childers was the real author of External Association and he seemed to be holding on to this with a kind of blind tenacity. He understood better than any of them the real status of Canada, but even though the British were offering Ireland that status with the specified exceptions of some defence and trade concessions, he argued those concessions essentially undermined that status. Even if the British dropped all the demanded concessions, he would still argue that Ireland would not have the same status as Canada because the Canadians essentially enjoyed their freedom as a result of their distance from Britain. Ireland, on the other hand, was close enough that British laws 'could be enforced against Ireland so as to override the fullest constitutional freedom nominally conferred'. But this would be a violation of the agreement, and if the British were going to violate it, they could just as easily violate External Association, as Ireland was still going to be as close to Britain.

Childers worked that day on a second part to his document contrasting the legal and constitutional status of Canada. But Collins no longer had any confidence in his judgment. 'Integrity of purpose is defeated at all times by those whose start rests elsewhere,' Collins wrote on 30 November. 'The advice and inspiration of C[hilders] is like farmland under water – dead. With a purpose, I think – with a definite purpose. Soon he will howl his triumph – for what it is worth.'

'I think also that Birkenhead's integrity of purpose is foiled in other quarters,' Collins continued. 'I can almost see the gloating that is so obvious among some of our opposites – whichever way it means trouble at home, an enjoyable spectacle for more people than one imagines.'

Chartres and Childers had come up with the phrase 'constitutional usage' to cover the *de facto* status of Canada. This was communicated to the British, and the term was included in the British draft treaty, which guaranteed that the Irish Free State the same status as Canada in 'law, practice and constitutional usage'. Collins objected to the oath being prescribed for Irish members of parliament. He suggested an alternative. There is no indication of who suggested it to Collins. Did he come up with it himself, or was it the result of Griffith's request that Childers and the others suggest an oath? The oath that Collins proposed on 30 November was:

I ... do solemnly swear to bear true faith and allegiance to the Constitution of the Irish Free State as by law established and that I will be faithful to His Majesty King George in acknowledgment of the Association of Ireland in a common citizenship with Great Britain and the group of nations known as the British commonwealth.

Such an oath would be explicitly in line with Childers' assessment of the *de facto* situation in Canada, where he contended that each 'Canadian owes obedience to his own constitution only'. The word 'faithful' was specifically included to denote equality between the monarch and those taking the oath, as opposed to the allegiance normally owed to one's sovereign. Although the oath involved common citizenship, which was tantamount to acceptance of indirect allegiance and also membership of the British commonwealth, the British rejected the proposal at this stage.

'Got my political life at stake,' Lloyd George said to Collins that night. Collins did not reply, but the following day he wrote to a friend, 'My life – not only political – is at stake.'

Griffith called a full meeting of the Irish delegation for 1 December. 'I want to hear all points of objections,' he said, 'so that nobody can say afterwards that all arguments were not fully heard.'

Childers noted that he did not want to create a scene at the meeting of the delegation by repeating some of his old arguments, so he confined himself to the defence terms, but got in a hassle with Griffith anyway. 'He flared at me with some vague charge of often before having said the delegation was going back on July 20th. I said on this occasion I had criticised on defence only. M.C. instead of backing me up, said he thought I implied a wider criticism and refused to withdraw when I asked him.' After the meeting Collins made what Childers considered 'a ghost of an apology'. Of course, there is no way of determining what Childers actually said, but it was significant that in referring to the draft treaty in his diary the previous night, he wrote, 'It is July 20th', with the addition of the *de facto* stipulation, the boundary commission scheme, and safeguards for Ulster, but without the right for the British to recruit in Ireland.

Before accepting the British terms the Irish representatives were obliged to consult the cabinet in Dublin in line with their instructions. Barton and Duffy, who were so opposed to the British terms, did not want the bother of returning to Dublin for consultations. But Griffith insisted that the whole delegation return for a meeting with the cabinet in line with their instructions. The negotiations had reached a critical stage and everyone knew that the conference was supposed to be concluded by the following Tuesday.

Arrangements were made for a cabinet meeting at the Mansion House on Saturday morning, 3 December 1921. Griffith returned to meet de Valera on Friday night, while Collins stayed on with Childers for some talks with the British on financial matters. De Valera broke off his tour of IRA units to return to Dublin on Friday. He insisted on driving all the way himself and was very tired when he reached Dublin at 10.30 that night. Griffith arrived about thirty minutes later and their meeting lasted for two hours.

'First of all I got a document from Mr Griffith which I said I will never sign,' de Valera recalled later. 'I will not sign it.' It was a strange thing for him to say, unless he was expecting to take over the leadership of the delegation at the last moment.

Griffith again emphasised that he was not going to break over the crown, but de Valera later told his authorised biographers that he was too tired at the time to argue the matter. So further discussion was postponed until the cabinet meeting next morning.

Meanwhile Collins was doing such an effective job of hiding his own attitude that Childers could not determine where the Big Fellow stood on the proposals. He and Childers set out for Dublin that evening and crossed from Holyhead on the mail boat, but it was delayed on route by an accident and had to return to port. As a result the mail boat did not dock until shortly before the cabinet was due to convene. A sleepless night was certainly not the best preparation for the arduous meetings that were to follow.

Chapter Fifteen

'AMENDMENTS WERE NOT MANDATORY'

Before setting out Collins had requested a meeting with the available members of the supreme council of the IRB while he was in Dublin but, because of the delay, he was unable to meet them as planned. Instead, he telephoned Seán Ó Muirthile from the Mansion House to pick up a copy of the draft treaty while the cabinet was meeting.

In addition to the cabinet members, Gavan Duffy and Duggan were invited to sit in on the meeting, as were Kevin O'Higgins and Childers, while Colm Ó Murchada attended as acting secretary to the cabinet.

At the outset each member of the delegation gave his views on the draft terms. Griffith explained he was in favour of accepting them, and he emphasised that he would not break on the question of the crown. Barton, on the other hand, argued against acceptance on the grounds that the proposals were not Britain's last word, that they did not really give full dominion status, and that there was no guarantee of unity. Gavan Duffy agreed with him, but Duggan concurred with Griffith.

There was come confusion about the attitude of Collins, who was obviously still trying to keep his views to himself, especially in the presence of Brugha and Stack. Childers noted in his diary that 'Collins was difficult to understand – repeatedly pressed by Dev but I really don't know what his answer amounted to'. Stack later recalled that 'Collins did not speak strongly in favour of the document at all'. But Ó Murchada described him as being 'in substantial agreement' with Griffith and Duggan in arguing that rejecting the 'Treaty would be a gamble as England could arrange a war in Ireland within a week'. Collins did say, however, that further concessions could be won on trade and defence, and he suggested the oath should be rejected.

At the president's invitation, Childers criticised the proposals. Confining himself to the defence clauses, he denounced them, saying that they meant the Free State's status would be less than that of a dominion.

Barton asked him if the dominions would support the Free State in any question involving status, seeing that any British infringement in Irish affairs might be seen as setting a precedent affording Britain the right to interfere in the domestic affairs of the other dominions.

'No,' replied Childers. So long as those defence clauses remained, he felt the Free State would not really be a Dominion at all. 'I said,' he recalled, 'we must make it clear that we had a right to defend ourselves.'

Griffith suggested consulting a constitutional lawyer to interpret the significance of the stipulation that the defence of Irish coastal waters would be undertaken 'exclusively' by the British. At this point Childers adopted a distinctly censorial tone.

'I said,' he wrote in his diary, 'two such lawyers had been brought by him to London and had been there for some time and could have been consulted.'

De Valera contended that the word 'exclusively' in the provision stipulating that 'the defence of the sea of the British Islands, including Ireland shall be undertaken exclusively' by British forces 'clearly meant a prohibition on us which could not be admitted', according to Childers. 'He said he differed from me in that he thought it natural for them to demand facilities on our coast as being necessary. I said I didn't disagree in this but we had to keep up our principles.'

'There was a very free expression of disagreement at the cabinet meeting,' according to Barton. But Childers noted that Brugha went over the top and created 'an unpleasant scene'.

Observing that Griffith and Collins had been doing most of the negotiating, Brugha asked who was responsible for the sub-conference set up in which some of the delegation were not in complete touch with what was happening. Someone replied that the British had invited Griffith and Collins to meet them, and Brugha remarked that the British had selected 'their men'.

Griffith was furious. He stood up and went to where Brugha was sitting and demanded that the remark be withdrawn, but Brugha refused at first. Collins, too, was angry, but he contained himself. 'If you are not satisfied with us,' he said to Brugha, 'get another five to go over.'

'Brugha had at last realised the situation but he took no steps to strengthen our hands or to join the delegation himself or to induce the President to do so,' according to Barton. 'He was serious, glowered and took no action.' But that was largely Barton's own fault, because he came to the defence of his colleagues. Not withstanding his own dislike of the sub-conference set-up, he said that Griffith and Collins had been negotiating with the 'knowledge and consent' of the full delegation.

Brugha therefore withdrew his remark, but Griffith insisted it be entered in the minutes. The damaged had been done and an air of tension prevailed throughout the rest of the day's discussions.

De Valera avoided personalities in criticising the draft treaty. He rejected it mainly on the grounds that the oath was unacceptable. 'The oath,' he later wrote, 'crystallised in itself the main things we objected to – inclusion in the empire, the British King as King of Ireland, Chief Executive of the Irish State, and the source from which all authority in Ireland was to be derived.' He also criticised the fact that Northern Ireland would be allowed to vote itself out of the Irish state. While he could have understood accepting dominion status in return for an end to partition, he complained that the proposals afforded neither one nor the other. He therefore suggested the delegation should return to London, try to have the draft treaty amended and, if necessary, face the consequence of war.

At 1.30 the cabinet broke for lunch. During the recess Collins had a hurried meeting with Ó Muirthile, who explained that their IRB colleagues had reservations about the oath, together with the defence and partition provisions of the British terms. He gave Collins an alternative oath acceptable to his IRB colleagues. As it was comparatively similar to the one already suggested by Collins to the British, it was likely the wording was actually suggested by somebody who was aware of the lines on which Collins was thinking.

The cabinet reconvened at three o'clock and Barton appealed to de Valera to join the delegation on the grounds that it was unfair to ask Griffith to break on the crown when he was unwilling to fight on the issue. The president later said that he was seriously considering the suggestion but was reluctant to go because, as he later explained, 'my going over would be interpreted as anxiety on our part and likely to give in. I did not want this interpretation to be placed on my action, and that extra little bit I wanted to pull them and hoped they could be pulled could not be done if I went and therefore I was balancing these.'

Griffith – who never lost an opportunity of declaring that he would not break on the issue of the crown – emphasised his own attitude. When as many concessions as possible had been gained, he said that he would sign the agreement and go before the Dáil, which was the body to decide whether it should be war or not.

'Don't you realise that, if you sign this thing, you will split Ireland from top to bottom?' Brugha interjected.

'I suppose that's so,' replied Griffith, obviously struck by the implication of the Brugha's words. 'I'll tell you what I'll do. I'll go back to London. I'll not sign the document, but I'll bring it back and submit it to the Dáil and, if necessary to the public.'

De Valera was satisfied with this. He later said that he would 'probably' have gone to London but for Griffith's undertaking not to sign the draft treaty. It never seemed to have occurred to him that he did not have the authority to join the delegation, seeing that he had not been selected as a plenipotentiary by the Dáil, as had the other members of the delegation.

Although various defects were pointed out in the draft treaty during the seven hours of discussion, the oath was the single item that evoked most criticism. In fact, with the exception of Griffith, every member of the cabinet advocated rejecting the oath.

Unfortunately, Ó Murchada's brief notes did not reflect much of the criticism. For example, he never even mentioned any contributions by W. T. Cosgrave. But about thirty minutes before the meeting broke up, Cosgrave actually declared that he would not 'take that oath'. There followed a discussion in which the cabinet was asked to suggest an alternative.

Brugha objected to any oath unless the British were, in turn, willing to swear to uphold the Treaty. De Valera also questioned whether an oath was necessary but, on being told that the British were insisting on one, he sought an acceptable formula to replace the oath in the draft treaty.

'It is obvious that you cannot have that or any like "and the King as head of the State and the Empire",' he said. 'You could take an oath of true faith and allegiance to the Constitution of Ireland.'

'I started trying to get some sort of oath,' de Valera explained afterwards. 'Here is the oath I refer to, "I, so and so, swear to obey the Constitution of Ireland and to keep faith with His Britannic Majesty, so and so, in respect of the Treaty associating Ireland with the states of the British commonwealth".'

'Nothing doing,' Brugha snapped, 'there is going to be no unanimity on such an oath as that.'

'Surely Cathal, you can't object to taking an oath if you agree to association,' de Valera said.

Stack agreed with the president, so he, too, tried to persuade Brugha that such an oath would be acceptable.

'Well,' Brugha sighed in resignation, 'you may as well swear.'

'At the end of the discussion on the oath,' Childers recalled, 'I expressly raised the point myself as to whether scrapping the oath in the draft meant scrapping of the first four clauses of the British draft, that is to say the clauses setting out dominion status.'

'Yes,' the president replied. Childers was, therefore, satisfied, but Collins never heard this exchange.

Before the meeting concluded some decisions were taken hurriedly. It was decided that the delegation should return to London with the same powers and instructions. If the oath were not amended, the draft treaty would be rejected regardless of the consequences. If this led to the collapse of the conference, Griffith was advised to say that the matter should be referred to the Dáil, and he was to try to blame the northern unionists for the impasse, if possible.

It was also decided that the trade and defence clauses should be amended, according to Childers, who noted that no specific suggestion was made about how to change the trade provisions. But the president did advocate that the British should be given 'two ports only' instead of the four they were demanding.

'All this amendment business was too hurried,' Childers noted in his diary, 'but it was understood by Barton, Duffy, and me that amendments were not mandatory.' They were 'only suggestions'. Later, de Valera emphasised this point himself in the Dáil.

'I did not give, nor did the cabinet give, any instructions to the delegation as to any final document which they were to put in,' he said.

Some writers have suggested that the fact the two elements of the delegation returned to London separately was evidence that the division between them was deeper than ever, but it seems the real reason was purely personal. After the meeting Childers returned to his home with Barton, and they had dinner there, and Childers saw his son Bobby to bed before heading back to London. Barton, Duffy and Childers took a boat from the North Wall, while Griffith, Collins and Duggan went on the mail boat from Dun Laoghaire.

Childers, Duffy and Barton talked together in a cabin until Cope arrived. 'He was all agog for information,' Barton recalled. 'We were in a similar state but we gave none and got none.' On the train to London, Diarmuid O'Hegarty arrived at Barton's sleeper to invite him to go for a chat with Tim Healy, who was unable to walk along the train. Barton and O'Hegarty then talked with Healy for a couple of hours. 'Healy expatiated on the dreadfulness of the crisis, the imminent risk of a renewal of war, and the generosity of the settlement the English were prepared to offer us,' Barton noted. 'I told him quite frankly and [O'] Hegarty supported me that he was on the wrong line and going full speed astern. He was furious at first but grew maudlin later and I left him and [O']Hegarty to finish their bottle.

'Next day Healy saw Lloyd George and afterwards came across to us where we had a long interview,' Barton continued. 'Later I met him in the hall and he told me that Collins was the only sensible man amongst us, possibly he told Lloyd George so too.'

'There's a job to be done and for the moment here's the place,' Collins wrote to Kitty upon his return to London. 'That's that.'

Childers began drafting an alternative to the British draft treaty, with help from Barton and later Gavan Duffy. 'The Cabinet gave us no written direction, no draft agreement, nothing but the hazy verbal headlines,' according to Barton. 'Griffith Collins and Duggan made no attempt to write anything or if they did, they did not show us the result of their deliberations which took place as was usual in some other room. When we were finished we requested them to come for a conference and presented them with copies of the proposals we suggested should now be sent to the British.

'On reading the document to our colleagues an extraordinary scene ensued,' Barton wrote. 'Griffith was very angry. He declared that the cabinet had been prepared to go much further towards agreement than we had indicated. That the terms we were proposing were stiffer than those already declared by the English to be impossible and that he was not going to stand for any such silly tactics.'

Collins objected to the inclusion of External Association. He thought the British guarantee about according the *de facto* status of Canada had been acceptable to the cabinet. He noted that nobody had talked about pressing for External Association at the cabinet meeting. He was right. There had been no such discussion, but the president had responded affirmatively when Childers asked if the suggested alterations to the oath also applied to the first three clauses of the British proposals. When Childers mentioned this exchange, Collins could not remember it, but Griffith confirmed that it had taken place.

Collins was understandably furious. Such an important issue – indeed, what ultimately became the vital issue – should not have been determined by a simple answer to an almost throwaway question from a secretary.

Part of Collins' confusion was undoubtedly contributed to by his recollection that de Valera had proposed an oath that was consistent with dominion status. Together with Griffith and Duggan, he recalled that the president had suggested that they could 'recognise the King of Great Britain as Head of the Associated States'. This could be interpreted to mean that the king was head of each state individually as well as the head of the combined association of states.

Barton and Childers contended, however, that de Valera had proposed recognising the king only as 'Head of the Association'.

Barton produced his notes, but these proved inconclusive because he had simply written 'Head of the Assoc'. Childers, on the other hand, actually recorded in his diary that the president had suggested 'King of the Associated States'. Moreover, Ó Murchada's notes were identical with the version remembered by Griffith, Collins and Duggan.

When de Valera later contended that he had said 'Association' and not 'Associated States', he found himself in the embarrassing position of confronting formidable evidence. He actually damaged his own case during a secret session of the Dáil by recalling what he had said a fortnight earlier.

'I do swear to recognise the King of Great Britain as Head of the Associated States,' he said. 'That is the way I expressed it verbally meaning the association of states.'

As this oath was rejected by the British, it is not really of much importance, except that the whole controversy does help to illustrate why Collins could have wondered whether Dublin was trying to advise or confuse the delegation. He was so annoyed over the confusion about reproposing External Association that he became quite obstreperous.

Childers essentially accused him of 'deliberately' trying to make the new document 'unreasonable' by insisting that 'Dev had said that only two ports [and] nothing else' could be conceded to the British. Childers took issue with Collins. 'I protested against making Dev's words ridiculous,' he noted.

'Collins declared that our proposals had already been discussed again and again with the English and turned down by them and he was not going to stultify himself by saying it all over again,' according to Barton. 'He stated that the proposals in the document were defeatist tactics and it was for those who wanted to break to present them. I do not remember what Duggan said but he probably echoed Collins as he always did. All three refused to present them at Downing Street.'

The other three had challenged them to go alone and present

their proposals. 'Duffy and I immediately accepted it,' Barton continued. 'I certainly realised and I suppose that Duffy did too that it was a hopeless kind of Balaclava charge as it was an obvious indication of a divided delegation, but as we had composed the document and as they challenged us to present it of course we accepted it, tho' knowing that we were going like lambs to the slaughter house. Directly we did accept Griffith jumped up and said he would go too. He had changed his mind and I had little doubt but that the reason was that he did not wish us to break or have words with the English.'

Collins refused to go and Duggan supported him. 'I did not attend this conference,' Collins wrote next day, 'for the reason that I had, in my own estimation, argued fully all points.' In addition, he had already shown his hand to the British by suggesting an oath that was consistent with Irish membership of the British commonwealth.

'Failure was foredoomed,' according to Barton. 'To succeed, our cause would have to have been pressed with vigour by all five of us.' Not one word was spoken in the car as the three of them set off for Downing Street. 'But when we got in front of the English,' he noted, 'Griffith played up like a man and fought as hard as we did.'

The British again flatly rejected External Association, as Collins predicted. The meeting actually broke up when Gavan Duffy blurted out that the Irish 'difficulty is coming within the Empire'. At that point the conference broke down. The two sides announced that they would submit their final proposals the following day and they would formally announce that the conference had collapsed.

As Duffy emerged from the conference room he whispered to Childers who was waiting outside, 'C'est fini.'

'I admire the way you stuck like a bulldog to the Ulster issue,' Barton said to Griffith as they were leaving Downing Street in a car. 'It may all be for the best yet.'

'For Duffy and myself it was a gloomy drive back to our house in Hans Place,' Barton wrote. 'Griffith was cynical, morose and insulting by turns. He twitted Duffy with his lack of discretion in having brought the conference to so abrupt a conclusion. Declared that we had undone all the good work that he and Collins had done in private negotiations and that not content with having to put forward proposals impossible for English acceptance we had been so inept as to cause a rupture on the very point which it had been our policy to avoid a break, namely on the crown and the Empire connection. We let him have his innings for a while, for I think we were both a bit crestfallen but before we reached our house we had turned the tables upon him by reminding him that two of our colleagues had run away from the most critical conference and therefore made its success impossible.'

The Irish delegation held a meeting at Hans Place. Griffith drafted a report of the meeting for de Valera and read it to his colleagues. Barton insisted that he add that Lloyd George had said the amendments in the latest Irish proposals were 'a complete going back on the discussions of the last week or so'. Collins objected strongly that this implied that Griffith and he 'had given way'. Barton refused to retract, but did not object when they contended the real meaning of the prime minister's complaint was that the latest proposals were merely a 'revision to amendments already discussed and rejected'.

While this report was being prepared, Griffith came back to say that 'he forgot to say that something had been said about the possibility of changing the form of the Oath'. Barton and Gavan Duffy had left Hans Place by then and Childers waited to check with them upon their return. Barton agreed to the inclusion although he could not remember the incident, but Gavan Duffy did remember it 'and said Birkenhead remarked it rather casually'.

'The negotiations were over then as we thought,' Barton

explained. He was despondent. 'Bob says all the dead fought for is lost,' Childers wrote to his wife. 'I say no – the dead died to prevent surrender.

'There can't be war on this,' Childers added. 'Our offer is too generous.'

'Duffy, Childers and I prepared to leave London next day but this was not to be,' Barton continued. 'The English must have noticed the significance of Collins' absence and at 2 a.m. Jones, the English Cabinet Secretary, came to Hans Place, unknown to the rest of us, and had a long private conversation with Griffith. What transpired at that Conference we shall never know but it is reasonable to suppose that Griffith informed the English that he and Collins had not said their last word, anyway Jones invited Collins to confer with Lloyd George again the next morning.'

Barton was right. Jones found Griffith 'labouring under a deep sense of the crisis'. The Irish chairman 'spoke throughout with the greatest earnestness and unusual emotion'. Collins and himself were in favour of the British terms, but needed something further to offer the Dáil. Their position would be simplified, Griffith said, if the British could get Craig to give 'a conditional recognition, however shadowy, of Irish national unity in return for the acceptance of the Empire by Sinn Féin'. If the British delegation could obtain an assurance that Northern Ireland would agree to unity, he said that Dublin would give all the safeguards the northern majority needed and the Boundary Commission could be scrapped. With a northern acceptance of unity, he was confident he could get the Dáil to accept a treaty with an oath that would be acceptable to the British. He added that Barton and the doctrinaire republicans could then be ignored, because ninety per cent of the gunmen would follow Collins.

Without the support of Collins, however, Griffith did not have a chance of getting the Dáil to accept the British terms. He therefore asked Jones to arrange a meeting so that Lloyd George could have a 'heart to heart' talk with Collins. Jones then left and arranged a meeting with the prime minister for the following morning, but Griffith had great difficulty persuading Collins to attend.

Collins was so annoyed over the confusion in Dublin that he was refusing to have anything further to do with the negotiations. It was not until just before the meeting with Lloyd George was due to begin that he finally relented and agreed to go to Downing Street. In fact, he had been so determined not to attend that he was some fifteen minutes late for the meeting, which was most uncharacteristic as he had a virtual obsession with punctuality.

During the meeting Collins emphasised he was 'perfectly dissatisfied' with the British terms regarding Northern Ireland. He said the British government should get the position clarified by pressing Craig for a letter specifying the conditions under which unity would be acceptable, or else rejecting it outright. At that point Lloyd George said, according to Collins:

that I myself pointed out on a previous occasion that the North would be forced economically to come in. I assented but I said the position was so serious owing to certain recent actions that for my part I was anxious to secure a definite reply from Craig and his colleagues, and that I was as agreeable to a reply rejecting as accepting. In view of the former we would save Tyrone and Fermanagh, parts of Derry, Armagh and Down by the Boundary Commission, and thus avoid such things as the raid on the Tyrone County Council and the ejection of the staff. Another such incident would, in my view, inevitably lead to a conflict, and this conflict, in the nature of things (assuming for instance that some of the Anglo-Northern police were killed or wounded) would inevitably spread throughout Ireland. Mr Lloyd George expressed a view that this might be put to Craig, and if so the safeguards would be a matter for working out between ourselves and Craig afterwards.

The prime minister was willing to consider objections to the financial, trade and defence clauses of the British draft treaty. He also offered to consider a new oath, if the Irish delegation accepted the clauses concerning dominion status.

'Finally,' Collins concluded his report, 'the conversation developed into a statement by Mr Lloyd George to the effect that were Clauses 1 and 2 accepted he would be in a position to hold up any action until we had, if we desired to do so, submitted the matter to Dáil Éireann and the country. I left it at that saying that unless I sent word to the contrary some members of the delegation would meet him at 2 o'clock.' Arrangements were then made for members of the two delegations to meet that afternoon.

Chapter Sixteen

'I MAY HAVE SIGNED MY ACTUAL DEATH WARRANT'

'Griffith now came to me and emphasised a point which certainly carried considerable weight with me,' Barton recalled. 'We had broken off negotiations on the connection with the Crown and Empire whereas it was definitely Cabinet policy to break on the Ulster question if we had to break at all. He made an urgent appeal to me to go again to Downing St. with him and Collins in order to learn how much nearer we could get to agreement on other points and to endeavour to shift the breakdown of negotiations from the Crown back to Ulster.'

'This was I knew the policy of our Cabinet,' Barton explained. 'I told Griffith that as regarded Ireland's inclusion under the British Crown my conscience would not permit me to trifle with the oath of allegiance I had taken. Griffith agreed and stated that he would not try to induce any man to violate a conscientious scruple but that if I went back again we would do our best to change the break from the Crown to Ulster and if we failed in that would get the acceptance or refusal of their terms referred back to the Dáil. I agreed to return on this understanding.'

Collins read his report of his private meeting with Lloyd George to the rest of the Irish delegation back at Hans Place, and Griffith, Collins and Barton then went to 10 Downing Street to meet with the prime minister, Chamberlain, Birkenhead and Churchill. From the outset Griffith tried to concentrate on the Ulster question by demanding that the Irish delegation should know whether Craig would accept or reject Irish unity. The British replied that Griffith was going back on his previous promise not to let them down on the Boundary Commission proposal.

'Collins said,' according to Barton, 'that for us to agree to any conditions defining the future relations of Great Britain and Ireland prior to Craig's giving his assent to the unity of Ireland was impossible, that to do so would be to surrender our whole fighting position. That every document we ever sent them had stated that any proposals for the association of Ireland with the British Commonwealth of Nations was conditional upon the unity of Ireland. That, unless Craig accepted inclusion under the all-Ireland Parliament, the unity of Ireland was not assured and that if he refused inclusion we should be left in the position of having surrendered our position without having even secured the essential unity of Ireland.'

Lloyd George became excited and accused the Irish of trying to use the Ulster question to break off the talks when the real difficulty was the opposition in Dublin to membership of the British commonwealth. He accused Griffith of going back on the promise of not repudiating the Boundary Commission proposal, and he produced the explanatory memorandum that Griffith had approved in November.

'What is this letter?' Barton whispered to Collins.

'I don't know what the hell it is.'

'Do you mean to tell me, Mr Collins that you never learnt of this document from Mr Griffith?' Lloyd George asked.

The memorandum outlining the Boundary Commission proposal was then passed across the table to Collins and Barton. Both were seeing it for the first time. Collins said nothing.

'I have fulfilled my part of the bargain,' the prime minister declared. 'I took the risk of breaking my party. You in Ireland often bring against us in England the charge of breach of faith. Now it is for you to show that Irishmen know how to keep faith.'

'I said I would not let you down on that, and I won't,' Griffith replied. He no longer felt able to break on the Ulster question, and he did not wish to break on the Crown, so he had little room to manoeuvre. 'I was determined not to break on the Crown as I told you at the Cabinet,' Griffith explained in his report to de Valera. 'The decision of peace or war had to be made.

'I said, provided we came to an agreement on other points, I would accept inclusion in the Empire on the basis of the Free State,' Griffith continued. The discussion changed to other subjects, and the British accepted the oath introduced by Collins that morning with only some minor verbal changes. They also offered other concessions such as dropping the stipulation that the British would 'exclusively' have the right to defend the seas around Ireland. The Irish could have vessels for both fishery protection and to combat smuggling, and the British conceded that defence provisions of the agreement would be reviewed in five years 'with a view to the undertaking by Ireland of a share in her own coastal defence'. Lloyd George also offered, as a final sweetener, to drop the British demand for free trade between the two countries, if the Irish delegation would agree to the rest of the proposals.

Griffith said he would sign the agreement. 'They asked me whether I spoke for myself or for the delegation,' Griffith wrote. 'I said I spoke for myself.'

'Do I understand, Mr Griffith, that though everyone else refuses, you will nevertheless agree to sign?' Lloyd George asked

'Yes, that is so, Mr Prime Minister.'

Collins and Barton remained silent.

'That is not enough,' Lloyd George said, sensing that he had the Irish delegation at his mercy. 'If we sign, we shall sign as a delegation and stake the life of the Government on our signature. Is the Irish delegation prepared to do the same?'

At this point Lloyd George knew that Barton was the one he had to convinced. He therefore turned to Barton.

'He particularly addressed himself to me,' Barton reported, 'and said very solemnly that those who were not for peace must take the full responsibility for the war that would immediately follow refusal by any delegate to sign the Articles of Agreement.'

'I have to communicate with Sir James Craig tonight,' Lloyd George said dramatically as he raised two envelopes. 'Here are the alternative letters which I have prepared, one enclosing the Articles of Agreement reached by His Majesty's government and yourselves, and the other saying that the Sinn Féin representatives refused the oath of allegiance and refused to come within the Empire. If I send this letter, it is war – and war within three days! Which letter am I to send? Whichever letter you choose travels by special train to Holyhead, and by destroyer to Belfast.

'The train is waiting with steam up at Euston. Mr Shakespeare is ready. If he is to reach Sir James Craig in time we must have your answer by ten p.m. tonight. You can have until then, but no longer to decide whether you will give peace or war to your country.'

'Neither Collins nor I made any reply,' Barton noted. They and Griffith withdrew to consider the next move.

'Michael Collins rose looking as though he was going to shoot someone,' Churchill recalled. 'I have never seen so much pain and suffering in restraint.'

As Collins left he was accosted by newsmen, who were aware that the deadline to inform Craig was approaching. They asked if the Irish delegation would be returning later that evening.

'I don't know,' Collins replied.

'Has the conference finished?'

'I don't know that either.'

Barton said it was eight-thirty when they left Downing Street. 'It was after eight-thirty when I heard the cars at the door of Cadogan Gardens,' Kathleen McKenna recalled. 'Collins, followed by his faithful men, rushed through the hall and dashed up the stairs.

'After a short time,' she continued, 'Broy came pounding down the stairs to my office. He said that Michael Collins was prepared to sign the Treaty that night, and that I should go to Hans Place where probably there might be need of my services. Broy said he would accompany me.'

On the way she became conscious of a menacing atmosphere. 'We were conscious that figures were loitering everywhere in the shadows,' Kathleen recalled. 'Three or four of them stepped out unexpectedly before us and without uttering a syllable blocked us. One flashed an electric torch in Broy's face and by its light I saw they had pistols. They scrutinised Broy thoroughly, passing the torch over his head, face and body, then silently slunk away.'

Collins arrived shortly afterwards at Hans Place with Tobin, Dolan and Charlie Russell, one of the pilots ready to fly Collins back to Ireland in case the talks broke down precipitately. 'They said the vicinity was bristling with Scotland Yard men,' McKenna noted.

There is some confusion about what Collins did when he arrived at Hans Place. 'Mick was impatient to find that the others were not down in the hall,' according to McKenna. 'He stalked nervously up and down the dining-room, then went to the end of it where there was a kind of buffet.' He sent somebody upstairs to say that he was below, but he did not go upstairs himself. She thought this might be because he had made up his mind about signing and did not want anyone to influence him to do otherwise.

'Instead he walked, like a wild beast in a cage, up and down the room, morose, silent and sullen, then plumped down on an ordinary dining-room chair – not an armchair – that happened to be in the centre of the room in exact line with that part of the stairs down which those who were to join him would have to come,' McKenna added. 'With his attaché case, and thrown over it his old grey-brown dust-coat, hanging down in one hand

and almost touching he carpet, and his other hand holding on his knee his felt hat, he fell into a profound sleep.

'As I gazed at him my heart ached with anguish at the thought of what this man's mental torture must be,' she continued. 'I realised full all the weight of responsibility placed by events beyond his control upon his young, generous shoulders.' She said that she was the only one that witnessed that scene.

Nobody else ever mentioned that Collins did not attend the meeting of the delegation. In his diary Childers noted that Collins said virtually nothing during the delegation's discussion, but there was the unmistakable impression that he was present at the meeting. Barton was quite definite in his notes that Collins was at the meeting.

At the outset 'Collins stated his willingness to sign and the ground slipt away from under my feet,' according to Barton. 'I had never even considered such a contingency.' The ultimatum was crucial in the ensuing discussion.

Geoffrey Shakespeare, who was waiting to take the letter to Craig, later wrote that he 'never understood why the Irish accepted the ultimatum at its face value. Why did they not call the bluff?'

Lloyd George was undoubtedly bluffing when he insisted that all the members of the Irish delegation had to sign the agreement. Collins must have known this.

First of all the prime minister had told Griffith and him the previous week that he planned to present Britain's final terms to Craig at the same time as they would be given to the Irish delegation. The British were apparently going to follow the same procedure used with the Versailles Treaty in 1919. It was given to the German delegation and published some weeks before it was actually signed. It was only to facilitate Griffith and Collins that the British handed over the draft treaty the previous Friday. Consequently they must have known that Lloyd George's schedule simply called for the British to send Craig a copy of their final terms by the next day – not necessarily a signed agreement.

Moreover, Lloyd George told Collins that morning that he would allow the draft treaty to be referred to the Dáil before signing, if the Irish delegation were prepared to recommend dominion status. In Griffith's case the ultimatum was insignificant because he had agreed to sign the Treaty before the ultimatum was issued, and it would have been out of character for Collins to desert him at that point. He had already agreed that the two of them were in the negotiations together to the bitter end. But he did not tell Barton that the threat of immediate and terrible war was probably a bluff. Instead, he went along with the bluff in order to ensure that all of the delegation signed, as this would make it easier to get the agreement accepted in Dublin.

Without Barton's vote, for instance, Collins realised there would be little chance of the cabinet accepting the Treaty, because de Valera, Brugha and Stack were likely to oppose it. If Barton joined them, then the majority of the cabinet would be opposed to the British terms and the Dáil would probably not be given any more say than it had with the July proposals, which were formally rejected in the name of Dáil Éireann before it even convened to discuss them.

Having been entrusted by the Dáil with the responsibility of negotiating an acceptable settlement, Griffith and Collins saw it as their duty to sign when they were convinced the terms would be acceptable not only to a majority of the Dáil but also a majority of the Irish people. Moreover, they thought an unwinnable war would inevitably follow the collapse of the conference.

'If Lloyd George did not wage immediate and terrible war upon rejection of his proffered terms he would appeal over our heads to the country with an offer of Dominion Home Rule along similar lines,' Griffith argued. 'The reception of that settlement was likely to expose the weakness of the really national elements and perhaps to reveal a persistent yearning for peace.'

'Unquestionably, the alternative to the Treaty, sooner or later was war,' Collins later wrote. 'To me it would have been a criminal act to refuse to allow the Irish nation to give its opinion as to whether it would accept this settlement or resume hostilities.'

Some notes drawn up by Collins during the latter stages of the London conference give a clear insight into his thinking. 'I am never of the opinion that the majority of the Irish people will be against such a treaty as we have in mind,' he observed. 'It is a question of greater influence – de Valera will command, I think, a large part of what was formerly the Volunteer Organisation.' Believing that there would be opposition in Dublin from 'those who have in mind personal ambitions under pretence of patriotism', Collins still thought that fifty-five to sixty per cent 'of all concerned' would support the Treaty.

Geoffrey Shakespeare realised the demand for the Irish delegates to sign that night was part of a bluff, but this did not mean that he thought they could have won further concessions, as has been inferred. 'Lloyd George was not bluffing in refusing further concessions,' Shakespeare wrote. 'He had gone to the limit, and there was nothing more to offer.' The prime minister was afraid, however, that if the 'Irish delegates went back without signing or expressing an opinion, the atmosphere in Dublin would have influenced them and the Treaty would have been lost.' Hence he issued the ultimatum.

That evening Shakespeare dined with Lloyd George. 'Either they sign now or negotiations are off,' the prime minister told him. 'If there is a break we will put into Ireland a large force and restore order. I told them as much and it is now up to them to choose between peace and war.'

Referring the final terms back to the cabinet in Dublin before signing was not at issue. Griffith, Collins and Barton were satisfied they had fulfilled their instructions in referring the draft treaty to the cabinet that weekend. None of them thought they had any further obligation to consult the cabinet in Dublin. They had been given full plenipotentiary powers 'to negotiate and conclude' an agreement, so the moment of truth had come. They had to make up their own minds.

'Would we, or would we not, come within the Community of Nations known as the British Empire?' That was the question the members of the Irish delegation had to answer, according to Griffith.

'The cabinet had advised the delegation to try the get the British draft treaty amended, especially in regard to the oath. 'We were all tired by the long, drawn-out negotiations, by the cabinet meeting in Dublin, the travelling, the meetings of the delegation, the rupture of the day before and then Griffith and Collins and I by the five hours meeting of that day,' Barton explained. 'We had got both draft and oath amended but not in any essential particular. Remember the indefiniteness of the decisions of our Cabinet, the refusal to listen to Duffy when he had gone over, the refusal of the other members to come to London. The cabinet had certainly told us that they were prepared to face a renewal of war but a situation had now arisen which they had never visualised. Griffith had gone over to the English. In Dublin he had declared that he would not break upon the question of the Crown and yet he was sent back as our leader. He had been outmanoeuvred, outwitted and smashed and he now proceeded to smash us.'

A copy of the revised British draft terms was delivered to Hans Place at nine o'clock and the Irish delegation then began its deliberations. 'Griffith, who was perhaps the most strung up amongst us, said he would be a murderer if such an opportunity were allowed to slip and the country be plunged back into a war of extermination,' according to Barton. Childers noted that Griffith 'spoke almost passionately for signing'.

While Childers observed that Collins said virtually nothing

during the 'long and hot argument', Barton described him as 'morose and violent by turns'.

'Up to this moment it had never occurred to us that Collins intended to follow the lead of Griffith but we had hardly started talking when he declared that it was his intention to sign also and Duggan, of course, followed suit,' according to Barton. 'It was as if the world fell in pieces around us. All three then turned upon Duffy and me.'

'Collins insisted that we knew nothing about the extremity the country was in or the exhaustion of the Volunteers,' Barton continued. 'I remember his stating that he was not going to throw the 2,000 volunteers who had done all the work back into war in which they would be slaughtered whilst the rest look on. Duggan asserted that he would be false to all those who died beside him at the barricades in 1916 if he refused such terms as were offered contrasted with those that we had proposed and which had been turned down.

'Collins was a member of the IRB, the watchdog of the Republican tradition,' Barton noted. 'His brilliant system had been rendered helpless by elimination of its key men. He knew that physical resistance, if resumed, would collapse and he was not going to be the leader of a forlorn hope. He intended to live to fight again.

'We had the most frightful battle in the delegation, among ourselves at which the most terrific things were said to Gavan Duffy and to me by Collins and Griffith and Duggan,' according to Barton.

'Barton,' said Duggan, 'you will be hanged from a lamp post in the streets of Dublin if your refusal to sign causes a new war in Ireland.'

Barton was shaken. He did not place any store in Duggan's opinions, but he did feel that 'Collins was in a better position to appraise our military position than anyone else'.

At different times Griffith, Collins and Duggan were on the

point of proceeding to sign without the others but Barton stalled them. The argument went on for so long that the delegation was still at Hans Place more than an hour after the time limit set by Lloyd George had expired.

'Three times they put on their hats and took their coats to go without us,' Barton recalled. 'The English had given us until 10 o'clock to decide.'

When eleven o'clock passed without any sign of the Irish representatives returning, the British became uneasy. 'We had doubts as to whether we would see them again,' the prime minister recalled afterwards. He realised that much depended on Collins. 'If only Michael Collins has as much moral courage as he has physical courage,' Lloyd George said to his colleagues, 'we shall get a settlement. But moral courage is a much higher quality than physical courage, and it is a quality that brave men often lack.'

Barton's signature was crucial. He had provided de Valera with the opportunity to use his own vote to exclude himself from the delegation, and without Barton's support it was possible that the cabinet could undermine any agreement. 'My dilemma was that whilst I knew the Cabinet and Ireland would face war under united leadership, I had no idea of what they would do when three of the principal leaders had "ratted",' Barton wrote. 'I was acting in a public capacity not a private one.' After some two hours of argument, Barton began to wilt.

'When three, including Collins, whom I had always looked upon as the pivot in our army, had agreed, what would the rest do when faced with war under divided leadership. Had I known Dev, Brugha and Stack better I would not have signed it.' His problem was that he did not know if de Valera would support him if he decided not to sign. He therefore asked to be allowed to consult privately with Childers.

As they left the room, did Collins just go downstairs to wait for the others? This could have been the scene that Kathleen McKenna witnessed of Collins asleep in the chair, while Childers and Barton talked together on a landing. Barton asked for the advice of his cousin. 'He seemed to be in great torture of mind,' Childers wrote to his wife Molly some hours later. 'I said I believed he should stick to principle,' Childers said, adding, 'Molly will be with us.'

This suddenly heaped even more pressure on Barton, because he thought that the women of Ireland, who had already suffered so much, were being given no say. He decided to sign in order that the Dáil would have a chance to consider the agreement.

'Well,' he said, 'I suppose I must sign.'

'At least stipulate that you sign under duress,' Childers said.

'We went in and he began with this which was contested by the others,' Childers continued. 'Then he hesitated and said he would sign *sans phrase*.' Gavan Duffy had been holding out, but he said he could not hold out if the other four agreed to sign. 'I cannot write more,' Childers concluded his letter to his wife. 'I feel as if my heart would burst.'

Barton privately told Childers some hours later that his 'allusion to Molly's support for a refusal to sign' had been the 'deciding element' in his decision to sign.

'Strange reason,' Childers exclaimed. He did not seem to understand that what Barton meant was that the allusion to Molly reminded him of all the women at home who would have no say at all unless he signed the Treaty. Childers was still convinced the main factor in Barton's decision was his 'belief that war was really imminent and inevitable – real war'. In other words, the remark about Molly Childers was just the last straw!

'What was perhaps the determining factor with me was that I had no idea whether having refused to sign and thereby flung the country lads into war,' Barton explained, 'I should not have been told when I returned that I had no justification for committing the country to war under divided leadership. This was an eventuality never dreamed of.'

'None of us even thought of using the telephone to try to

resolve the difficulty,' Barton admitted. Griffith and Collins stressed that they were plenipotentiaries and they 'would possibly have resented the idea' of contacting Dublin.

Barton also admitted that they did not think of their instructions. 'Not one of us, not even Erskine Childers thought of the instructions that had been given us before we left Dublin for the first time that the final draft or the document about to be signed must be brought home for confirmation,' Barton explained. 'If Duffy, Childers or I had stumbled upon that fact in our memories we could have found justification for our refusal and the Articles of Agreement would have had at most three signatures only, if any. Nobody thought of the instructions.'

There were suggestions later that Hazel Lavery persuaded Collins to sign the Treaty that night. If Collins met her that evening, it had to be sometime after eight-thirty and before nine o'clock. Some believed that she not only persuaded Collins to sign but also drove him back to Downing Street that night. This was apparently based on Sir John Lavery's memoirs. He wrote that: 'Michael Collins stood firm to the last minute. He seemed to have lost his temper. Even I, whose head was never really out of the paint-pot, could see that he who loses his temper in argument is lost, and told him so, but I failed to convince him. Eventually, after hours of persuasion, Hazel prevailed. She took him to Downing Street in her car that last evening, and he gave in.'

But he did not have even half an hour in which she could have persuaded him and anyway, he returned to Downing Street with Griffith and Barton that night. The suggestion made was that Hazel blackmailed him by supposedly threatening to divulge that Collins was the father of Moya Llewelyn-Davies' son, Richard. No evidence was ever produced to support the theory. If Hazel had blackmailed him in such a manner, would he likely have retained the friendship with her afterwards? The way Collins operated he would have been much more likely to have had her shot. Collins signed the Treaty because it was a compromise that provided the means to achieve what he desired. At the last cabinet meeting in Dublin, the only objection that he raised to the Treaty was the oath, which had since been substituted with one that he had submitted. He had been so annoyed over the attempt to press for External Association the previous day that he refused to go to Downing Street, and it was he who had first suggested a Boundary Commission to redraw the border if the north refused to come within a united Ireland. There was no argument that night about the Ulster clauses, because they believed the Boundary Commission would undermine Northern Ireland. 'If the North refuses to come in, we will have a boundary commission, and they will lose half their territory, and they cannot stay out!' Griffith had repeatedly proclaimed, according to Barton. 'Over and over again he made that statement.'

'We agreed that islands, such as West Belfast, would vote themselves into Southern Ireland, and we agreed that it would be administratively impossible,' Barton added. 'Voting in or out would have to be by contiguous areas.' They had badly miscalculated but they did not realise it at the time. Collins was satisfied that he had got the compromises that he desired on the major issues. On what grounds would he have refused to sign?

If it had been so important that all of them sign that night, however, why did Duggan and Gavan Duffy not sign that night? They were not even at Downing Street. Having everybody sign the document was clearly not that important.

When Collins signed around 2.20 on the morning of 6 December, he was aware of the likely consequences for himself. Immediately after the signing, Birkenhead turned to Collins. 'I may have signed my political death warrant tonight,' he said.

'And I may have signed my actual death warrant,' Collins replied.

Somewhat distraught Childers was waiting outside in the

lobby. 'My chief recollection of these inexpressible, miserable hours,' he wrote, 'was that of Churchill in evening dress, moving up and down the lobby with his loping step and long strides and a huge cigar, like a bowspit, his coarse heavy jowls making him a very type of brutal militarism.'

Within minutes the Irish delegates emerged from Number 10 Downing Street looking very tired and grave.

'Have you anything to say?' a reporter asked Collins.

'Not a word,' he replied sharply.

Chapter Seventeen

'THE FIRST REAL STEP?'

'Think – what have I got for Ireland?' Michael Collins wrote just hours after signing the Treaty. 'Something which she has wanted these past seven hundred years. Will anyone be satisfied at the bargain? Will anyone? I tell you this, early this morning I signed my death warrant. I thought at the time how odd, how ridiculous – a bullet may just as well have done the job five years ago.

'I believe Birkenhead may have said an end to his political life,' Collins continued. 'With him it has been my honour to work. These signatures are the first real step for Ireland. If people will only remember that – the first real step.'

'In the creation of the Irish Free State we have laid a foundation on which may be built a new world order,' Collins told an Associated Press correspondent that day. This, of course, was pure hyperbole.

Just because Ireland was supposedly being accorded the *de facto* status of the Dominions was hardly grounds for thinking that the British commonwealth would become a League of Free Nations in which even the United States would participate. This showed little understanding of American politics. Yet Collins now declared that 'Ireland would be a link to join America and Britain. And with America in this League of Free Nations, what country would wish to stay outside?'

Gavan Duffy did not sign until many hours later, and Duggan never signed the British copy. He returned to Dublin with the Irish copy of the Treaty and it was necessary to cut his signature from a dinner menu he had autographed. It was then attached to a document before it was photographed by the media. The affixed signature is obvious in the photograph. The whole thing was so hurried that they had not given the Treaty its intended title. The copies initially signed has merely described it 'Articles of Agreement'.

'We noticed the following day that this document didn't bear the words "Treaty between Great Britain and Ireland". We immediately arranged for it to be put in.' The title of the document was therefore altered to read. 'Treaty between Great Britain and Ireland' as the title and 'Articles of Agreement' the subtitle on the second line.

Harry Boland issued a particularly positive statement in the United States. 'After centuries of conflict the Irish nation and the British have compromised their difference,' he announced. 'A treaty of peace has been signed and an agreement reached between the representatives of the Irish nation and the representatives of the British Empire, an agreement which restores Ireland to the comity of nations.'

Boland later claimed that the actual terms of the Treaty had not been published when he issued that statement, but they had been published on 8 December when he issued a further statement attacking Cohalan and Diarmuid Lynch of the Friends of Irish Freedom for criticising the Treaty. Of course, de Valera's views were not known, but when they did become known, all of them changed sides.

De Valera was in Limerick when he first heard that the Treaty had been signed. His initial reaction was one of delight, according to himself. Because of Griffith's promise not to sign the draft treaty the previous Saturday, the president assumed the British must have capitulated.

'I never thought that they would give in so soon,' he remarked to those with him.

It was only that evening as he was about to attend a cultural gathering in Dublin that Eamon Duggan and Desmond Fitzgerald arrived from London with a copy of the Treaty, which Duggan handed to the president. When de Valera showed no interest in the document, Duggan asked him to read it.

'What should I read it for?' de Valera asked.

'It is arranged that the thing be published in London and Dublin simultaneously at eight o'clock and it is near that hour now,' replied Duggan.

'What,' said the president, 'to be published whether I have seen it or not?'

'Oh well, that's the arrangement.'

Having read the terms of the Treaty de Valera summoned a meeting of the available members of the cabinet. 'I am going to pronounce against the Treaty,' he declared. He added that he intended to demand the resignations of Griffith, Collins and Barton from his government upon their return. Stack and Brugha agreed with him, but Cosgrave objected.

'I don't agree with that,' declared Cosgrave, insisting that the plenipotentiaries should be allowed to explain what had happened, before any pronouncement was made. 'I saw a look of peace and satisfaction pass over de Valera's face,' Cosgrave noted, convinced that the president welcomed the objection that allowed him to hold his hand until the whole cabinet could meet.

A full meeting was called for 8 December, 1921, and a press release was prepared. 'In view of the nature of the proposed treaty with Great Britain,' it read, 'President de Valera has sent an urgent summons to members of the cabinet in London to report at once so that a full cabinet decision may be taken.'

Desmond Fitzgerald, the minister for publicity, was surprised at the tone of the release. 'This might be altered Mr President,' he said entering the cabinet room. 'It reads as if you were opposed to the settlement.'

'And that is the way I intended it to read,' de Valera said. 'Publish it as it is.'

Fitzgerald was amazed. 'I did not think he was against this

kind of settlement before we went over to London,' he whispered to Stack.

'He is dead against it now anyway,' replied Stack. 'That's enough.'

It was like a cry of triumph. Fitzgerald thought Stack was gloating that he and Brugha had persuaded the president to abandon his more moderate views while the delegation was in London.

Michael Staines said that he appealed to de Valera in the presence of both Brugha and Stack not to issue the statement. 'I said it was for the Dáil to decide that; that it was not the Dáil cabinet sent them to London and I said that the Dáil Cabinet should not have asked them to report to the Dáil Cabinet at all but that they should have reported to the Dáil itself.'

Many people though de Valera would be in favour of the terms of the Treaty, in view of his moderate pronouncements during the summer when he made it clear that he was no doctrinaire republican. Before the London conference de Valera had repeatedly called for 'the status of a dominion', and the plenipotentiaries had returned with essentially 'dominion status'. Thus they had a right to expect the president's support, but Collins knew it would not be forthcoming.

If Fitzgerald had doubts that de Valera would have been in favour of such terms beforehand, these were probably dispelled the following week when the president indicated that he would have rejected the Treaty if he had been consulted in advance. 'I would have said, "No",' he explained, 'though I might not have said "No" before. I would have said "No" in the circumstances because I felt I could have said "No" with advantage to the nation.'

On arriving in Dublin on the day after the signing, Collins asked Tom Cullen how his own men viewed the Treaty.

'Tom, what are our fellows saying?' he asked.

'What is good enough for you is good enough for them,' Cullen replied.

Although this represented the attitude of many people, there were already ominous signs. The previous evening in London the delegation had been given a tumultuous send off by Irish exiles. Childers actually noted that he was 'nearly crushed to death' by the enthusiastic crowd. So Collins found it 'in a sense prophetic' that there was no welcoming crowd and 'no signs of jubilation' on reaching Dublin next morning. Instead, the few people about 'seemed strangely apathetic'.

'This lack of jubilation among the people was dispiriting enough,' Collins continued, 'but it was nothing compared with the open hostility we faced in the cabinet drawing-room of the Mansion House.' De Valera was waiting there, looking gaunt and depressed, while Stack was in a blazing mood and Brugha was 'the personification of venom'.

The ensuing cabinet meeting, which recessed three times, lasted through the afternoon and into the late evening. Frank Gallagher was in the next room with the press, and he said he frequently talked loudly in an effort to cover 'the raised voices' in the cabinet room.

De Valera accused the delegation of breaking its instructions by not consulting the cabinet before signing. They had consulted the cabinet the previous Saturday, but Griffith had said that he would not sign the Treaty.

Collins, Barton and Gavan Duffy all said that the issue of referring the Treaty to Dublin had never arisen. 'They had not thought of it,' they said, according to Childers, who clearly did not think of it either.

The president said that he would have gone to London but for the misunderstanding over Griffith's promise. 'I would have gone and said "go to the devil, I will not sign".'

The merits and drawbacks of the Treaty were examined, but not in any great detail, according to Stack, who noted that the main topic of discussion was the circumstances under which the plenipotentiaries signed the agreement. Griffith refused to 'admit duress by the British', which was indisputably true in his case, seeing that he had agreed to sign before Lloyd George issued his infamous ultimatum. Collins, on the other hand, said that if there had been duress it was only 'the duress of the facts'.

'I did not sign the Treaty under duress,' he later wrote, 'except in the sense that the position as between Ireland and England, historically, and because of superior forces on the part of England, has always been one of duress.' He added that 'there was not, and could not have been, any personal duress'. But both Barton and Duffy said they had been intimidated into signing.

They admitted that Lloyd George had not attempted coercion in the sense of physically threatening them. 'The form of duress he made use of,' according to Barton, 'was more insidious and in my opinion, a more compelling duress, for Mr Lloyd George, knowing already from Mr Griffith himself that he was prepared to sign, demanded that every other delegate should sign or war would follow immediately, and insisted that those who refused to sign must accept the responsibility.' As far as Barton was concerned, his refusal to sign would have meant going against the wishes of the majority of the delegation, and accepting 'personal responsibility for the slaughter to ensue' without having a chance 'to consult the President, the cabinet in Dublin, the Dáil, or the people'.

Barton 'strongly reproached the President', according to Childers. De Valera 'vacillated from the beginning' and he had even turned down a chance to go to London at the last moment when he asked him to go on Saturday. The disaster was, Barton declared, 'we were not a fighting delegation'.

The cabinet vote was the first crucial vote. 'All hung on Cosgrave's vote,' Childers noted.

The cabinet voted to endorse the Treaty by the narrowest margin possible. Griffith, Collins, Barton and Cosgrave lined up in favour, while the president, Brugha and Stack were in opposition. Barton was personally opposed to the agreement, but he felt bound to vote for it, seeing that he had agreed to recommend it to the Dáil by signing it in London.

Kevin O'Higgins, who did not have a vote in cabinet, said that while the Treaty should never have been signed, it should nevertheless be supported because it was important to preserve a united front. Diarmuid O'Hegarty, the cabinet secretary, even interrupted to make a strong appeal to the president not to oppose the Treaty, but Childers called for a protest in the Dáil against 'the irrevocable step of signing away independence'.

'Supposing Ulster came in on the Treaty,' de Valera was asked, 'would you agree to it?' He replied that it was the one consideration that might affect his judgment. 'This surprised me,' Childers wrote.

Although repeatedly pressed, de Valera rejected the suggestion that he not speak out publicly. Speaking 'at great length', he explained that he had been working for unity by seeking a form of association that people like Brugha and Stack could accept, but that had been thrown away without the permission of the cabinet. Still 'he did not despair of winning better terms yet', according to Childers.

Stack appealed to the delegation 'not to press the document on the Dáil'. At one point he turned to Collins: 'You have signed and undertaken to recommend the document to the Dáil,' he said. 'Well, recommend it. Your duty stops there. Your are not supposed to throw all your influence into the scale.'

If the agreement were rejected, Stack argued, they would be in an even stronger position than before. 'Will you do it?' he asked.

'Where would I be then?' Collins snapped, according to Stack.

The cabinet was irrevocably split. De Valera announced he would resign if the Dáil accepted the Treaty, while both Griffith and Collins said they would do the same if it were rejected. In the interim, however, it was decided that all should carry on until the Dáil could vote on the agreement.

Following the meeting de Valera issued a proclamation to the Irish people. 'The terms of the agreement are in violent conflict with the wishes of the majority of the nation as expressed freely in successive elections during the past three years,' he declared. 'I feel it is my duty to inform you immediately that I cannot recommend the acceptance of this Treaty either to Dáil Éireann or to the country. In this attitude I am supported by the Ministers for Home Affairs and Defence.

'The greatest test of our people has come,' he concluded. 'Let us face it worthily, without bitterness and above all without recriminations. There is a definite constitutional way of resolving our political differences – let us not depart from it, and let the conduct of the Cabinet in this matter be an example to the whole nation.'

When the cabinet rejected the July proposals, the Dáil was given no say on the British terms. De Valera just informed the British that their offer had been rejected by the Dáil. After the cabinet approved of the Treaty on 8 December, however, the president announced that it must 'be ratified by Dáil Éireann no less than by the British Parliament in order to take effect'. Because of the differences in the cabinet he insisted that the Treaty could not be submitted 'as a cabinet measure', which would be 'the usual course'. He added, 'the motion for ratification will now be introduced by Mr Griffith as Chairman of the Delegation'.

Though the first hurdle in the ratification process had been cleared, Collins was obviously troubled after the cabinet meeting. He called at Batt O'Connor's home, where he had been a frequent visitor during the terror, but now he was unsure of his welcome. When O'Connor opened the door, Collins did not walk in as usual but stood on the doorstep 'with a strange expression' as he waited to be invited in.

'Come in,' said O'Connor somewhat puzzled. 'What are you waiting for?'

'I thought you would have no welcome for me, Batt.' Of course, he was welcome, but he was so upset that he was unable to relax. Too agitated to sit down, he strode around the room, gesturing animatedly with his hands flailing the air. Should the Treaty be defeated, he said that he would move back down the country. 'I will leave Dublin at once,' he said bitterly. 'I will go down to Cork. If the fighting is going to be resumed, I will fight in the open, beside my own people down there. I am not going to be chivvied and hunted through Dublin as I have been for the last two years.'

'You have brought back this Treaty,' O'Connor argued. 'It is a wonderful achievement. The people want it. They must at least be given the chance to say what they think of it. Then if they reject it (only they will not reject it) you will have done your part, and will have no responsibility for the consequences.'

'I will accept their verdict,' Collins declared.

Next day de Valera met Childers, Barton and Duffy and explained that he planned to draw up an alternative to the Treaty. It was a 'revelation' to Childers to find that the president 'was thinking more of one which could get extremist support' rather than looking to the middle ground. 'His nerve and confidence are amazing. Seems certain of winning.' He noted that de Valera intended to put up terms for a 'real peace – not a sham'.

When the supreme council of the IRB met to consider the Treaty on 10 December, Collins chaired the meeting at which Liam Lynch was the only dissenting voice. Lynch was sorry that he felt conscientiously compelled to differ with Collins, but he nevertheless felt that his opposition would not strain their friendship.

'I admire Mick as a soldier and a man,' Lynch wrote. 'Thank God all parties can agree to differ.'

Although the supreme council endorsed the Treaty, three

other members not present at that meeting – Harry Boland, Joe McKelvey and Charlie Daly – all subsequently opposed the Treaty. It was decided that IRB members who were Dáil deputies would be free to vote as they saw fit. The IRB was not going to try to compel its members to vote for ratification.

Griffith and Collins were undoubtedly helped by the negative reaction to the Treaty in Belfast. Sir James Craig expressed 'grave dissatisfaction and alarm' to the Stormont parliament. Its members were irate that the Treaty had been signed with representatives of Sinn Féin representing the whole island. Northern Ireland was included without even consulting its representatives.

'We protest against the declared intention of your Government to place Northern Ireland automatically in the Irish Free State,' Craig wrote to Lloyd George. 'It is true that Ulster is given the right to contract out, but she can only do so after automatic inclusion in the Irish Free State.' Among the defence provisions, for instance, Belfast Lough was mentioned as one of the four Treaty ports to be retained by the British.

'What right has Sinn Féin to be recognised as parties to an agreement concerning the defences of Belfast Lough, which touches only the loyal counties of Antrim and Down?' Craig asked indignantly.

He could hardly have been reassured when Andrew Bonar Law expressed the belief that the Boundary Commission clauses would lead to the transfer of Fermanagh and Tyrone to the Irish Free State. And Lloyd George seemed to confirm the assessment himself in the House of Commons.

'There is no doubt,' the prime minister said, 'certainly since the Act of 1920, that the majority of the people of the two counties prefer being with their Southern neighbours to being in the Northern Parliament. Take it either by constituency or by Poor Law Union, or, if you like, by counting heads, and you will find that the majority in these two counties prefer to be with their Southern neighbours – What does that mean? If Ulster is to remain a separate community, you can only be means of coercion keep them there, and although I am against the coercion of Ulster, I do not believe in Ulster coercing other units.'

'Our Northern areas will be so cut up and mutilated that we shall no longer be masters in our own house,' Captain Charles C. Craig, the northern prime minister's brother complained. He was utterly vitriolic about the Treaty, as was Sir Edward Carson. In his diary Field Marshal Sir John French described the Treaty 'as a complete surrender'. He depicted the oath as 'farcical', and he concluded, 'The British Empire is doomed.'

At the outset de Valera had merely asked the British to stand aside and let the Irish settle the partition issue between themselves. When the British signed the agreement with Sinn Féin on behalf of the whole island without even consulting the unionists, the latter felt distinctly betrayed.

The debate at Westminster began on the same day as in the Dáil, but it was passed by an overwhelming majority just two days later, by 401 votes to 58. It enjoyed the support of most of the coalition, the Liberals, the Labour Party and even Bonar Law. The opposition was somewhat stronger in the House of Lords, where the Treaty was still passed by 166 votes to 47.

Chapter Eighteen

'I HAVE BEEN CALLED A TRAITOR'

There was a great air of anticipation on 14 December 1921 when the Dáil convened in the main hall of University College at Earlsfort Terrace, Dublin. Collins was the first minister to arrive in the chamber. 'He was, as usual, smiling and good humoured and, with his moustache shaved off in the last twenty-four hours, he looked more boyish than ever,' according to *The Irish Times*.

The division within the cabinet immediately manifested itself in the seating arrangement, which saw de Valera, Brugha and Stack positioned to the left of the speaker, while Griffith, Collins and the other members of the delegation took up their seats across the floor. Most members of the general body sat facing the speaker, with the public gallery behind them, while some 110 journalists from around the world were crammed together at the other end of the hall behind the speaker's chair.

Following the roll call there was supposed to be a motion to go into private session, but de Valera, who was dressed in a brown suit for a change, rose to say a few words first. It was but a foretaste of what was to come during the following days. Whenever he wanted to say something he just interrupted as if he had a right to determine procedure himself. During the thirteen days of public and private debate, he interrupted the proceeding more than 250 times. It was, no doubt, a measure of his standing that he was allowed to interrupt so often. Many of those interruptions were admittedly very brief interjections, but some were quite lengthy.

His opening remarks were patently dishonest. Speaking in

Gaelic, he said that his command of the language was not as good as he would like and he would therefore speak in English, because he would be better able to arrange his thoughts. Then he proceeded to tell the Dáil in English that he was not going to continue in Gaelic because some of those present could not understand the language. He quoted the instructions to the plenipotentiaries and noted that they had not fulfilled the provision stipulating that the 'complete text of the draft treaty about to be signed' would be submitted to the cabinet in Dublin and a 'reply awaited'.

Collins rose to refute the suggestion that the members of the delegation had exceeded their authority, or violated their instructions. They 'did not sign a treaty', he argued but merely signed a document 'on the understanding that each signatory would recommend it to the Dáil for acceptance'. The document would not effectively become a treaty until it had been ratified.

A vital consideration in signing, as far as Collins was concerned, was the fact that there was so little difference between what the rest of the cabinet wanted and what the British were offering. In order that the circumstances would be better understood he wanted the fullest possible disclosure of all documents in relation to the negotiations. He was therefore annoyed when the president acted selectively in reading the secret instructions given to the delegation without even mentioning their credentials.

Standing with hands in his pockets, Collins faced the speaker and spoke slowly but firmly. 'In repose his eyes glimmer softly with humour,' according to John F. Boyle of the *Irish Independent*. 'When roused they narrow – hard, intense and relentless. He speaks like this. One or two words. Then he pauses to think. His speech does not flow like a stream as it does in the case of Eamon de Valera. Yet not from one word is firmness absent.'

'If one document had to be read,' Collins said with his jaw set determinedly and his voice vibrant with the intensity of his feelings, 'the original document, which was a prior document, should have been read first. I must ask the liberty of reading the original document which was served on each member of the delegation.'

'Is that the one with the original credentials?' de Valera asked.

'Yes,' replied Collins.

'Was that ever presented?' the president asked. 'It was given in order to get the British Government to recognise the Irish Republic. Was that document giving the credentials of the accredited representatives from the Irish Government presented to, or accepted by, the British delegates? Was that seen by the British delegates or accepted by them?'

It was a dramatic moment as de Valera stood there facing Collins across the floor. The credentials had not been given to the British, but the important point, as far as Collins was concerned, was that they were given to the delegates by de Valera himself. Collins was not therefore about to get sidetracked on the issue.

'May I ask,' he said almost jocularly to the speaker, 'that I be allowed to speak without interruption?'

'I must protest,' the president insisted. But the speaker called for order. 'The little incident ended in a ripple of relaxation, and some applause. De Valera sat down,' according to the *Irish Independent*.

Continuing with dramatic effect Collins read the credentials signed by the president himself. Those specifically stated that the delegates had been conferred with plenipotentiary powers 'to negotiate and conclude' a treaty with Britain. Collins did not stress the words 'negotiate and conclude', but the reading of the terms of reference seemed to create a profound impression on all those present in the hall.

From his 'slow, measured tones', Collins gradually built himself into 'a crescendo of anger and indignation' as he repeated that the credentials should have been read along with the instructions so that members of the Dáil would be in a position to judge the issue on its merits. He said that he had refrained from trying to influence members of the Dáil before it met to consider the agreement, even though he knew that he was being vilified by opponents of the agreement.

'I have not said a hard word about anyone,' he emphasised as he rapped the table in front of him, 'but I have been called a traitor.'

'By whom?' de Valera asked.

The atmosphere was electric as the Big Fellow ignored the question. 'If there are men who act towards me as a traitor I am prepared to meet them anywhere, any time, now as in the past,' he continued. 'It was a challenge – not uttered with provocative emphasis but with deep feeling,' according to Boyle.

People were heard to murmur throughout the room. De Valera sat staring at Collins while ministers and deputies became restless. But then the tension dissipated as Collins changed the subject and continued in a more ordinary tone. Even though he was opposed to a private session, he said he would accept one.

'If there is anything, any matter of detail, if, for instance, the differences as they arose from time to time, should be discussed first in private, I am of the opinion that having discussed it in private I think we ought then to be able to make it public,' he said. In short they could discuss these matters privately to clear up any misunderstandings, but then they should be free to explain their own points of view. 'I am willing to go as far as that, that is only detail. But on the essentials I am for publicity now and all along.'

The debate drifted as various members argued whether or not to go into private session. Although de Valera wanted one, Brugha objected, thereby demonstrating that sincerity and independence which even Collins admired. Suddenly the president revived the controversy over the credentials.

'Do you wish to lay stress on the word conclude?' de Valera asked Collins.

Collins looked up and replied promptly and emphatically, 'No, sir, no.'

'What is the point then of raising the original credentials, if the word "conclude" did not mean that when you had signed it was ended?' the president asked. But nobody asked why de Valera had included the word in the first place.

Griffith settled the issue by pointing out that 'whether they had full power to make this Treaty on this nation', they had not tried to do so. Neither they nor the British signatories had bound their nations by the signatures. 'They had to go to their parliament,' he said, 'and we to ours.'

'Deputies sensed the underlying meaning of this momentous phrase, and there was relieved applause,' according to the *Irish Independent* reporters. 'One felt that they were glad at being thus told so bluntly by the Chairman of the Delegation of Plenipotentiaries that they had the fullest and most perfect freedom of actions in the discussion over ratification. Eamon de Valera for the first time smiled – not a mocking or an ironical smile but one that illuminated his grave and austere features.'

After the Dáil went into private session, the president again referred to the powers of the delegation. Although some people were confused about those powers, he left no doubt that the delegation had the right to sign the agreement. 'Now I would like everybody clearly to understand,' he said, 'that the plenipotentiaries went over to negotiate a Treaty, that they could differ from the cabinet if they wanted to, and that in anything of consequence they could take their decision against the decision of the cabinet.' He stressed the same point in the Dáil at least five other times during the debate. He also said on 14 December, for instance, 'The plenipotentiaries, I repeat, had a perfect right to disagree with the cabinet and a perfect right to sign.' Three days later he said, 'The plenipotentiaries got full powers if they wanted to sign on their own responsibility.' Moments later, he said, 'The plenipotentiaries had full power to sign whether we liked it or not.' By using the term 'plenipotentiaries', de Valera said they realised the delegates had 'full power to negotiate and to take responsibility for negotiating and signing'. Earlier during the public session, he had said, 'If there was a definite difference of opinion, it was the plenipotentiaries had the responsibility of making up their own minds and deciding on it.'

In short, de Valera's position was that the delegation had a right to sign but should not have done so in view of the undertaking given by Griffith at the cabinet meeting not to sign the draft treaty. 'I think it only right to say there was a document there and Mr Griffith said he would not sign that document and a different document was signed,' Collins admitted. If this was the case, however, the new document should have been submitted to the cabinet in accordance with the instructions. There could be no doubt that Griffith had broken the undertaking involved either in his acceptance of the instructions or his declaration at the cabinet meeting on 3 December that he would not sign the draft terms being discussed.

De Valera was annoyed that they had not only signed without consulting him again but also published the text of the agreement. 'They not merely signed the document but, in order to make the *fait accompli* doubly secure,' de Valera wrote, 'they published it hours before the President or their colleagues saw it, and were already giving interviews in London and proclaiming its merits and prejudicing the issue at the time it was being read in Dublin.'

The president was clearly irritated that the plenipotentiaries had not taken their lead from him. 'I was captaining a team,' he told the private session on the first afternoon of the debates, 'and I felt that the team should have played with me to the last and I should have got the chance which I felt would put us over and we might have crossed the bar in my opinion at high tide. They rushed before the tide got to the top and almost foundered the ship.'

'A captain who sent out his crew to sea, and tried to direct operations from dry land!' Collins remarked to those about him.

'I am excusing myself to the Dáil as the captain of the ship and I can only say it is not my fault,' de Valera continued. 'Had the Chairman of the delegation said he did not stand for the things they had said they stood for, he would not have been elected.' Here the president's argument was a patently disingenuous. He knew well where Griffith stood when he proposed him for the delegation, and that was why he sent Childers to keep an eye on him.

During the afternoon Collins called several times for the release of various documents relating to the latter stages of the negotiations so deputies could determine for themselves the difference between the signed terms and what the others wanted. In particular, he argued that the counter proposals, which were presented to the British on 4 December, should be 'put side by side' with the Articles of Agreement. Otherwise people were likely to think that de Valera, Stack and Brugha had been standing for an isolated republic, whereas Collins himself believed the difference was not worth fighting over.

De Valera had come prepared to explain exactly what he wanted. He produced his own alternative, which Collins dubbed Document No. 2, and the name stuck. The president made the startling admission that it was 'right to say that there will be very little difference in practice between what I may call the proposals received and what you will have under what I propose. There is very little in practice but there is that big thing that you are consistent and that you recognise yourself as a separate independent State and you associate in an honourable manner with another group.' He contended that if the Dáil stood by his counter proposals, the British would 'not go to war for the difference. In other words, both Collins and de Valera were saying that the difference was not worth fighting over.

'I felt the distance between the two was so small that the British would not wage war on account of it,' de Valera explained. 'You may say if it is so small why not take it. But I say, that small difference makes all the difference. This fight has lasted through the centuries and I would be willing to win that little sentimental thing that would satisfy the aspirations of the country.'

Document No. 2 included External Association on the lines of the proposals put forward by the delegation during the final weeks of the London conference. There was no oath in the new document, but there was a stipulation that 'for the purposes of the Association, Ireland shall recognise His Britannic Majesty as head of the Association'. Britain would be afforded the same defence concessions, except that instead of stipulating that the two countries would reconsider the defence clauses in five years, the alternative stated that coastal defence would be handed over 'to the Irish Government, unless some other arrangement for naval defence was agreed upon by both Governments'. The partition clauses were also included practically verbatim in the alternative document, except that there was a declaration to the effect that 'the right of any part of Ireland to be excluded from the supreme authority of the National Parliament and Government' was not being recognised.

In other words, de Valera explained, the alternative would not 'recognise the right of any part of Ireland to secede', but for the sake of internal peace and in order to divorce the Ulster question from the overall Anglo-Irish dispute, he was ready to accept the partition clauses of the Treaty, even though he found them objectionable from the standpoint that they provided 'an explicit recognition of the right on the part of Irishmen to secede from Ireland'.

'We will take the same things as agreed on there,' the president told the Dáil. 'Let us not start to fight with Ulster.'

Collins welcomed Document No. 2 because it confirmed his contention that the delegation had practically achieved its aim. 'The issue has been cleared considerably by the document the President has put in,' he explained. The alternative was basically in line with the proposals put forward by the delegation during the latter stages of the conference.

'We put this before the other side with all the energy we could,' Collins said. 'That is the reason that I wanted certain vital documents and these will show that the same proposals that the President has now drafted have been put already.' Consequently he thought it would be pointless trying to get the British to accept Document No. 2. They would not even listen to any delegation that went back and tried to substitute the alternative for the Treaty. He predicted the British would say, 'You can go to the devil; you can't speak for anyone: you can't deliver the goods.'

De Valera appeared to confirm this assessment of his own proposals. 'No politician in England would stand by them,' he admitted. 'Because they would have the same difficulty in legally ratifying this proposed Treaty that I hold our delegates have in ratifying it here constitutionally. It would not be a politician's peace but a people's peace.' He subsequently made the same statement in public.

After the cabinet accepted the Treaty, de Valera essentially argued that this meant nothing, that it was a matter for the Dáil, but at the end of the third day of the private session, he recognised that a majority of the Dáil were likely to support the Treaty. 'I know that most of you will vote for ratification of the Treaty,' he admitted. But he already seemed to be saying that this did not matter either, because it was really a matter for the people. 'The Republic will not be disestablished until it is disestablished by the will of the people,' he said. 'This assembly cannot ratify a Treaty which takes away from the Irish people the sovereignty of the Irish people,' he emphasised the following morning.

In some respects Collins actually believed the Treaty was better than Document No. 2, but he was keeping his views to himself until the public session resumed. 'Anything I have to say will be said in public,' he told the Dáil on the first afternoon of the private session. 'In my opinion no good purpose is served by making speeches in the private session that can be made in the public session.'

Describing the External Associations clauses of the alternative as a dangerously loose paraphrase of the Treaty, Collins later complained that Ireland would be committed to an association so vague that Britain might be able to press for control of Irish affairs as a matter of common concern amongst the countries of the British commonwealth. Ireland would not have the same status as the dominions, with the result that the dominions would not have a vested interest in ensuring that the Dublin government would not be forced to make special concessions to Britain. Such concessions would not establish a precedent for relations between Britain and the dominions as would be the case under the terms of the Treaty. Thus Collins believed that Document No. 2 'had neither the honesty of complete isolation' nor the advantages of 'free partnership'. He admitted there were restrictions in both the Treaty and the president's alternative. 'But,' he added, 'the Treaty will be operative, and the restrictions must gradually tend to disappear as we go on, more and more strongly solidifying and establishing ourselves as a free nation.'

De Valera quickly realised that he had made a tactical error in introducing Document No. 2. He therefore withdrew the document at the end of the private session.

Collins found the debate a particular strain. 'In a few days I may be free from everything and then we can see how the future goes,' he wrote to Kitty Kiernan at the end of the second day. 'It's a dreadful strain and it's telling a good deal on me.' He was still writing on similar lines at the end of the private session on 18 December.

'All this business is very very sad – Harry has come out strongly against us. I'm sorry for that, but I supposed that, like many another episode in this business, must be borne also. I haven't an idea of how it will all end but with God's help all right. In any event I shall be satisfied.'

Chapter Nineteen

'I AM A REPRESENTATIVE OF IRISH STOCK'

When Collins entered the Dáil for the resumption of the public session the following Monday, 19 December 1921, something was obviously wrong. He was not smiling as usual. Instead he looked sour and he slammed his attaché case down on the table in front of him before taking his seat.

On opening the session the speaker announced that the president wished to inform the Dáil that Document No. 2 was 'withdrawn and must be regarded as confidential until he brings his own proposal formally'. Griffith and Collins objected vociferously before the speaker made it clear that he was not ruling on the issue. Each individual deputy would be free to decide whether or not to comply with de Valera's request.

Griffith formally proposed the motion 'That Dáil Éireann approves the Treaty between Great Britain and Ireland, signed in London on December 6th, 1921.' In the course of his speech he complained about not being able to refer to Document No. 2 and also the fact that some people were representing themselves as having 'stood uncompromisingly on the rock of the Republic – the Republic, and nothing but the Republic'.

'It has been stated also here that,' he continued, 'the man who won the war – Michael Collins – compromised Ireland's rights. In the letters that preceded the negotiations not once was a demand made for recognition of the Irish Republic. If it had been made we knew it would have been refused. We went there to see how to reconcile the two positions and I hold we have done it.'

The Treaty was seconded by Seán MacEoin. Then de Valera spoke. 'I am against this Treaty because it does not reconcile Irish national aspirations with association with the British Government,' he declared. 'I am against this Treaty, not because I am a man of war, but a man of peace. I am against this Treaty because it will not end the centuries of conflict between the two nations of Great Britain and Ireland.'

The president, who never even alluded to the partition question, kept his remarks very general as he contended the Treaty was 'absolutely inconsistent with our position; it gives away Irish independence; it brings us into the British Empire; it acknowledges the head of the British Empire, not merely as the head of an association but as the direct monarch of Ireland, as the source of executive authority in Ireland'. Basically the oath was the only aspect of the Treaty to which he took specific exception during his speech.

De Valera's opposition to the oath was by no means straight-forward. He had already told the private session that he had suggested that the Irish people could swear 'to keep faith with his Britannic Majesty'. Moreover during the Dáil debate he told an American correspondent, Hayden Talbot of the Hearst newspaper chain, that his problem was not with swearing to be 'faithful to the King'. He did not find the word 'faithful' objectionable at all because he said it could be taken in the context of 'the faithfulness of two equals' to uphold a bargain. His real problem with the oath was in swearing 'allegiance to the constitution of the Irish Fee State as by law established'. This, he argued, would be tantamount to swearing direct allegiance to the crown, seeing that the law which would establish the Free State constitution would be enacted by the British parliament in the name of the crown. The Provisional Government, which would take over the administration of Ireland from the British, would not be set up by the Dáil, but by the southern Irish parliament established under the partition act passed at Westminster. Thus the Provisional Government would derive its authority from the British king in whose name parliament had passed the partition act in the first place. In addition the Free State constitution, which would be drafted by the Provisional Government, would be enacted at Westminster, with the result that if the British had the acknowledged right to enact the Irish constitution in the name of their king, then it would automatically follow that they could amend the constitution if they wished. They would, in effect, be legally able to act in the king's name to interfere in Irish affairs at will.

Stack then seconded de Valera's opposition to the Treaty. In the course of his speech he bragged about being the son of a Fenian. As was mentioned earlier Moore Stack had been arrested in 1886 and sentenced to ten years in jail. While incarcerated he wrote to the crown authorities explaining that some colleagues had previously suspected him of informing and he proceeded to outline all he purported to know about the Fenian organisation. While researching a biography of Austin Stack more than a century later, Fr J. Anthony Gaughan would find this letter after it was opened under the existing hundred-year secrecy rule. 'Some experienced person should be instructed to see me when it is probable that many things which do not occur to me may be elicited on a personal interview,' Moore Stack added. Of course, it would be wrong to blame the behaviour of the father on the son, especially as he was not even born at the time, but Austin Stack was on dubious ground when he invoked the patriotism of his father in the fight against the Treaty.

Collins did not speak until immediately after a lunchtime break. As the Dáil reassembled there was a great buzz of excitement and expectation. 'At the back of the hall visitors, clergymen and telegraph messengers crushed forward to hear,' according to the *Freeman's Journal*. 'A Japanese journalist was wedged in the crowd, and three coloured gentlemen from Trinidad – medical students – leant forward to view the scene' when Collins rose to continue the debate. He was the focus of everyone's attention. 'His flashing eyes, firm jaw, and thick black hair, through which he ran his fingers from time to time, were all revealed under the dazzling light of the electoliers.'

'Mr Collins was passionate, forcible, and at times almost theatrical,' according to *The Irish Times*. Although he had a prepared speech before him, he rarely consulted it. Now and again he would rummage among his papers, feel his smooth chin, or toss his hair with one of his hands. At times he stood erect and at other times he leaned forward. He spoke slowly until aroused by the intensity of his conviction, and then vibrating with emotion, the words would come in a torrent.

Early in the address he complained that a deputy had suggested the delegation had broken down before the first bit of British bluff. 'I would remind the deputy who used that expression,' the Big Fellow said indignantly, 'that England put up a good bluff for the last five years here and I did not break down before that bluff.'

'That's the stuff,' someone shouted, while the gathering applauded.

Collins said that he was recommending the Treaty as one of the signatories. 'I do not recommend it for more than it is,' he emphasised. 'Equally I do not recommend it for less than it is. In my opinion it gives us freedom, not the ultimate freedom that all nations desire and develop to, but the freedom to achieve it.'

As a result of the guarantee of the 'constitutional status' of dominions like Canada and South Africa, he contended that those countries would be 'guarantors of our freedom, which makes us stronger than if we stood alone'. He admitted that allowing Britain to retain four ports was a 'departure from the Canadian status', but he felt the Free State's association with the dominions on an equal footing would ensure that Britain would not use the ports 'as a jumping off ground against us'. He also admitted the partition clauses were 'not an ideal arrangement, but if our policy is, as has been stated, a policy of non-coercion, then let somebody else get a better way out of it'. He had planned to compare the Treaty with Document No. 2 but explained that in deference to the president's request, he would not make use of his prepared arguments.

'Rejection of the Treaty means that your national policy is war,' Collins continued. 'I, as an individual, do not now, nor more than ever shirk war. The Treaty was signed by me, not because they held up the alternative of immediate war. I signed it because I would not be one of those to commit the Irish people to war without the Irish people committing themselves.' This was a rather ironic statement coming from him in the light of his own role in deliberately trying to precipitate a state of general disorder back in 1919.

According to one seasoned parliamentarian, Collins' speech was 'worthy of a lawyer as well as a politician. It was big enough for a trained statesman. I was surprised by its precision and detail, and rhetoric,' Tim Healy wrote. Interspersing the speech with some wry humour Collins observed that one deputy had complained the Free State could not enjoy the same freedom as Canada because that freedom was largely dependent on that country's distance from Britain. 'It seems to me,' Collins continued alluding to the same deputy, 'that he did not regard the delegation as being wholly without responsibility for the geographical propinquity of Great Britain to Ireland.'

The speech also contained what may well have been a subtle effort to depict some of his leading opponents as something less than fully Irish. 'I am a representative of Irish stock,' Collins said. 'I am the representative equally with any other member of the same stock of people who have suffered through the terror in the past. Our grandfathers have suffered from war, and our fathers or some of our ancestors have died of famine. I don't want a lecture from anybody as to what my principles are to be now. I am just a representative of plain Irish stock whose principles have been burned into them, and we don't want any assurance to the people of this country that we are not going to betray them We are one of themselves.'

Few people would have failed to notice that some of the leaders on the other side of the floor, like the American-born de Valera with his Spanish father, or Childers and Brugha with their English backgrounds – were not able to boast of such strong Irish ancestry.

It was a trying day for Collins, who afterwards explained to Kitty that it was 'the worst day I ever spent in my life'. He wrote that 'the Treaty will almost certainly be beaten and no one knows what will happen. The country is certainly quite clearly for it but that seems to be little good, as their voices are not heard.'

According to Desmond Ryan, who witnessed the proceedings as a journalist, the debate developed into 'one long wrestle between ghosts and realities with all the stored up personal spleen of five years flaming through the rhetoric'. He concluded the two groups in the Dáil appeared 'to hate each other far more than they ever hated the Black and Tans'.

Numerous speakers argued that the various dead heroes would never have accepted the Treaty, but Collins decried the practice. 'Out of the greatest respect for the dead,' he complained, 'we have refrained from reading letters from relatives of the dead. We have too much respect for the dead.' He thought that deputies should not presume to speak for those deceased, though he was understanding when Kathleen Clarke, the widow of one of the 1916 leaders, told him that evening that she was going to vote against the Treaty because she believed her late husband would have wished to do so.

'I wouldn't want you to vote for it,' Collins told her. 'All I ask is that if it is passed, you give us the chance to work it.'

With Christmas approaching and no likely end to the debate in sight, Collins proposed that the Dáil recess on 23 December until 3 January 1922. He realised that this would have the advantage of allowing the deputies from around the country to consult their constituents. Even de Valera had admitted the majority of the people were in favour of the Treaty. Countess Markievicz seconded the recess motion.

Seán MacEntee proposed an amendment for the debate to continue 'until we finish, and that there be no adjournment over Christmas. Instead of seeing any national advantage I see a grave national danger in adjourning.' The amendment was seconded and a vote taken, with de Valera, Brugha, Stack and Childers voting to continue the debate, but the amendment was defeated by 77 votes to 44. The substantive motion proposed by Collins was then put and carried by acclamation.

During that recess the press, which was solidly behind the Treaty, encouraged local bodies to endorse the agreement, and more than twenty county councils responded in a unanimous show of support. But the struggle for ratification was to become a long, drawn-out affair. Labour Party leaders took the initiative during the recess to try to avoid a division in the Dáil on the question of the Treaty. They suggested the Dáil allow the Treaty to become operative by passing legislation to establish the southern Parliament as a committee of the Dáil so that the Provisional Government would also derive its authority from the Dáil. De Valera's strongest objections could be surmounted in this way and the Irish people would be given an opportunity of evaluating the Treaty in practice.

From a practical standpoint Collins really did not care whether Irish freedom was symbolically derived from the British or anyone else, so long as that freedom was real. He therefore welcomed the Labour Party initiative. 'I think there is the basis of something that can be hammered into an agreement,' he told the Labour Party representatives on 23 December. Griffith, too, was hopeful on Christmas Day, but de Valera rejected the plan two days later.

Nevertheless Collins was not prepared to forget about the initiative so easily. When the Dáil reconvened on 3 January 1922, he suggested the Treaty be accepted without a division and the Dáil then authorise the establishment of the Provisional Government so that it could demonstrate the extent of the country's freedom. 'If necessary,' he said to those across the floor, 'you can fight the Provisional Government on the Republican question afterwards.'

'We will do that if you carry ratification, perhaps,' the president replied, spurning the suggestion.

Interviewed that evening, Collins explained that he was not asking his opponents to do anything dishonourable:

> They are not asked to abandon any principle; they may, if need be, act as guardians of the interests of the nation – act as guarantors of Irish requirements, and act as censors of the Government of the Irish Free State. The Government of the Irish Free State may have difficulties in carrying on and in fulfilling promises contained in the Treaty. If these promises are less in their working out than we who are standing for the Treaty declare, then there is a glorious opportunity for the present opponents of the Treaty to show their ability to guard the Irish nation and to act on its behalf. At the present moment we ask not to be hampered, and if we do not achieve what we desire and intend, we shall willingly make room for the others, and they will have no more loyal supporters than ourselves. This is the one way of restoring unity in the Dáil and to preserve [it] as a body truly representative of the Irish people.

However, de Valera had plans of his own. Next day he released a revised version of Document No. 2, which some rather derisively called Document No. 3. The six partition clauses of the Treaty had initially been included in Document No. 2, but those had since been dropped and replaced by an addendum stipulating, 'we are prepared to grant to that portion of Ulster which is defined as Northern Ireland in the British Government of Ireland Act of 1920, privileges and safeguards no less substantial that those provided for in the "Articles of Agreement"'.

The president gave notice of his intention to move it as an amendment to the resolution calling for the approval of the Treaty, even though it had already been agreed that there could be no amendments until the Treaty had been voted on first. This raised the spectre of extending the already drawn-out debate further by allowing each of the more than one hundred deputies to speak again – this time on the amendment.

Collins argued that the vote should be taken on the Treaty first, and he was supported by Kevin O'Higgins, but the president was determined to get his own way. Each person was supposed to speak on the Treaty only once, with the exception of Griffith, who had the right to start and wind up the debate as the proposer of the motion. But de Valera spoke virtually at will.

Despite having spoken already and having submitted and withdrawn Document No 2, he now tried to submit an amended version. 'It is not within any member's power to do such a thing without the unanimous consent of this House, and I entirely object to it,' Griffith complained. 'A document has been put into our hands this evening that is not Document No. 2.'

'You are quibbling,' de Valera responded. 'The Minister for Foreign Affairs is quibbling now.'

'The President is a touchy man,' a backbench deputy interjected. 'He jumps up very quickly when one puts his own interpretation on this document. Is it in order for the President to call the Minister for Foreign Affairs a quibbler?'

'I say that the word "quibble" has been used here several times,' the president explained. 'If ever it was once true it is in this case, because there is nothing changed but in the setting up – a slight change to have it in final form.'

'Document No. 2 consisted of twenty-three clauses and an appendix,' Griffith observed. 'This new document consists of seventeen clauses. Six clauses are omitted.'

'I am responsible for the proposals and the House will have

to decide on them,' de Valera declared. 'I am going to choose my own procedure.'

The Dáil was staggered. Griffith rose and responded in a cold, intent manner. 'I submit it is not in the competence of the President to choose his own procedure,' he declared. 'This is either a constitutional body or it is not. If it is an autocracy let you say so and we will leave it.'

'In answer to that I am going to propose an amendment in my own terms,' the president maintained. 'It is for the House to decide whether they will take it or not.' He seemed to want to 'hurl another few words across the floor, but the soothing hand of a supporter from the bench behind tapping him gently on the shoulder had a calming effect'. The undignified spectacle was thus mercifully ended and the Dáil recessed for the evening.

Griffith was so annoyed at de Valera's conduct that he gave a copy of the original Document No. 2 to the press. Nine backbenchers representing various shades of opinion – among them Seán T. O'Kelly, Liam Mellows, Paddy Ruttledge, Eoin O'Duffy, and Michael Hayes – met at O'Kelly's home in an effort to find a formula that would prevent a complete split within Sinn Féin. With only Mellows dissenting, they came up with a proposal in line with the idea that opponents should abstain from voting against the Treaty and allow the Provisional Government to function drawing its powers from the Dáil, while de Valera would remain as president in order 'that every ounce can be got out of the Treaty'.

Griffith and Collins accepted the plan that night, but O'Kelly was unable to contact de Valera. Unfortunately the atmosphere next morning was poisoned by a savage attack on de Valera in the *Freeman's Journal*, whose political correspondent accused him of 'arrogating to himself the rights of an autocrat'.

'It seems as though he wanted to wreck the Dáil before a vote could be taken, and then carry the devastating split as far as his influence could reach, throughout the length and breadth of the land,' the correspondent continued. 'The worst disaster which has befallen Ireland since the Union is imminent, and can only be averted by the deputies who love their country more than they love Mr de Valera, refusing to share his terrible responsibility.'

In the same issue there was also a vitriolic editorial denouncing him for a 'criminal attempt to divide the nation' by pressing 'an alleged alternative' that was not really an alternative at all. The editorial continued:

It contains all the articles for which the Treaty has been assailed by the 'ideal orators of Dáil Éireann'.

Only it is much worse.

It agrees to Partition, but unlike the Treaty, it abandons Tyrone and Fermanagh to Orange domination.

The Document is the answer to all the criticism of the Treaty.

What then is the explanation?

Is it Mr de Valera's vanity?

Apparently, he cannot forgive the Irishmen who have made the Treaty for their success.

And for this he is ready to sacrifice the country.

He has not the instinct of the Irishman in his blood.

It is the curse of Ireland at this moment that its unity should be broken by such a man acting under the advice of an Englishman who has achieved fame in the British Intelligence Service.

Document No. 3 is largely the work of Mr Erskine Childers.

Mr Childers won his spurs as a fighter against the South African Republic.

His next achievement was his 'Riddle of the Sands', a record of British spying on the German coast.

As a Flight Commander of the Navy he fought against Roger Casement's ally.

These are the men for whom the nation is to put aside Arthur Griffith, Michael Collins, and Richard Mulcahy.

When the fight was on Mr de Valera and Mr Erskine Childers

fell accidentally into the hands of the military.

They were immediately released.

That was the time there was £10,000 for the corpse of Michael Collins.

The Irish people must stand up, and begin their freedom by giving their fate into the hands of their own countrymen.

Whether or not Collins had wished to draw attention to the president's foreign background in his own Dáil speech a fortnight earlier, he quickly disassociated himself from the *Freeman's Journal* attack. He not only denounced it in the Dáil but also complained to the editor that he did not want his 'name associated with any personal attack on those who are opposed to me politically in the present crisis'.

De Valera remained deeply irritated by the attack. Flatly rejecting the backbench initiative, he insisted that Document No. 2 be accepted instead.

Next morning, 6 January 1922, the Dáil went back into private session to consider the backbench initiative, but the president was adamantly opposed. 'I am going to settle all this thing by resigning publicly at the public session,' he stated, banging the table in front of him. 'I am not going to connive at setting up in Ireland another government for England.'

Erskine Childers believed that Harry Boland, who had returned from the United States the previous day, persuaded de Valera to announce his resignation and force an election of a president before any vote on the Treaty.

Chapter Twenty

'THE MAN WHO WON THE WAR'

The public session reconvened in an air of expectation on the afternoon of 6 January. The president began by announcing his resignation in the course of a truly extraordinary speech. 'Even in his happiest moments Mr de Valera has scarcely surpassed himself in declaratory power,' one reporter noted. The remarkable address claimed the full attention of the whole Dáil.

De Valera began slowly and deliberately, but his voice became charged with emotion as he defended his alternative. 'Now, I have definitely a policy,' he explained, 'not some pet scheme of my own, but something that I know from four years' experience in my position – and I have been bought up among the Irish people. I was reared in a labourer's cottage here in Ireland.'

The Dáil applauded. This was obviously the president's answer to the snide questioning of his credentials as an Irish man by the *Freeman's Journal*. 'I have not lived solely amongst the intellectuals,' he continued. 'The first fifteen years of my life that formed my character were lived among the Irish people down in Limerick; therefore, I know what I am talking about; and whenever I wanted to know what the Irish people wanted I had only to examine my own heart and it told me straight off what the Irish people wanted.' Consequently, he said, he knew that the Irish people did not want the Treaty, and he was determined to wreck it. He announced his resignation as president and said the Dáil would have 'to decide before it does further work, who is the be the Chief Executive in this Nation'. And he was going to stand for re-election.

'If you elect me and do it by a majority,' he said, 'I will throw out that Treaty.' This was a naked attempt to turn the whole Treaty issue into a personal vote of confidence. 'It looked like a last effort to reach the hearts of the deputies and obscure their judgment in a storm of emotion, passion, and personal attachment – in a word, anything but the consideration of the Treaty on plain, matter-of-fact lines,' the political correspondent of the *Freeman's Journal* wrote. 'The Strangers Gallery was left gasping. Everything considered, it was a sensation of the first magnitude.

'Even in his happiest moments Mr de Valera has scarcely surpassed himself in declaratory power,' the report continued. 'His address last evening claimed devoted attention. Coolness, calmness and solemnity; passion, emotion and that fire that outsteps passion, characterised his remarkable speech.'

His tactics provoked so much criticism that he felt compelled to withdraw his resignation, but not before making some self-righteous remarks. It was then proposed and seconded that the standing orders should be suspended to discuss the crisis caused by the president's resignation. Collins was enraged.

'The other side may say what they like, and they may put in any motion they like, and they may take any action they like, but we must not criticise them. That is the position that we have been put into,' he declared. 'We will have no Tammany Hall methods here. Whether you are for the Treaty or whether you are against it, fight without Tammany Hall methods. We will not have them.' He went on to complain that the backbench initiative to avoid a division had been frustrated by 'three or four bullies'.

De Valera objected to the use of the term bullies and the speaker asked Collins to withdraw the remark. There followed an uneasy silence. Collins seemed to seek inspiration from the papers in front of him. Almost a minute passed before he responded.

'I can withdraw the term,' he said slowly and deliberately, 'but the spoken word cannot be recalled. Is that right, sir?'

A showdown with the speaker had been averted. Deputies laughed and the gathering applauded. But Brugha, who felt that he was one of those alluded to as a bully, was unhappy with the way the remark was withdrawn.

'I don't know to whom he referred when he mentioned this word "bullies",' Brugha said. 'Possibly he may have referred to me as being one of them. In the ordinary way I would take exception and take offence at such a term being applied to me, but the amount of offence that I would take at it would be measured by the respect or esteem that I had for the character of the person who made the charge. In this particular instance I take no offence whatever.'

If the standing orders were suspended, however, Brugha said that Collins and the others should be free to discuss Document No. 2.

'In that case I am satisfied,' Collins replied.

But Griffith was not. He accused the president of violating the agreed procedure. 'He agreed that I should wind up the discussion,' Griffith explained. 'I have listened here for days – during all that time – to arguments and attacks on my honour and the honour of my fellow-delegates and I have said nothing. I have waited to wind up this discussion.

'Why we should be stopped in the middle of this discussion and a vote taken on the personality of President de Valera I don't understand,' Griffith continued. 'And I don't think my countrymen will understand it.'

'I am sick and tired of politics,' de Valera responded, 'so sick that no matter what happens I would go back to private life. I have only seen politics within the last three weeks or a month. It is the first time I have seen them and I am sick to the heart of them.' Depicting himself as straight and honest in the face of the twisted dishonesty of his opponents, he continued, 'It is because I am straight that I meet crookedness with straight dealing always. Truth will always stand no matter from what direction it is attacked.'

Of course, it was disingenuous of de Valera to feign innocence about the seamier side of politics. He had been up to his neck in such politics while in the United States and, arguably, he had more political experience than anyone else in the Dáil. In fact, he refuted his assertion of innocence in the same speech by referring to his American experiences.

'I detest trickery,' de Valera said. 'What has sickened me most is that I got in this House the same sort of dealing that I was accustomed to over in America from other people of a similar kind.' It was particularly significant he should compare his critics in the Dáil with his opponents in the United States, because there was a remarkable similarity between his attitude towards the Treaty and his actions during the Republican Party's National Convention at Chicago in June 1920.

'It was a case of Cohalan and his machine over again,' de Valera wrote to McGarrity.

'Insinuations about me have hurt me,' he told the Dáil. 'I am straight with everybody and I am not a person for political trickery; and I don't want to pull a red herring across. If there is a straight vote in this House I will be quite satisfied if it is within forty-eight hours.'

'One of the most irritating features of Mr de Valera's behaviour at this time,' Piaras Beaslaí wrote, 'was that, having used every device of a practical politician to gain his point, having shown himself relentless and unscrupulous in taking every advantage of generous opponents, he would adopt a tone of injured innocence when his shots failed, and assume the pose of a simple sensitive man, too guileless and gentle for this rough world of politics.'

Maybe Collins would have been willing to allow the debate to be diverted, but Griffith was not about to allow it. It was a political ploy to defeat the Treaty by turning it into a personal vote of confidence in de Valera.

Just as he knew there was no realistic chance of securing diplomatic recognition in the United States in 1920, de Valera had already admitted to the Dáil that no British politician would now be prepared to accept his alternative proposals in Document No. 2.

For the Dáil to have accepted the president's suggestion that the Treaty be rejected and Document No. 2 presented to the British instead would have been as foolhardy as he was naive if he really believed that the propaganda campaign advocated by him had any more chance of success than the pathetic failure of his comparatively similar effort to win over the American electorate in 1920.

A successful campaign in 1922 would have needed the sympathetic understanding of at least some sections of the press, and there was little chance of securing this, seeing that the only organs which opposed the Treaty had done so on the grounds that the agreement was too generous towards Sinn Féin. Not one Irish daily newspaper supported de Valera's position. A total of 328 statutory public bodies – county councils, urban councils, rural councils and borough corporations – had already voted openly in favour of the Treaty, while only five came out against it. Moreover, there was little prospect of getting international support because even American opinion was strongly in favour of the settlement.

Next day *The New York Times* carried an editorial that was highly critical of de Valera:

Apparently he essayed a Napoleonic or Cromwellian stroke in resigning, at the same time that he demanded re-election with all power placed in his hands; but when this failed, he talked and acted like a hysterical schoolgirl. Whatever happens in Ireland, de Valera seems to have hopelessly discredited himself as a leader. Narrow, obstinate, visionary and obviously vain, he has now, in his representative capacity, wrought immense harm to the Ireland of his professed entire devotion.

Harry Boland admitted that 'the great public opinion of America is on the side of this Treaty'. Indeed, he added, the American press had adopted 'a unanimous attitude in favour' of it. There was even strong support among some of de Valera's supporters in the United States.

The president of American Association for Recognition of the Irish Republic had, for instance, come out in favour of the agreement. Boland had done so also, but he told the Dáil on 7 January that he had issued his statement before the Treaty was published in the United States. He said that he had made the mistake of assuming the Treaty would be favourable because de Valera had assured him nothing less than External Association would be acceptable. But this did not explain why, after the terms were published, he actually denounced Cohalan and Diarmuid Lynch, the secretary of the Friends of Irish Freedom, for criticising the agreement. The latter pair of them had, ironically, been among the first to denounce the Treaty, but they subsequently supported it after they learned de Valera was opposed to it. Such vicissitudes certainly lent credence to the idea that personalities figured largely in the controversy.

At one point during his address Boland turned to Collins. 'Is this, in your opinion a final settlement of the question between England and Ireland?'

'It is not,' Collins replied.

After Boland finished, Joe McGrath spoke and told how Boland had told him back in August that he was going to America on de Valera's behalf 'to prepare the American people for something short of a Republic'.

De Valera objected that what he meant was that instead of 'an isolated Republic' that External Association would have to be accepted. 'It was because I was honest and wanted to be honest with the American people that I said that an isolated Republic would have to be changed into some sort of association,' he added.

Stripped of its polemical distortions and insinuations, the debate centred on bizarre irrelevancies. Despite the national significance and momentous implications of the Treaty, it was painfully obvious that personalities were playing an inordinate role in determining how people were lining up on the issue. On the one side people were backing de Valera, while on the other side they were gathering behind Collins.

It was the personality of Collins which loomed largest during the closing speeches. Winding up the debate on the anti-Treaty side, Cathal Brugha delivered a speech that quickly turned into a tirade against the Big Fellow, whom he described as 'merely a subordinate in the Department of Defence'.

'Brugha is a little man, with a slight limp and a singularly immobile face,' *The Irish Times* reported. 'He speaks quietly weighing every word before he utters it, and makes little or no attempt to secure rhetorical efforts. But his speech was saturated with bitterness. He heaped scorn Cosgrave, Duggan and most of all Collins.'

Amid cries of 'Shame' and 'Get on with the Treaty', Brugha complained that Collins had originated the stories that there was a price on his head, and the press had built him into 'a romantic figure' and 'a mysterious character' which he was not. But it was Griffith's reference to Collins as 'the man who won the war' that was most irritating to Brugha, who actually questioned whether Collins 'had ever fired a shot at any enemy of Ireland'.

Shortly after Brugha had finished Arthur Griffith wound up the debate. He made no apology for his earlier reference to Collins: 'I said it and I say it again; he was the man that made the situation; he was the man, and nobody knows better than I do how, during a year and a half, he worked from six in the morning until two next morning. He was the man whose matchless energy, whose indomitable will carried Ireland through the terrible crisis; and although I have not now, and never had, an ambition about either political affairs or history, if my name is to go down in history I want it associated with the name of Michael Collins. Michael Collins was the man who fought the Black and Tan terror for twelve months until England was forced to offer terms.'

The Dáil erupted with a roar of approval and thunderous applause. It was without doubt the most emotional response of the whole debate. Having listened to Brugha's invective in embarrassed silence, deputies jumped at the opportunity of disassociate themselves from those bitter remarks.

Griffith speech was described by *The Irish Times* as 'by far the most statesmanlike utterance that has been made in the Dáil'. He made some telling points in favour of the Treaty.

'The principle I have stood for all my life is the principle of Ireland for the Irish people. If I can get that with a Republic, I will have a Republic; if I can get that with a monarchy, I will have a monarchy. I will not sacrifice my country for a form of government,' he concluded. 'I say now to the people of Ireland that it is their right to see that this Treaty is carried into operation, when they get for the first time in seven centuries, a chance to live their lives in their own country and take their place among the nations of Europe.'

As the proposer of the resolution calling for the Dáil's approval of the Treaty, Griffith was supposed to have the last word before the vote was taken, but de Valera again violated the procedure.

'Before you take a vote,' he said, 'I want to enter my last protest – that document will rise in judgment against the men who say there is only a shadow of difference.' He was obviously calling on deputies to reject the Treaty in favour of his own Document No. 2.

'Let the Irish nation judge us now and for future years,' cried Collins.

The clerk of the Dáil began calling the role in the order of constituencies. Having been elected from Armagh, it fell to Collins to cast the first vote. With a faint smile he rose, paused momentarily, and answered slowly 'Is toil.'

The clerk continued through the other names, with deputies voting either 'Is toil' or 'Ní toil'.

When the names of the deputies from Cork were reached, Collins was again called upon to vote, but he declined to do so on the grounds that he had voted already. Likewise, when de Valera was called upon to vote for his second constituency, he declined, by shaking his head slowly and smiling across at Collins. But Griffith protested against the disenfranchisement of his second constituency.

It took about ten minutes to complete the voting and another couple of minutes before the announcement was made that the Treaty had been approved by sixty-four votes to fifty-seven. There was no real demonstration within the hall, but when news filtered outside there was a wave of enthusiastic cheering in the street, where a crowd of some hundreds had gathered. The cheering continued for some minutes and seemed to stir those inside the chamber.

'It will, of course, be my duty to resign my office as Chief Executive,' de Valera said. 'I do not know that I should do it just now.'

'No,' cried Collins.

'There is one thing I want to say,' the president continued. 'I want it to go to the country and to the world, and it is this: the Irish people established a Republic. This is simply approval of a certain resolution. The Republic can only be disestablished by the Irish people. Therefore, until such time as the Irish people in regular manner disestablish it, this Republic goes on.'

Collins called for a committee of public safety to be set up by both sides of the Dáil to preserve order. Some people thought de Valera was going to respond favourably until Mary MacSwiney intervened to denounce the vote just taken 'as the grossest act of betrayal that Ireland ever endured'.

'There can be no union between representatives of the Irish Republic and the so-called Free State,' she declared.

De Valera announced he would like to meet 'all those who voted on the side of the established Republic' the following afternoon, and Collins repeated his appeal for 'some kind of understanding' between the two factions 'to preserve the present order in the country'.

'I would like my last word here to be this,' de Valera responded. 'We have had a glorious record for four years, it has been four years of magnificent discipline in our nation. The world is looking at us now.'

At this point he broke down, buried his head in his hands, and collapsed sobbing into his chair. It was a very emotional scene. Women were weeping openly and Harry Boland was seen with tears running down his cheeks, while other men were visibly trying to restrain their tears.

Aftermath

'AMIDST THE RUINS'

Following the Dáil's acceptance of the Treaty, Collins sought to implement it as quickly as possible as a means of enlisting popular support. Convinced of the Treaty's enormous possibilities, he believed he could win over sceptics by demonstrating that the agreement could be used as a stepping-stone to complete independence.

At every step, however, he was confronted by the determination of his opponents. De Valera had first stated that the Treaty was a matter for the cabinet, but when the cabinet approved it, he said it was a matter for the Dáil, and when it became apparent that the Dáil would approve it, he contended that only the Irish people could ratify it.

'The resolution recommending the ratification of a certain treaty is not a legal action,' he told the meeting of anti-Treaty deputies at the Mansion House on 8 January 1922. 'That will not be completed until the Irish people have disestablished the Republic which they set up of their own free will.' Of course, it was the Dáil which proclaimed the Irish Republic.

De Valera announced his resignation as president, but said he intended to run again on a platform of no co-operation in implementing the Treaty. While some journalists may have taken his earlier threat to retire from politics seriously, J. L. Garvin of *The Observer* refused to believe it. In a widely circulated article that was reprinted in *The New York Times,* he described the president as 'a Robespierre who would send the dearest of his former friends to the guillotine for a formula and eat his dinner afterwards with self-righteousness.'

Collins called for a committee of public safety, made up of representatives from both sides of Sinn Féin, to replace the president until a general election could be held, but de Valera rejected this as unconstitutional. 'This assembly must choose its executive according to its constitution,' he insisted.

Kathleen Clarke proposed de Valera for re-election 'as President of the Irish Republic'. But Collins was ready for the move. 'We expected something like this,' he said. 'We would have been fools if we had not anticipated it.' If de Valera were re-elected, he warned, 'everybody will regard us a laughing stock'.

If re-elected, De Valera said he would 'carry on as before' and ignore Treaty. 'I do not believe that the Irish people, if they thoroughly understood it, would stand for it,' he added. It was not just his arrogance that critics found offensive, but also the smug, self-righteous way in which he sought re-election. It was as if he was saying that he wished to go back to private life but, because he was more intelligent than most Irish people and could see things that they could not understand, he would condescend to serve them. 'Remember,' he said, 'I am only putting myself at your disposal and at the disposal of the nation. I do not want office at all.'

'I do not ask you to elect me,' he said, re-emphasising the point moments later. 'I am not seeking to get any power whatever in this nation. I am quite glad and anxious to get back to private life.'

If de Valera was re-elected, Collins said that he would quit. 'I will go down to the people of South Cork and tell them that I did my best, that I could bring the thing no further.'

'There is only one man who can lead us properly and keep us all together,' Brugha interjected. 'If Eamon de Valera did not happen to be President who would have kept Arthur Griffith, Michael Collins and myself together?'

'That is true,' replied Collins. 'It is not today or yesterday it started.'

'I only wish to God we could be brought together again under his leadership,' Brugha continued. 'I only wish it was possible.'

'It is not, though,' said Collins.

Griffith depicted the president's tactics as a 'political manoeuvre to get round the Treaty'. It was an attempt to exploit the emotions of deputies. 'There is no necessity for him to resign today,' Griffith added. 'His resignation and going up again for re-election is simply an attempt to wreck this Treaty.'

As nobody else had been nominated for president, Stack argued that de Valera 'has been re-elected unanimously'.

'Well, I am voting against anyway,' Collins insisted. He tried to nominate Griffith, but the Speaker ruled the Dáil would have to vote on de Valera's nomination first.

As the roll was called de Valera declined to vote in an apparent effort to dramatise that he personally did not want the office. This might easily have been a very costly gesture, because the vote was extremely close. He was only defeated by 60 votes to 58. If just one deputy had voted in favour instead of against de Valera, his own vote would have given him victory by 60 votes to 59.

The difficulties of implementing the Treaty in the face of obstructionist opposition became apparent when Collins proposed Griffith as 'President of the Provisional Executive', rather than as president of the Dáil or of the Irish Republic. Article 17 of the Treaty stipulated that 'a meeting of members of Parliament elected for constituencies in Southern Ireland' should meet to select a Provisional Government – all the members of which had to signify in writing their acceptance of the Treaty.

The Dáil could authorise the establishment of the Provisional Government so that it would have continuity from the Irish people. This would make no practical difference, but de Valera was adamant that the Dáil could not transfer any of its authority, or do anything to implement the Treaty, without the prior approval of the Irish people. He was insisting that until the Treaty was ratified there would have to be two Irish governments – the Dáil executive, which would be recognised under Irish law, and the Provisional Government, which would take over the administration at Dublin Castle and would thus only be recognised under British law.

In effect, that argument was about whether Griffith could call himself chairman of the Provisional Government as well as president of the Dáil. It was ironic that de Valera, of all people, should be so obstinate over the title, seeing that he had changed the title from *priomh aire* to president back in 1919 without even informing, much less consulting, his colleagues. It was more than two years before he asked the Dáil to regularise the constitutional position with an oblique amendment in August 1921.

The wrangle over the Griffith's title was not resolved until next day when de Valera was given his own way. 'If I am elected,' Griffith told the Dáil, 'I will occupy whatever position President de Valera occupied.'

'Hear, hear,' exclaimed de Valera. He had won his point. 'I feel that I can sit down in this assembly while such an election is going on.' But minutes later, however, he changed his mind and announced that he was walking out of the Dáil 'as a protest against the election as President of the Irish Republic of the Chairman of the Delegation who is bound by the Treaty'. He and his supporters left the chamber in what could only be described as a contemptuous insult towards what he insisted was the sovereign assembly of the nation. It was all the worse in the face of the conciliatory attitude adopted by his opponents.

Collins was indignant. 'Deserters all!' he shouted at those leaving. 'We will now call on the Irish people to rally to us. Deserters all!'

Countess Markievicz turned and shouted back: 'Oath breakers and cowards.'

'Foreigners – Americans – English,' snapped Collins.

'Lloyd Georgeites,' cried Markievicz. Mary MacSwiney also shouted something but her words were drowned out amid cries of 'Up the Republic' and the counter taunts of those remaining in the chamber. The sordid spectacle was mercifully ended as the last of the dissidents left the chamber.

Griffith was then elected without further opposition. He proceeded to call a meeting of the southern parliament, but in obvious deference to the de Valera group, he did not do so as president of the Dáil, but as chairman of the delegation that negotiated the Treaty. The southern parliament was a smaller body than the Dáil, because everyone elected to Stormont was entitled to sit in the Dáil. In practice this made little difference because all the deputies who took their Dáil seats, with the one exception of Seán Milroy – a pro-Treaty deputy from County Fermanagh – had been elected in the 26 counties.

Members of the second Dáil had been elected under the machinery to set up the southern parliament, which was supposed to set up the Provisional Government. It was therefore summoned, but only pro-Treaty deputies and the unionists elected at Trinity College turned up at the Mansion House on Saturday, 14 January 1922. The gathering promptly approved the Treaty without a division. The appointment of an eight-man Provisional Government under the chairmanship of Collins was approved. The Dáil cabinet had agreed this in advance. They were just going through the motions of duplicating everything to satisfy both de Valera and the British. It was really only a cosmetic exercise. Others might have highlighted the significance of the occasion with some kind of ceremonial address, but not Collins.

'We did not come here to speak, but to work,' he said. The whole thing was over in forty-five minutes.

Ever since the establishment of the Dáil there had been two administrations in Ireland – the Dáil and the crown regime at Dublin Castle. In theory this arrangement was continuing with Collins and the Provisional Government taking over at Dublin Castle. With the exception of Griffith and Mulcahy, members of the Dáil cabinet were appointed to the same portfolios in the Provisional Government, so the two administrations were effectively combined under the dual leadership of Griffith and Collins. They had worked well together while de Valera was in the United States, and again during the Treaty negotiations. Hence the dual set-up established to placate de Valera was never likely to be more than a minor inconvenience.

When Collins went to Dublin Castle to receive his commission as chairman of the Provisional Government from the lord lieutenant, he was uncharacteristically late. As he alighted from a taxi an official approached him looking at his watch. 'Mr Collins,' he said, 'you're seven minutes late, and you have kept the Lord Lieutenant waiting.'

'You people are here 700 years,' Collins replied. 'What bloody difference will seven minutes make now that you are leaving?'

There was a kind of ceremonial changing of the guard, as Irish soldiers marched in and British soldiers marched out. The Big Fellow, who was obviously uncomfortable at the thought of receiving his commission from the representatives of the British king, put his own spin on the events, not just by keeping the lord lieutenant waiting, but more especially by issuing a formal statement afterwards: 'Members of *Rialtas Sealadacht na hÉireann* [Provisional Government of Ireland] received the surrender of Dublin Castle at 1.45 p.m. today,' he announced. 'It is now in the hands of the Irish nation.' Thereafter the events of the day would be remembered as 'the surrender of Dublin Castle'.

One of the more surprising aspects of the Treaty was the paucity of opposition to the partition clauses. Most of the Dáil seem to accept the interpretation of Collins that if Stormont did not agree to be subservient to the Dáil, the Boundary Commission would transfer so much territory that Northern Ireland would become an unviable economic entity, and partition would be ended one way or another. Why did people so readily accept this interpretation?

For one thing, Lloyd George had indicated during the Treaty debate in the House of Commons that if Stormont did not agree to a united Ireland, counties like Fermanagh and Tyrone could only remain within Northern Ireland by force, and he made it clear that he was opposed to such force. Moreover, Collins indicated privately that he had received some kind of informal assurance from the British during the negotiations.

During the Treaty debate in the Dáil, for instance, Collins used to meet regularly with IRB colleagues like Seán Ó Muirthile, Joe McGrath and P. S. O'Hegarty. One evening O'Hegarty mentioned he was surprised at how the anti-Treaty people were essentially ignoring the partition issue.

'It's an astonishing thing to me,' he said, 'that in the attack on the Treaty practically nothing is said about partition, which is the one real blot on it.'

'Oh, but that is provided for,' Ó Muirthile replied. 'Didn't you know?'

'How is it provided for?' O'Hegarty asked. 'Ulster will opt out.'

'Before they signed,' Ó Muirthile explained, 'Griffith and Collins got a personal undertaking from Smith [Birkenhead] and Churchill that if Ulster opted out they would get only four counties and that they would make a four-county government impossible.'

O'Hegarty looked over at Collins, who grinned. 'That's right,' he said.

De Valera and Collins soon began travelling to political rallies throughout the country at which the Treaty was the main issue. At a rally in Cork on Sunday, 19 February, de Valera raised the political temperature. 'If the Treaty was signed under duress,' he said, 'the men who went to London broke faith with the Irish people. If it was signed without duress they were traitors to the cause.' The following weekend he addressed rallies in Limerick and Ennis.

Collins and Griffith responded with a massive rally near Trinity College, Dublin, the following Sunday, 5 March. Collins accused de Valera and his supporters of exploiting the situation. 'They are stealing our clothes,' Collins said. 'We have beaten out the British by the means of the Treaty. While damning the Treaty, and us with it, they are taking advantage of the evacuation.'

'The arrangement in regard to North-East Ulster is not ideal,' he said. 'But then the position in North-East Ulster is not ideal. If the Free State is established, however, union is certain.' Rejecting the Treaty, on the other hand, would 'perpetuate partition'. Behind the scenes Collins was contributing to the unrest in northern Ireland by secretly supplying the IRA in the north with weapons as the British armed the forces of the Provisional Government. He even connived at the kidnapping of unionists to be held as hostages against the execution of three men in Derry, whose sentences had actually been commuted hours earlier.

The sectarian outrages were on both sides. In a three-week period during February, 138 people were killed – 96 Catholics and 42 Protestants. In Milewater Street, Belfast, a bomb was thrown among teenagers playing in the street, killing five of them. 'In my opinion,' Churchill wrote to Collins, 'it is the worst thing that has happened in Ireland in the last three years.'

Andy Cope assured London that members of the Provisional Government 'are doing their best' in difficult circumstances. 'Collins has had great difficulty in holding in certain sections of the IRA who were out for hostages,' Cope wrote.

During March and early April, Collins travelled from Dublin to political rallies in Cork, Skibbereen, Waterford, Castlebar, Wexford, Naas and Tralee. The first of his rallies outside Dublin was fittingly in Cork city, where he was greeted by a large crowd at Glanmire Station and taken through the city in triumph, behind a number of bands, much to the annoyance of some armed republicans. They tried to disrupt the proceedings by firing shots in the air as he being driven through Patrick's Street.

Armed republicans also held up special excursion trains from

Fermoy, Newmarket and Youghal. They kidnapped the drivers and firemen, leaving the passengers stranded. But a crowd of about 50,000 people turned up for a rally on Grand Parade.

'While the captain was away from the ship – that time in America – there was a hurricane blowing,' Collins said. 'The helm has been left by the captain in the hands of those very same incompetent amateurs who afterwards, in the calm water, had the ship on the rocks, and while he was away, somehow or other, we steered safely through those troubled waters, the roughest through which the ship of the Irish nation had to be navigated in all her troubled history.'

De Valera responded in Carrick-on-Suir and in Thurles on St Patrick's Day, that if the Treaty were ratified they would have 'to wade through Irish blood, through the blood of the soldiers of the Irish government, and through, perhaps, the blood of some members of the government in order to get Irish freedom.' He was widely blamed for inciting the IRA, but he was, in fact, rapidly losing his sway over the organisation.

Some militants, like Rory O'Connor, the director of engineering, had little time for de Valera any more. O'Connor openly declared that he was 'no more prepared to stand for de Valera than for the Treaty'. On 30 March O'Connor led a raid on the offices of the *Freeman's Journal*, where they wrecked the printing equipment, and issued a statement justifying their actions. Although de Valera later said that he personally 'heartily disagreed' with O'Connor, he nevertheless publicly defended O'Connor's outrageous behaviour in a series of press interviews.

'The threat of war from this government is intimidation operating on the side of Mr Griffith and Mr Collins as sure and as definite as if these gentlemen were using it themselves, and far more effective, because it is indirect and well kept in the background,' de Valera argued.

'If we proceed to fly at each other's throats,' Collins told a rally in Wexford on 9 April, 'the British will come back again to restore their Government, and they will have justified themselves in the eyes of the world. They will have made good their claim that we were unable and unfit to govern ourselves. Would not Mr de Valera, then, pause and consider where his language, if translated into action, was hurrying the nation? He had much power for good or evil. Could he not cease his incitements – for incitement they were, whatever his personal intentions. Could he not strive to create a good atmosphere instead of a bad one?'

The Roman Catholic Archbishop of Dublin, Edward Byrne, invited leaders of both sides to a peace conference in Dublin on 12 April. The attendance included Griffith, Collins, de Valera, Brugha, the archbishop and the respective lord mayors of Dublin and Limerick – Laurence O'Neill and Stephen O'Mara. No progress was made but the two sides agreed to meet again after Easter.

In the early hours of Good Friday, 14 April, Rory O'Connor and a group of anti-Treaty IRA occupied the Four Courts and a number of other buildings in Dublin. Between 300 and 400 men were estimated to be involved in the operation. O'Connor announced that scrapping the Treaty was the only way of avoiding civil war.

The similarity with the start of the Easter rebellion, six years earlier, was unmistakable. Although de Valera was assumed to be behind the takeover, he had nothing to do with it. In fact, he was not even informed in advance. Nevertheless he did nothing to disabuse the public misconception.

A Labour Party deputation that called on him later that day, found him particularly unreceptive to their pleas for peace. 'We spent two hours pleading with him, with a view to averting the impending calamity of civil war,' one member of the deputation later recalled.

'The majority have no right to do wrong,' de Valera told them. 'He repeated that at least a dozen times in the course of the interview,' according to one of those present. He refused to accept he had a 'duty to observe the decision of the majority until it was reversed'.

By the time the archbishop's peace conference reconvened at the Mansion House on the following Thursday, the atmosphere had been further poisoned. Brugha accused Griffith and Collins of being British agents. When the archbishop demanded that the accusation be withdrawn, Brugha agreed but explained that he considered those who did the work of the British government to be British agents.

'I suppose we are two of the ministers whose blood is to be waded through?' Collins asked.

'Yes,' replied Brugha quite calmly. 'You are two.'

'Civil war is certain,' Harry Boland wrote, 'unless Collins and Company see the error of their ways and come to terms with their late colleagues.' Collins eventually relented and concluded an election pact with de Valera on 20 May. The two wings of Sinn Féin would put forward a united panel of candidates in ratio with their existing strength in the Dáil and, if victorious, the party would form a kind of coalition government in which there would be a president elected as usual and a minister of defence selected by the army, along with five other pro-Treaty and four anti-Treaty ministers. This was supposed to remove the Treaty as an election issue.

Griffith was particularly cool towards the election pact. He pointedly stopped addressing Collins as 'Mick', but called him 'Mr Collins' instead.

Collins stoutly defended the pact in London. When Austen Chamberlain pressed him to disavow the IRA's campaign, he replied that he would not 'hold the hands of the northern government when Catholics were being murdered'. He was 'in a most pugnacious mood' according to Tom Jones, who noted that the Big Fellow 'talked on at a great rate in a picturesque way about going back to fight with his comrades'. He accused the British of being 'bent on war', because they were doing nothing about the situation in Belfast. Jones noted that Collins went 'on and on at great length about the Ulster situation'.

Collins had 'become obsessed' with Northern Ireland, according to Lloyd George, who found himself in the unenviable position of trying to placate the volatile personalities of both the Big Fellow and Churchill. He felt 'there was a strain of lunacy in Churchill,' and he said that 'Collins was just a wild animal – a mustang'. When someone suggested that negotiating with Collins was like trying to write on water, Lloyd George interjected, 'shallow and agitated water'.

'We ought to remember the life Collins had led during the last three years,' Eamonn Duggan explained, according to Jones. 'He was very highly strung, and over-wrought, and sometimes left their own meetings in a rage with his colleagues.'

Collins tried to exclude the Treaty oath from the new constitution and he played down the role of the king, seeing that the *de facto* role of the king was not defined in Canada or even Britain. The British feared 'Collins might appoint a charwoman' to the post of governor-general, Jones noted. 'I see no great objection if she's a good one,' he added, 'but others may take a different view of what is fitting.'

The British insisted on the inclusion of the Treaty oath in the constitution, because they argued its omission could be seen as a violation of the Treaty. Griffith had no intention of defending the republican symbols of the draft constitution to the point of breaking with the British, with the result that Collins had to back down. The oath was incorporated into the constitution and the Treaty itself was scheduled to the document, with the stipulation that in any conflict between the Treaty and the constitution, the Treaty would take precedence.

The text of the constitution was only released on the eve of the election. As a result the Irish people did not have a chance to see it until it was published in the daily newspapers on election day, which fulfilled the strict letter of an earlier commitment by Collins that the constitution would be published before the election. Of course, critics were effectively denied the chance of explaining the document before polling. By then Collins had also run roughshod over the spirit of the election pact.

Speaking in Cork on the eve of the election, he virtually asked voters to support others, rather than vote for anti-Treaty candidates on the Sinn Féin panel. He appealed to the people of Cork, 'to vote for the candidates you think best'. He pointedly added, 'You understand fully what you have to do, and I will depend on you to do it.'

Of the sixty-five pro-Treaty Sinn Féin candidates, fifty-eight were elected, while only thirty-five of the anti-Treaty people were successful. Even that exaggerated the anti-Treaty support, because sixteen of them were returned without opposition. Where the seats were contested, forty-one of forty-eight pro-Treaty candidates were successful, while only nineteen of forty-one anti-Treaty candidates were elected.

The popular vote painted an even bleaker picture for the anti-Treaty side, which received less than 22 per cent of the first preference votes cast. No anti-Treaty candidate headed the poll in any constituency and Sligo-Mayo East was the only constituency in the whole country in which a majority of voters supported anti-Treaty candidates. The total vote of the pro-Treaty Labour Party's eighteen candidates was only 1,353 votes short of the combined total of the forty-one anti-Treaty candidates who faced opposition. Labour candidates actually won seventeen of the eighteen seats they contested.

In Dublin, anti-Treaty Sinn Féin only won one of the eighteen seats in the city and county. In the city they lost four of their five seats. Only Seán T. O'Kelly won re-election, and they failed to win any seat in the remainder of County Dublin, where Patrick Pearse's mother lost out, even though she was the only anti-Treaty republican seeking election in the six-seat constituency.

There was absolutely no doubt that the people were in favour of the Treaty. 'Labour and Treaty sweep the country,' Harry Boland noted in his diary.

With the exception of his prediction of the outcome of the Boundary Commission, Collins would later be proved right about the Treaty, but he did not live to see it.

Shortly after getting back into power in 1932, de Valera pledged to remove any symbol that was 'incongruous with the country's status as a sovereign nation'. 'Let us remove these forms one by one,' de Valera said at Arbour Hill on 23 April 1933, 'so that this State that we control may be a Republic in fact and that, when the time comes, the proclaiming of the Republic may involve no more than a ceremony, the formal confirmation of a status already attained.'

When the Republic was declared in 1949, it amounted merely to a change of name. The country had already demonstrated that it was a republic in fact. The Treaty had provided stepping-stones for the Irish Free State to attain the desired freedom for that part of the island, which was what the Treaty controversy and the civil war were about. Ironically, it was de Valera who proved that Collins was right.

Bibliography

Manuscript Sources:

Barton, Robert C. Papers, National Archives of Ireland.
  – Witness Statement 979, Bureau of Military History, NAI.

Broy, Eamonn. Witness Statement 1,285. Bureau of Military History, NAI.

Childers, R. Erskine. Papers and Diaries, Trinity College, Dublin.

Collins, Michael. Papers, in possession of the late Liam Collins, Clonakilty, Co. Cork.

Dáil Éireann Files in DE 2 series, State Paper Office, Dublin.

De Valera, Eamon. de Valera Papers, UCD Archives, Dublin.

Devoy, John. Papers, National Library of Ireland, Dublin.

Gavan Duffy, George. Papers, NAI.

Gavan Duffy, George. Witness Statement 381. Bureau of Military History, NAI.

Johnson, Thomas. Papers, National Library of Ireland, Dublin.

Kennedy, Tadhg. Witness Statement, 135. Bureau of Military History, NAI.

Knightly, Mike. Witness Statement 833. Bureau of Military History, NAI.

McGarrity, Joseph. Papers, National Library of Ireland, Dublin.

Mulcahy, Richard. Papers, University College, Dublin.

Napoli, Kathleen (nee McKenna). Papers, National Library of Ireland, Dublin.
  – Witness Statement, 643. Bureau of Military History, NAI.

O'Mara, James. Papers, Natioal Library of Ireland, Dublin.

Stack, Austin. Papers, Private Source.

Published Material:

Barton, Robert. *Why Collins Signed*, interview with R. Murdoch, Sunday Press, 26 September 1971.

Beaslai, Piaras. *Michael Collins and the Making of a New Ireland,* Dublin, 1926.

Birkenhead, Frederick, 2nd Earl of. F. E.: *The Life of F. E. Smith, First Earl of Birkenhead,* London, 1960.

Bowman, John. *De Valera and the Ulster Question*, 1917–1973, Oxford, 1982.

Boyle, Andrew. *The Riddle of Erskine Childers,* London, 1977.

Brasier, Andrew and Kelly, John. *Harry Boland: A Man Divided,* Dublin, 2000.

Brennan, Robert. *Allegiance,* Dublin, 1950.

Callanan, Frank. *T. M. Healy*, Cork, 1998.

Chamberlain, Austen. *Down the Years,* London, 1935.

Childers, Erskine. *The Framework of Home Rule*, London, 1911.

Churchill, Winston S. *The Aftermath,* London, 1929.

— *Thoughts and Adventures*, London, 1932.

Clarke, Kathleen. *Revolutionary Woman: My Fight for Ireland's Freedom*, Dublin, 1997.

Collins, Michael. *The Path to Freedom,* Dublin, 1922, reprinted Cork, 1968.

— *Arguments for the Treaty,* Dublin, 1922.

Colum, Padraig. *Arthur Griffith,* Dublin, 1959.

Coogan, Tim Pat. *Michael Collins: A Biography*. London, 1990.

— *De Valera: Long Fellow, Long Shadow,* London, 1993

Cowell, John. *A Noontide Blazing: Brigid Lyons Thornton, Rebel, Soldier, Doctor*, Dublin, 2005.

Cronin, Seán. *The McGarrity Papers,* Tralee, 1972.

Curran, Joseph M. *The Birth of the Irish Free State,* 1921–1923, Alabama, 1980.

Dáil Éireann. Private Sessions of Second Dáil, Dublin, n.d.

— *Official Report: Debate on the Treaty between Great Britain and Ireland.* Dublin, 1922.

de Burca, Padraig and John F. Boyle. *Free State or Republic?* Dublin, 1922.

de Valera, Eamon. *Speeches and Statements by Eamon de Valera, 1917–1973*, ed. M. Moynihan, Dublin, 1980.

de Valera, Terry. *A Memoir*, Dublin, 2004.

Doherty, Gabriel and Keogh, Dermot. *Michael Collins and the Making of the Irish State*, Cork, 1998.

Dwyer, T. Ryle. *Eamon de Valera*, Dublin, 1980.

— *Michael Collins and the Treaty: His Differences with de Valera*, Cork, 1981.

— *De Valera's Darkest Hour: In Search of National Independence, 1919-1932*, Dublin and Cork, 1982.

— *Michael Collins: The Man Who Won the War*, Cork, 1990.

— *De Valera: The Man and the Myths*, Dublin, 1991.

— *Big Fellow, Long Fellow: A Joint Biography of Collins and de Valera*, Dublin, 1998.

— *Tans, Terror and Troubles: Kerry's Real Fighting Story*, Cork, 2001.

— *The Squad and the Intelligence Operations of Michael Collins*, Cork, 2005.

Figgis, Darrell. *Recollections of the Irish War*, London, 1927.

Fitzpatrick, David. *Harry Boland's Irish Revolution*, Cork, 2003.

Forester, Margery. *Michael Collins: The Lost Leader*, London, 1971.

Foy, Michael T. *Michael Collins's Intelligence War: The Struggle Between the British and the IRA 1919–1921*, Stroud, Gloucestershire, 2006.

Gallagher, Frank. *The Anglo-Irish Treaty*, London, 1971.

Gaughan, J. Anthony. *Austin Stack: Portrait of a Separatist*. Tralee, 1977.

Griffith, Arthur. *Arguments for the Treaty*, Dublin, 1922.

Griffith, Kenneth and O'Grady, Timothy E. *Curious Journey: An Oral History of Ireland's Unfinished Revolution*, Cork, Dublin, 1982.

Hart, Peter. *Mick: The Real Michael Collins*, London, 2005.

Hayes, Michael. *Dáil Éireann and the Irish Civil War*, Studies, Spring, 1969.

Healy, T. M., *Letters and Leaders of My Day*, London, 1928.

Jones, Thomas. *Whitehall Diary, Vol. III: Ireland, 1918–25*, London, 1971.

Kee, Robert. *Ireland: A History*, London, 1981.

Lloyd George, David. *Is it Peace?*, London, 1923

Longford, Earl of, and Thomas P. O'Neill. *Eamon de Valera*, Dublin, 1970.

Macardle, Dorothy. *The Irish Republic, London*, 1968.

MacBride, Seán. *That Day's Struggle: A Memoir, 1904–1951*. Dublin, 2005.

MacDowell, Vincent. *Michael Collins and The Brotherhood*, Dublin, 1997.

Macready, General Sir Neville. *Annals of an Active Life*, London, 1924.

Maher, Jim. *Harry Boland: A Biography*, Cork, 1998.

Makey, James. *Michael Collins: A Life*, Edinburgh and London, 1996.

McColgan, John. *British Policy and the Irish Administration, 1920–22*, London, 1983.

McCoole, Sinéad. *Hazel: A Life of Lady Lavery, 1880-1935*, Dublin 1996.

Murphy, Brian. *John Chartres: Mystery Man of the Treaty*, Dublin 1995.

McKenna, Kathleen Napoli. *In London with the Treaty Delegates, Capuchin Annual*, 1971, pp. 313–332.

Nicholson, Harold. *King George V*, London, 1952.

O'Brien, William. *Forth the Banners Go*, Dublin, 1969.

O'Broin, Leon. *Revolutionary Underground, The Story of the Irish Republican Brotherhood, 1858–1924*, Dublin, 1976.

— *Joseph Brennan, 'Civil Servant Extraordinary'*, Studies, Spring, 1977.

— *Michael Collins*, Dublin, 1980.

— *In Great Haste: The Letters of Michael Collins and Kitty Kiernan*, Dublin, 1983.

— *W.E. Wylie and the Irish Revolution, 1916-1921,* Dublin, 1989.

O'Connor, Batt. *With Michael Collins in the Fight for Irish Independence,* London, 1929.

O'Connor, Frank. *The Big Fellow: Michael Collins and the Irish Revolution,* rev. ed., Dublin, 1965.

Ó Cuinneagáin, Mícheal. *On the Arm of Time: Ireland 1916–1922,* Donegal, 1992.

O'Hegarty, P. S. *A History of Ireland Under the Union, 1801–1922,* London, 1952.

O'Higgins, Kevin. *Civil War and the Events which Led to It,* Dublin, 1922.

O'Malley, Ernie. *Army Without Banners,* London, 1967.

Osborne, Chrissy. *Michael Collins Himself,* Cork, 2003.

Pakenham, Frank. *Peace by Ordeal,* rev. ed., London, 1967.

Regan, John M. *The Irish Counter-Revolution, 1921–1936: Treatyite Politics and Settlement in Independent Ireland,* Dublin, 1999.

Riddell, Lord. *Intimate Diary of the Peace Conference and After, 1918–1923,* London, 1933.

Ring, Jim. *Erskine Childers,* London, 1996.

Ryan, Meda. *Michael Collins and the Women in his Life,* Cork, 1996.

Salvidge, Stanley. *Salvidge of Liverpool,* London, 1934.

Shakespeare, Sir Geoffrey. *Let Candles Be Brought In,* London, 1949.

Stevenson, Frances. *Lloyd George: A Diary,* New York, 1971.

Sturgis, Mark. *The Last Days of Dublin Castle: The Diaries of Mark Sturgis, ed. Michael Hopkinson,* Dublin, 1999.

Talbot, Hayden. *Michael Collins' Own Story,* London, 1923.

Taylor, Rex. *Michael Collins,* London, 1958.

Valiulis, Maryann Gialanella. *Portrait of a Revolutionary: General Richard Mulcahy and the Founding of the Irish Free State,* Dublin, 1992.

Winter, Ormonde. *Winter's Tale,* London, 1955.

Younger, Calton. *Ireland's Civil War,* London, 1968.

Index